The Descendants of Hans Michael Wallick
In the American Civil War

One Family's Journey Through
The War of the Rebellion

Michael David Wallick

Revised Edition

ISBN-13: 978-1468086447

ISBN-10: 1468086448

Front cover: Officers and non-commissioned officers of the 1st Massachusetts Volunteer Cavalry, Companies C and D. This photograph was taken during the 1864 siege of Petersburg, VA.

All photographs and reproductions in this volume are from the author's collection, The Library of Congress or unless stated otherwise, in the public domain.

Dedication

This book is dedicated to all the Wallick men who served their country during the American Civil War. Most of these men were volunteers, leaving home, family and loved ones to fulfill what they believed to be their obligation as a good citizen of the United States of America. Some were quite old when they volunteered while others must have lied about their age when they enlisted. Perhaps all had different motives to join in the fight. Some were quick to enlist, such as William F. Wallick, who enlisted the week after the Confederates attacked Fort Sumter. Others, like Michael Wallick (who enlisted at forty-four years old and had a wife, five children and an Indiana farm to manage), must have carefully weighed the choice to volunteer, calculating the personal and financial sacrifices to be made when joining the Union army. One soldier served nearly four years and a few only seven days. One soldier was drafted and four never returned home. But I believe all these Wallick men, to a greater or lesser degree, understood that they were fighting for our national unity and the future greatness of our country.

Table of Contents page

From Indiana

Miami County

Daviess County

DeKalb County

From Ohio

Tuscarawas County

Holmes County

Maps

Foreword

I am a seventh-generation descendant of Hans Michael Wallick and I have always had a love for history. In the fall of 2008, my love for history merged with a new interest in genealogy when I was asked if I knew anything about my ancestors in the American Civil War. I had to admit that I had never looked into the subject, but having been previously bitten by the "ancestry bug," my curiosity was piqued and I began my investigation. What started as a mere pastime one evening soon became an all-consuming passion. I tried to discover as much as possible about my distant Wallick cousins and their service in The War of the Rebellion. To my complete surprise, these Wallick soldiers were present in many of the war's most famous battles and campaigns, from the Union's first great victories at Forts Henry and Donelson to the war's concluding Grand Review of the Armies in Washington, D.C. The descendants of Hans Michael Wallick were involved throughout the entire conflict. Gettysburg, Chancellorsville, the Wilderness, Shiloh, Stones River, Vicksburg, Chickamauga, the "March to the Sea"- all had Wallicks engaged in some capacity, sometimes with two or three cousins on the same battlefield. After four years of full-time study, with countless hours of reading, cyber-searching and traveling thousands of miles to walk dozens of battlefields, I have put to paper all I have learned about these wonderful men and their service in the Union army.

This volume serves as both a narrative history and a reference book. As a narrative it tells the history of the Wallick soldiers and what they did while serving in the Union army (to date, no Wallicks from the Hans Michael linage are known to have served in the Confederate army). I have also included what little is known about the soldier's pre and post-war years. Each biography begins with a summary of the soldier's vital statistics, such as his regiment, rank, place of enlistment, birthplace, age, occupation, family lineage, etc. This is followed by a few paragraphs describing what little may be known about the soldier's antebellum years. A synopsis of his military service is then stated. The heart of the biography is the soldier's wartime chronology, giving greater detail to his personal experiences and regimental activities during the war. Frederick Dyer's, *A Compendium of the War of the Rebellion*, plus the soldiers' regimental histories and compiled military service records are the core resources used in this section. Here, I write in the historical present tense to describe all the events. I have read some history books written in such a manner and found that I was more forcefully drawn into the action when reading in the present tense. At the conclusion of each biography there is a brief epilogue about the veteran.

When using this work as a reference book, the reader can access information quickly when looking for battles, places or events where Wallicks served. Most of our nation's battlefields and historic sites have interpretive markers and monuments. To discover if any of the Wallick soldiers were engaged on a given battlefield, all one needs to do is refer to Appendix II - Orders of Battle, which lists all the major engagements where Wallick regiments fought. This tells how the chain-of-command was organized. By consulting the Order of Battle, then reading the battlefield's interpretive markers, one can determine where a soldier's unit was located during the engagement. It is my hope that the reader will examine these biographies before visiting a national military park and discover which Wallicks were present during the battle so they may better appreciate their ancestors' participation in the conflict.

The creation of this book has given me the opportunity to reflect on just how critical that era was for our nation and appreciate the unique qualities of the men who fought in that terrible war. These were truly extraordinary individuals. Through my writings I have grown quite fond of these men, wishing I could spend a weekend with them to discuss their many adventures while serving in the Federal army. I suppose that is a longing most historians develop when writing about their deceased subjects. There are far too many questions left unanswered about the military and civilian service of these men for this to be considered an exhaustive study. However, with the limited resources that are available, I hope I am able to convey to the reader some of each soldier's character and personality when telling his story. It is my sincere desire that by reading these short vignettes one may appreciate the sacrifices this generation had to endure to keep us united as a nation.

The Patriarch - Michael Wallick *or* Hans Michel Walck

Hans Michel Walck was a German immigrant who landed in Philadelphia and stepped into his "New World" on September 26, 1732. He came from the small village of Waldangelloch, Germany, and arrived from Rotterdam on the ship *Mary*. Michel was just one of many thousands who left "the old country" during the eighteenth century in order to forge a new life in the fledgling American Colonies. He settled in York, Pennsylvania, where the spelling of his name was anglicized to M-i-c-h-a-e-l W-a-l-l-i-c-k (and so it will be spelled throughout this narrative). There is some evidence that he may have been a carpenter or wood worker and sometime before 1740 he met and married another German immigrant, Frederica Esther Schultz. It was in York that Michael bought his first property and raised his family. To the best of our knowledge, Hans Michael and Frederica had five children, four sons and a daughter-Johannes, Michael, Christian, Philip and Sarah. It is from three of these sons, Johannes, Michael and Philip that twenty-five federalized soldiers from the Union army can trace their lineage.

The necessity for nicknames in the Wallick Family Tree: In any large-sized family tree certain given names are repeated in multiple generations and it is sometimes necessary to develop a system that will distinguish one generation from another. For example: Patriarch Hans Michael Wallick (born c.1709) had a son named Michael (b. 1740), who had a son named Michael (b. 1775), who had a son named Michael (b.1817). This Michael IV fought in many major engagements with the 27th Indiana Volunteer Infantry during the Civil War. To help keep all the Michaels' identities separated, prefixes to their given names are used which tell where these forefathers are buried, i.e., Michael the IV is buried in Daviess County, Indiana, so he is referred to as "Daviess" Michael; his father is buried in Bunker Hill Cemetery, Tuscarawas County, Ohio, so he is "Bunker Hill" Michael; his father is buried in Bedford County, Pennsylvania, so he is "Bedford" Michael. His father was Hans Michael, and we don't know where Hans Michael is buried. The same problem is true in the Wallick family for the given names George, Benjamin, John and Philip. Sometimes their unique trade, such as "Boat Builder" George (b. 1796), identifies the ancestor.

Key to the Ancestral Tree Nicknames
(see opposite page)

1. "Strasburg" George — buried in Grandview Cemetery, Strasburg, Ohio.

2. "Peru" Benjamins Jr. & Sr. — buried in Reyburn Cemetery, Peru, Indiana.

3. "Boat Builder" George — boat builder for the Ohio Erie Canal- buried in 4th Street Cemetery, Dover, Ohio.

4. "Bedford" Michael — buried in Bedford County, Pennsylvania, unknown cemetery.

5. "Bedford" John — buried in Bedford County, Pennsylvania, unknown cemetery.

6. "Guthrie" Michael — buried in North Oak Grove Cemetery, Guthrie County, Iowa.

7. "Kansas" Benjamin — buried in Evergreen Cemetery, Atchison County, Kansas.

8. "Bunker Hill" Michael — buried in Bunker Hill, Cemetery, Tuscarawas County, Ohio.

9. "Daviess" Michael — buried in Raglesville Cemetery, Daviess County. Indiana.

10. "Coshocton" Philip — buried in Keene Presbyterian Cemetery, Coshocton County, Ohio.

11. "Holmes" Henry — buried in Monroe Lutheran Cemetery, Holmes County, Ohio.

12. "Switzerland" Philip — buried in Switzerland County, Indiana, unknown cemetery.

These nicknames are used in the book, *Hans Michael Wallick's Descendants in America, 1732-2012*, written by Scott Alan Wallick, ISBN-13: 978-1466433076 ISBN-10: 1466433078

Ancestral Tree for the Wallick Civil War Soldiers

Those who served are in **bold** type

All are descendants of Hans Michael Walck/Wallick (c.1707-67)

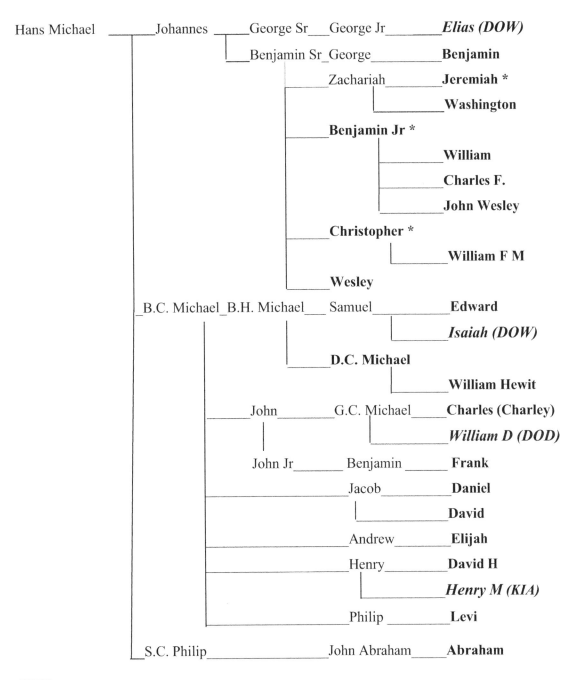

<u>KEY</u>

B.C. Michael- son of Hans Michael, buried in **B**edford **C**ounty, PA.

B.H. Michael- son of B.C. Michael, buried in **B**unker **H**ill, Cemetery, Winfield, Ohio.

D.C. Michael- son of B.H. Michael, buried in **D**aviess **C**ounty, Indiana.

G.C. Michael- son of John, buried in **G**uthrie **C**ounty, Iowa.

S.C. Philip buried in **S**witzerland **C**ounty, Indiana.

*Members of federalized militia that served only one week (July 10-17, 1863).

KIA- killed in action   *DOW*- died of wounds   *DOD*- died of disease

Index to Battles and Events

(in chronological order)

Map 1   Wallick Soldiers in the Eastern Theater of the War.

1st Kernstown - Henry, William F.   **Gettysburg** - Michael   **Spotsylvania** - Elias

Buckton Station - Michael   **Monocacy Junction** - Elias   **Washington D. C.** Hewit, Charles F.

Cedar Creek - Edward   **Opequon** - Elias, Edward   **The Wilderness** - Elias

Chancellorsville - Michael   **Petersburg** - Elias

Cold Harbor - Elias   **Richmond** - Michael (POW), William (POW)

Map 2 Wallick Soldiers in the Deep South and Western Theaters of the War.

Atlanta - Michael, Charles F.

Bentonville - Hewit, Charles F.

Cahaba - Elijah (POW)

Cedar Bluff - William

Chattanooga - Isaiah, Levi, Charles F.

Chickamauga - Isaiah, Levi, Charles F.

Chickasaw Bayou - Charley

Columbia – Hewit, Charles F.

Ft. Henry & **Donelson** - Levi

Ft. Wagner - Henry

Nashville - William

Perryville - Levi, William, Charles F.

Port Gibson – Charley, Abraham

Resaca - Michael, Charles F.

Savannah - Hewit, Charles F.

Shiloh - Isaiah, Levi, William

Stones River - Isaiah, Levi, William

Vicksburg - Charley, Daniel, Abraham

Acknowledgements

A number people deserve special recognition for lending their advice and contributing to this collection of Wallick biographies. I want to first thank my brother, Dr. Scott Alan Wallick from Seattle, Washington, for presenting this challenge to me and encouraging me to honor all the Wallicks who fought in the American Civil War. This has been a labor of love for me and it would have been impossible to create this volume without Scott's knowledge and expertise in our family's ancestry. In addition, if it were not for his steadfast pursuit of the Wallick genealogy through DNA testing, the number of soldiers included in this account would be greatly diminished. The use of DNA science proved that eight Wallicks from Miami County, Indiana, two from Hardin County, Ohio, and one from Albia, Iowa, were indeed descendants of Hans Michael Wallick. The details and results of the tests are included in Scott's book, *Hans Michael Wallick's Descendants in America, 1732-2012*. With the inclusion of these soldiers, our family's involvement in the war is considerably expanded. I regularly called on Scott for help in points of genealogy, formatting techniques and the creation of maps when writing these stories. I also appreciate all the editorial advice my sister-in-law, Lorna Wallick, gave me when preparing this work.

I am deeply indebted to Jeffery Wallick from Los Angeles, California, whose research on the Hans Michael Wallick family was invaluable to me when composing these biographies. Jeff's exhaustive work made it possible for me to concentrate on just writing about the family's participation in the war and not have to conduct a genealogical search for each soldier. The hours, months and years he spent in libraries studying local histories, courthouse records and other evidence is to be greatly admired. I consulted his work first before I began a soldiers' biography.

Nancy Matson of the Miami County Historical Society Museum in Peru, Indiana, was very willing to share all she knew about the large Wallick collection that is housed in that museum. She was a great resource for all the Miami County Wallicks who fought in the war and she even allowed me to handle and read the original William Wallick diary that he wrote while incarcerated in Libby Prison. That was a great treat! She also allowed me to take a copy of the Charles F. Wallick diary transcript, which is reproduced in Appendix I. I certainly appreciate all the cooperation and kindness she provided when Scott and I visited Peru, Indiana.

There are a number of people who supplied pictures and documents that helped augment what I could tell in these soldiers' stories. Thank you to James Wallick of Yreka, California, for providing pictures of Michael Wallick and his son, Hewit. These pictures are especially meaningful to me because these two soldiers are my closest relatives who fought in the War of the Rebellion. Michael is my great-great-granduncle. The two pictures of William Wallick in uniform are from the Craig Dunn collection of Kokomo, Indiana. I spent time with Craig one afternoon and he shared with me his great array of Civil War memorabilia and gave me some very helpful hints on how to research the Indiana Volunteer Infantry (IVI) regiments. Michael Wood graciously provided the picture of Charles Wallick, which was taken near the turn of the century at a reunion of the 16th Ohio Volunteer Infantry (OVI). Mary Wallick Stierhoff was kind enough to provide me the compiled military service records of her great-grandfather, Edward Wallick, and his brother, Isaiah. She also gave me the "Remembrance" transcript, which describes a meeting between Isaiah and one of his brothers-in-arms. The transcript was found in the Hardin County Historical Society. I am very appreciative of Lisa Marquise for her willingness to share her family's history and the photograph of Abraham and Mary Wallick. Abraham is a new soldier in this second edition and he brings some unique backstories to his biography. In addition, I would be remiss if I did not acknowledge Ron Wallick of Whidbey Island, Washington, who has been so supportive of my work and supplied all he could in the way of pictures, documents and resources. And after my lengthy sabbatical from writing, Ken Bandy of Beloit, Ohio, helped reignite my passion to complete this revised edition. Ken is one of the most Civil War savvy individuals I have ever met. He is also extremely well-read on the history of the era and being a past reenactor, he has an experiential knowledge of how the soldiers lived and fought. But most of all I want to thank my wife, Diane, who has encouraged me throughout this project and helped me with some of the technical points of writing. She has traveled this Civil War journey with me as much as anyone. Her love and patience I have tested yet her support has remained unwavering; for all of that, I am extremely thankful.

In Memoriam

Those who paid the ultimate price while in the service of their country had their names written in the Roll of Honor on state documents and monuments. Four Wallick soldiers died in the war, all from the State of Ohio. Three of them are listed in Ohio's Roll of Honor but for some unknown reason, Henry M. Wallick was omitted. It is an unfortunate oversight for he, without question, should be included in that list.

Roll of Honor

William D. Wallick, 67th Ohio - Died of disease in Cumberland, Maryland - February 26, 1862.

Isaiah Wallick, 49th Ohio - Died of wounds at Missionary Ridge, Tennessee, - November 27, 1863.

Henry M. Wallick, 67th Ohio - Killed in action at Chester Station, Virginia - May 10, 1864. Burial site unknown, body probably never recovered from the battlefield.

Elias Wallick, 126th Ohio - Died of wounds at the Battle of Opequon Creek, Virginia, - September 23, 1864.

William D. Wallick
Antietam National Cemetery
Buried as an Unknown Soldier

(see biography for explanation)

Isaiah Wallick
Chattanooga National Cemetery

Elias Wallick
Winchester National Cemetery

Prisoners of War

Michael Wallick, 27th Indiana - POW from May 23, 1862 - September 18, 1862. Captured at Buckton Station, Virginia. Incarcerated at Belle Island and Libby Prison, Richmond, Virginia. Paroled, exchanged and then rejoined his regiment.

William Wallick, 51st Indiana - POW from May 3, 1863 - February 9, 1864. Captured near Rome, Georgia. Tunneler and one of 109 officers who escaped from Libby Prison on the night of February 9, 1864. He then rejoined his regiment.

Elijah Wallick, 102nd Ohio - POW from September 24, 1864 - March 16, 1865. Captured at Fort Athens, Alabama. Incarcerated at Cahaba Federal Prison, Cahaba, Alabama. Paroled and released at the close of the war.

Introduction

No other event in American history changed the very essence of our nationhood as did our great Civil War. The Wallicks who fought in this "War of the Rebellion" (as it was referred to by the northern victors) were part of a unique generation who forged a new national identity, without the curse of slavery. It is unfortunate that a fratricidal conflict had to take place to keep our collective states together. This confrontation eventually changed how we perceived ourselves as a country, for before the war one would say, "The United States **are**…..etc." But after the war the verb changed, from plural to singular, and everyone began to say, "The United States **is**…..etc.", as we do today. The Civil War is what made us one nation, indivisible. The inherent good in remaining united instead of splitting into two countries is a given now for most Americans. This account of the American Civil War is told with an admitted bias toward Unionism, for all the Wallick soldiers were members of the Federal army.

Twenty-five Wallicks were mustered into Federal service during the war. Twenty-two served one hundred days or more and three, due to some unusual circumstances, served only seven days. From this collection of men there were two who recorded some of their wartime experiences in diaries. We have the original diary written by Captain William Wallick of the 51st Indiana Volunteer Infantry (IVI) from Peru, Indiana, and a partial transcript of a diary written by his brother, Corporal Charles F. Wallick of the 87th IVI. These two men give us a glimpse into what life was like as a soldier in the Union army and, in William's case, as a prisoner of war. These eyewitnesses write first-hand accounts of their regimental actions and personal experiences. William's diary was written from the spring of 1863 through the winter of 1864. Charles wrote from April 1864 to April 1865, however, there is a six-month gap in the middle of his transcript. The original leather-bound diary was lost at some point in history and the person who transcribed Charles' diary left the transcription unfinished. William and Charles have two very different writing styles and excerpts from their diaries will be included in the biographies when it helps facilitate the telling of their stories. William's original diary can be found in the Miami County Historical Society Museum in Peru, Indiana.

Since all the Wallick soldiers fought for the North, the names of the battles in this book are those used by the Federal forces. The Civil War was so divisive that the North and South couldn't even agree upon what to call their battles! In general, the North named their battles after natural features, such as rivers, creeks or a ridge. The South named their battles after man-made places, such as towns or a residence. Therefore, in the North we have the battles of Bull Run, Stones River and Antietam Creek, while the same battles in the South are called Manassas Junction, Murfreesboro and Sharpsburg. There were a few battles where both the North and the South came to an agreement, such as the battles of Gettysburg and Chickamauga.

There are some battles and events where we **know** Wallick soldiers were engaged in the action and at other times we must **assume** they were present. There is always the possibility that a soldier was uninvolved for some unknown reason. The following biographies are a combination of known incidents of involvement and assumed participation, taking for granted that the soldier was healthy enough to be "effective" and take part in the activities of his regiment and company. Usually, no roll call was recorded just before a unit entered battle. Different companies in the regiment may have had different responsibilities or a soldier may have been absent due to sickness or an undocumented temporary assignment.

When reading these biographies, it will be helpful to have an understanding of army unit sizes during the Civil War. Theoretically, a company at full strength was 100 men, a regiment 1,000, a brigade 4,000, a division 12,000, and a corps anywhere from 20,000 to 30,000 men. However, those numbers rarely reflected the actual size of Civil War units. Most regiments operated between forty to sixty percent of optimum size once they were in the field. Disease, desertions and battle casualties depleted the ranks quickly, so it would not be unusual during the war for a company to consist of just 50 men, a regiment 300 or less, a brigade 2,000, a division 4,000 to 6,000 and a corps 12,000 to 15,000 men. At the battle of Gettysburg some regiments barely numbered 200 men.

There will be terms and phrases used throughout this book that were commonly understood in nineteenth-century military parlance, but may need a little explanation today.

Mustered in- When a soldier enlisted in a volunteer regiment, he became part of a state unit with the governor serving as its commander-in-chief. In order for the volunteer regiments to be under the command of the United States Government, the governor had to relinquish some of his authority and the men had to be officially sworn into Federal service. This was called "being mustered in." Once done, the regiment was under Federal control and the army could deploy the unit as it saw fit. In the early years, when there was a glut of volunteers anxious to serve, it could take months between a soldier's enlistment and his regiment being mustered in. Later in the war, when the ranks needed to be filled quickly, it could happen within days if not immediately.

parole and exchange of prisoners of war- At the beginning of the war both Federal and Confederate governments agreed to the European system of parole and exchange of prisoners of war. When an enemy combatant was captured, he was given the opportunity to swear an oath that he would not rejoin his unit nor take up arms against the enemy until he was officially "exchanged." Parole was supposed to be granted to the men within 10 days of capture, and then the soldiers were free to go on their own recognizance or confine themselves to a detention camp run by their own government. For a time this worked well, but as the war progressed, the system began to break down for military and political reasons. An exchange of prisoners was based on the value of the rank. For example: 1 private was worth another private, 2 privates were worth a corporal or sergeant, 4 privates were worth a lieutenant, 6 privates were worth a captain and so on until 46 privates were worth a commanding general. Once the soldier was exchanged, he could rejoin his unit and resume hostilities. There were two primary places of exchange for the opposing sides. In the east was Aikens Landing (today the site of Varina, Virginia, a plantation house just south of Richmond), and in the west, Vicksburg, Mississippi.

compiled military service records- By 1886, it became evident to the War Department that a system was needed to help collect and organize information about a soldier's military service and medical records. The aging veteran population caused the number of pension and benefits applications to explode. What developed was a system of abstracts on index cards that stated the volunteer soldier's date of mustering-in, pay roll, physical description, hospital and prison records, plus other materials. Much of the information was gathered from company roll call books. Every soldier who served in the Civil War had a jacket-envelope that stated his name, rank, and unit. Inside are the card abstracts plus other documents that might have been saved from the war. Some Wallick soldiers have just the bare minimum information in their compiled military service record. Officers' records generally have more information than enlisted men. First Lieutenant Henry M. Wallick (who was killed in action at the Battle of Chester Station) has a great deal of personal information and military correspondence in his compiled military service record. The same can be said of Captain William Wallick. The compiled military service records for all Wallick soldiers can be ordered from the National Archives, Washington, D.C.

From Indiana

William Wallick - 51st Indiana Volunteer Infantry, Co. G

Rank: 2nd Lieutenant, promoted to Captain

Place of enlistment: Miami County, Indiana - October 8, 1861

Mustered into Federal service: December 31, 1861

Service time: 3 years, 2 months, 11 days

Born: November 4, 1832 - Tuscarawas County, Ohio

Age at enlistment: 27 years old

Civilian occupation: carpenter

Family Lineage: William, son of "Peru" Benjamin Junior, son of "Peru" Benjamin Senior[1], son of Johannes, son of Hans Michael Wallick

Captain William Wallick

Craig Dunn Collection

William Wallick was a carpenter in the spring of 1861 when Rebel artillery opened fire on Ft. Sumter. That fall, as sectional passions continued to escalate and the Union army reeled from its defeat at Bull Run, William decided to put aside his trade for three years and enlist in what eventually became known as Company G of the 51st Indiana Volunteer Infantry (IVI). He, like many others in the north at that time, answered President Lincoln's call for 300,000 more volunteers to put down the southern rebellion. In October, the twenty-seven-year-old William left his wife, Mary (whom he called Molly), and newborn daughter Flora to march off with scores of other men from Miami County to serve their President and country. Early in the war his regiment was either directly involved or put in supporting roles in some of the greatest battles in the west- Shiloh, Perryville and Stones River. However, it was while he was deployed in northern Alabama, in the spring of 1863, that he became entangled in one of the most remarkable adventures of the entire Civil War.

William was part of Colonel Abel Streight's ill-fated and poorly conceived "Raid to Rome" (Georgia) that took place in the spring of 1863. One of the problems from the beginning of the expedition was its reliance on mules for transportation. Because of the hilly terrain in northern Alabama, it was thought that mules would serve the brigade better than horses, mules being more sure-footed than horses on steep slopes. However, the braying of the 700 animals, as they meandered through the hill country, made the Rebels fully aware of every movement the brigade made. The Confederates made great fun of Colonel Streight's "Lightning Mule Brigade" and joked about chasing after the "Jackass Cavalry." On May 3, 1863, Colonel Streight, along with most of his 1,700 man brigade, fell victim to the wiles of Confederate General Nathan Bedford Forrest and were forced to surrender to him a few miles east of Cedar Bluffs, Alabama, near what is today the little hamlet of Lawrence. The

---

[1] As with the given name Michael, there are so many Benjamins in the Wallick family tree that it is necessary to distinguish these patriarchs, who is buried in Peru, Indiana, from all the other Benjamins in the Wallick clan.

men were taken to Atlanta and from there were sent on to two Richmond, Virginia, prison camps- Belle Island for the enlisted men and Libby Prison for William and his fellow officers.

William was the second member of the Wallick clan sent to Libby Prison during the war[2] and he kept a diary of his nine-month ordeal, which survives today.[3] Conditions at Libby were harsh for all the incarcerated officers and they were constantly trying new means of escaping. William was a tunneler in a plan to burrow out of the prison basement and vanish into the streets of Richmond. On February 9, 1864, William and 108 comrades succeeded in tunneling out of Libby. He spent five days and nights in the swamps of Virginia evading Confederate patrols. Eventually, he and fifty-eight other officers made their way safely back to their own regiments (the remainder of the escapees were recaptured by the Confederates). After the war, William presented numerous lectures about his escape and survival from hunger, cold, and the dangerous tidewater swamps of northern Virginia.

After a long recuperation and furlough back in his hometown of Peru, Indiana, William returned to his regiment in Nashville, Tennessee. In May, many of his regimental brothers reenlisted as veterans but he, along with some others, just wished to go home. He had been promoted to captain during his incarceration at Libby and fulfilled the rest of his duty with the 51st IVI, but eventually he resigned his commission. William was discharged December 17, 1864, the day after the Battle of Nashville. The 51st was heavily engaged in that battle but William was not part of it. He and those who were about to be discharged remained in camp, preparing for their departure home.

William Wallick with the 51st Indiana Volunteer Infantry

1861

OCT 8   William enlists in the 51st Indiana Volunteer Infantry and then commissioned a second lieutenant.

DEC 14   The regiment is mustered into Federal service at Camp Morton, Indianapolis.

DEC 15 - DEC 31   The 51st IVI is moved to Louisville, then to Bardstown, KY.

1862

51st Indiana Infantry Monument Shiloh National Military Park.

JAN - FEB 6   William has duty at Bardstown in the defense of the Bluegrass State.

FEB 7 - MAR 29   The 51st IVI is marched to Nashville, TN, where they perform garrison duty and guard the Nashville Railroad.

MAR 30 - APR 6   The regiment moves to Savannah, TN, in preparation for the Federals advance down the Cumberland River.

APR 6   Battle of Shiloh   William and the 51st Regiment are in a supporting role guarding the troop supply wagons. Today, the regiment has a very imposing monument near the Visitor's Center, mainly to declare that it was under the command of brigadier general and future president, James A. Garfield. The monument's location is very prestigious and the stone quite handsome. William begins to suffer with his first bout of what then was called sciatic rheumatism of the left hip, leg and knee. This severely impairs his ability to walk and will become a chronic disability the rest of his life.

---

[2] Michael Wallick of the 27th Indiana was captured May 23, 1862 during an engagement at Buckton Station, VA. and sent first to Libby Prison, then to Belle Island, which is located in the middle of the James River in downtown Richmond.
[3] The diary of William Wallick is housed in the Miami County Historical Society Museum in Peru, Indiana.

MAY - SEP   The regiment participates in General Buell's campaign in middle Tennessee and northern Alabama, then pursues General Bragg into Kentucky.

OCT 8   Battle of Perryville   The 51st regiment is held in reserve but close enough to hear the sounds of battle.

NOV - DEC   The regiment is deployed in and around Nashville and begins an advance toward Murfreesboro, TN.

DEC 31 - JAN 2, 1863   Battle of Stones River   The 51st is at the far left of the Union line and is ordered to cross Stones River when suddenly they are attacked by the enemy. The command to cross the river is rescinded and the regiment is then ordered to defend their new position. They fight continuously throughout the afternoon but eventually are forced to retreat to the same rear area as where distant cousins Isaiah and Levi Wallick have retreated, west of today's Visitor's Center and south of Asbury Road. On January 1st there is an all-day lull in the battle as both the Union and Confederate armies adjust and strengthen their lines. The next day, January 2nd, William and his regiment are moved on the battlefield to the Union left and engage the Confederates in some brief but heavy fighting. By January 3rd the battle is over and the 51st is ordered to occupy Murfreesboro. At one point in the battle William has an artillery shell explode so close to him that he suffers life-long hearing lose in his left ear.

1863

JAN - FEB   Duty in and around Ft. Rosecrans at Murfreesboro, TN.

FEB 20   William begins his diary. **(William Wallick's Diary-WWD)** He writes of himself, *"Lieutenant Wallick takes command of his company on the 20th of February, 1863."* At first William's diary entries are very few and brief but by mid-March he offers more details concerning his regiment, the weather and letters to his wife Molly. He is captured in early May and his entries during his incarceration become very short, but regular...until they start digging out of prison. By the beginning of January, 1864, there is a noticeable difference in the frequency and quality of information in his writing. The daily, whiny mantra-*"Still in this Hell and no prospect of getting out soon..."* ceases. William, being one of the tunnelers, didn't have time to write or whine while he was preoccupied with escaping. Also, during this time, his diary is more upbeat and he is much less despondent. In this biographical sketch the focus of his diary will be limited to the dates of his capture, imprisonment and escape. He writes in a very *free* form, paying little attention to spelling or punctuation. Some of these shortcomings have been corrected here to help the reader.

APR 19 - May 1   Colonel Streight (William's commanding officer) with 1,700 men, leave Nashville, TN, to begin their "Raid on Rome," GA, in order to destroy the Western & Atlantic Railroad. The raid turns into a disaster.

MAY 2   *WWD*   *"We march hard all day. The rebs attack us and kill Colonel Wethermerz and several others."*

MAY 3   William Wallick is captured   Colonel Streight's entire brigade is captured just east of Cedar Bluff, AL, by General Nathan Bedford Forrest and his troop of 322 cavalrymen. General Forrest tricks Colonel Streight into believing that the Confederates confronting him are a much larger force than the Federals by simply parading his troops in a partially concealed circle over a nearby ridge. Although vastly outnumbering the Confederates, Colonel Streight is deceived and surrenders his entire command.

Monument to General Nathen Bedford Forrest.
This monument commemorates the capture of Colonel Streight and his 1,466 men by General Nathan Bedford Forrest's 322 cavalrymen. It was erected in 1939 by the United Daughters of the Confederacy and is located four miles east of Cedar Bluffs, AL, on SR 9, near the hamlet of Lawrence, AL.

MAY 3   WWD   *"We are fired into 20 miles from Rome, Georgia. We surrender and go to Rome. We are treated hard."*

MAY 5   WWD   *"We take the cars to Atlanta, Georgia, 65 miles away. We get there at night, get the courthouse for quarters. We get supper at 10:00 at night."*

MAY 7   WWD   *"Some prospect of getting away. We are now confined to the room entirely. Something is afloat. We have all we want to eat. The weather is still cold, I wish I could send a letter home. The citizens are not allowed to see us. The boys fare hard."*

MAY 14   WWD   *"We travel all day in North Carolina. We have a hard trip of it. Nothing much to eat... We get to Petersburg at night. Stop all night."*

MAY 16   WWD   *"...we arrive at Richmond. Searched and put in prison but thank God all in good spirits."*

MAY 20   WWD   *"Still in Libby Prison but in good spirits. Some hope of getting out soon. Here I sit and look out on the James River, I feel unwell today."*

Libby Prison, Richmond, Virginia.

The Confederate government converted the Libby & Son Ship Chandlers & Grocers Warehouse in downtown Richmond into a prison for captured Union officers. Conditions at Libby Prison were harsh, even by Civil War standards. The three-story prison held 1,200 men in eight 103 by 42 feet over-crowded, vermin-infested and drafty rooms. Many deaths occurred due to poor sanitation and nutrition. Colonel Thomas E. Rose of the 77th Pennsylvania was placed in Libby Prison after he was captured at the Battle of Chickamauga on September 19, 1863. Rather than endure the conditions in the prison, Colonel Rose planned to escape by tunneling from the prisoner's kitchen cellar across a 50-foot-wide vacant lot and up into a shed on the other side of a fence bordering the lot. By making a hole in the back of a fireplace on the first floor, Rose was able to gain access to an unused section of the cellar.

With makeshift tools he and a few fellow prisoners, including William Wallick, toiled for weeks and carved a narrow tunnel under the empty lot. However, the first tunnel soon became flooded due to its proximity to the James River, rendering it unusable. A new tunnel was then started and on the evening of February 7, 1864, Colonel Abel D. Streight, now the commanding officer of the prisoners, declared the new tunnel finished. As senior officer involved in the project he demanded to be the first to escape. Unfortunately, when he broke through the ground he found that he was still several feet from the fence and overheard the guards discussing the strange sounds coming from the ground. Miraculously, the hole in the ground remained undiscovered as the prisoners worked furiously for two more days to extend the tunnel.

This is just one of many versions of the escape. Variations of this account were told and disputed for years after the war. However, there is little disagreement about the following facts:

During the evening of February 9th, Colonel Rose, along with Colonel Streight and some of his men, crawled through the tunnel made by the prisoners and disappeared into the streets of Richmond. At morning roll call it was discovered that 109 prisoners were missing, making it the largest mass prison escape of the war. Fifty-nine of them, including William and Colonel Streight, made it back to Union camps, two drowned while crossing streams, and the other 48, including Colonel Rose, are recaptured.

William continues his story…

MAY 22 *WWD* *"Still in prison at Libby, much out of heart this morning. Still hopes of getting away soon. There is an exchange made but none of us of the Provisional Brigade [those captured at Cedar Bluffs] get to go."*

JUN 1 *WWD* *"Still in prison. We look for a boat. We think we shall leave this Hell on Wednesday evening. The prospect of getting out is hard. I pay one dollar for six eggs. I have my dinner today for the first time in prison."*

JUN 9 *WWD* *"Still in this Hell and no prospect of getting out soon."*

JUN 19 *WWD* *"Some prospect of getting out."*

JUL 3 *WWD* *"Still in Hell and no prospect of getting out soon..."* This one sentence is entered day after day for weeks during his captivity.

OCT 22 *WWD* *"Still in Hell and no prospect of getting out soon. Two letters from father and one from mother."*

NOV 4 *WWD* *"Beautiful weather this morning. Still in prison and but little prospect of getting out. I'm 30 yrs old today."*

DEC - JAN 1 There are a few entries in William's diary in December and they say much the same as before. However, by New Year's Day there is a dramatic change in his daily journal.

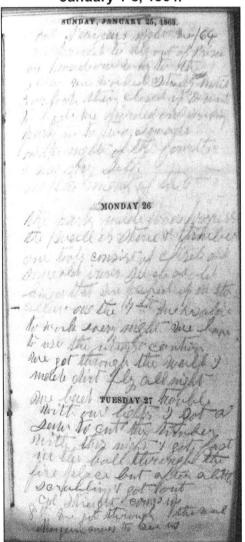

A page from William Wallick's diary, January 1-8, 1864.

1864

JAN 1 *WWD* *"On New Year's night '64 we proceed to dig out of prison. We made our way to the cellar. We worked steady until 3 o'clock then closed up and went to bed. We divided our working party into two squads."*

JAN 4 *WWD* *"On the night of the fourth I dug myself."*

JAN 6 *WWD* *"On the night of the 6th the party made good progress. The wall is stone and timber. Our tools consist of a chisel and some old irons such as old hinges that we picked up in the cellar.*

JAN 7 *WWD* *"On the 7th we resolve to work every night. We have to use the utmost caution. We got through the wall. I made dirt fly all night. We have troubles with our lights* (the candles lacked oxygen in the tunnels). *I got a saw to cut thru timber with. This night I got forst* [forced] *in the hole through the fireplace but after a little scrambling I got out. Col. Streight comes up."*

JAN 8 *WWD* *"We get through the wall. Morgan comes to see us."* This man, Morgan, is Confederate General John Hunt Morgan, who made a famous raid into southern Indiana and Ohio in the summer of 1863. Five Wallicks from Peru, IN, were mustered into Federal service and helped pursue General Morgan and his daring Rebel raiders into Ohio. Their story can be read in "The Seven Days Soldiers" on page 49, He was eventually captured and sent to the Ohio State Penitentiary in Columbus. Morgan escaped that institution by tunneling out of the stone walled fortress on November 27, 1863.

Miami County Historical Society

He returned to the South and received a hero's welcome because of his exploits. It is interesting that William refers to the General's visit, since the Union prisoners are about to escape from Libby the same way General Morgan escaped his Yankee captors, through tunneling.[4]

JAN 11 *WWD* *"We redouble our efforts."*

JAN 12 *WWD* *"We have much to contend with."*

JAN 16 *WWD* *"The work still goes on, the weather may stop our work."*

JAN 23 *WWD* *"We have trouble and cannot work because of the men and officers make so much noise they are arrested and stand 3 hours. We had to postpone work."*

JAN 24 *WWD* *"We work all day. Captain Hamilton and Colonel Rose are down all day."*

JAN 25 - 27 *WWD* *"Our work lays still."*

JAN 28 - 29 *WWD* *"We lay still. Major Bates walks out today. Captain Porter out today."*

JAN 30 *WWD* *"Three officers walk out . Our work lays still. We shall move soon. Major Bates is captured".*

FEB 1 *WWD* *"Our work is pushed along fast."*

FEB 2 *WWD* *"The rebs count us all the time. We think we shall go out Thursday night* [February 4th].*"*

FEB 3 *WWD* *"The work is now finished. Today our tunnel measures 33 feet. This morning the Rebels put flour in the cellar* [this postponed work for a few days].

FEB 5 - 8 *WWD* *"The work still goes on, out the 9th. We are about through."*

FEB 9 *WWD* *"We shall leave here tonight* [late that evening they escape]. *We have a hard time of it. We wade the Chickahominy* [River]. *Spend the day in a swamp. I suffer with cold. I long for night to come so that we can travel."*

FEB 11 *WWD* *"We camp at a hill at the* [illegible]. *Thursday we travel in the marshes."*

FEB 12 *WWD* *"Friday we travel all day and night. Get to Williamsburg Saturday* [February 13th].*"*

FEB 13 *WWD* *"We get dinner. We go down to Yorktown. We meet with much hospitality at Yorktown."*

FEB 14 *WWD* *"We get to Fort Monroe... We meet with much hospitality. We go to General Butler's quarters. We take the boat to Baltimore."*

William is the first prisoner to reach Fortress Monroe and tell of the successful mass escape from Libby Prison. The former POW is then granted a furlough home to rest and recuperate from his incarceration.

FEB 15 *WWD* *"Arrive at Baltimore. I suffer with sore feet. At Baltimore we take breakfast. Take the train for Washington at 8 o'clock. Staying in Washington tonight."*

FEB 16 - 18 *WWD* *"We take the train for home* [to Peru, IN] *at 6 o'clock. On the 17th stay at Harrisburg* [PA]. *18th stay all day at Bayard__* [?].*"* Thus ends the prison diary of William Wallick.

---

[4] One will notice in the photograph of William's diary that the printed dates have been scribbled out and do not correspond to the actual dates of his writings. William dated his entries within the text of his diary and did not follow the printed page.

APR   William's furlough is extended 30 days due to severe bronchitis and nephritis (inflammation of the kidneys).

MAY 2   William returns from his furlough and joins his regiment in Tennessee. He has been promoted to captain June 30, 1863, while a prisoner of war. William is the highest-ranking officer of all the Wallicks who fought in the American Civil War.

MAY 30   Captain William Wallick takes command of Company G. Regimental historian, William R. Hartpence, recalls an incident in Captain Wallick's company in his book, *History of the Fifty-First Volunteer Infantry*:

> *One day "Mother" Richeson and Alex Ward of Co. G, got into an altercation, and kept it up until the other boys prevailed on **Captain Wallick** to make them step out in front of the company, and "have it out." On the Captain's invitation, they both stepped promptly to the front, and, with their haversacks and accouterments on, went at it like tigers, till they had it out. From that moment on one never heard a word from either of them.*

JUN - SEP   The 51st is deployed to Chattanooga, TN. Distant cousin Levi Wallick has provost duty there.

OCT   William sees action at Dalton, GA, and pursues General Hood into Alabama.

NOV 30   Battle of Franklin   The 51st is held in reserve and supports the Federal army in its withdrawal toward Nashville, TN.

DEC 15 - 16   Battle of Nashville   William's regiment is heavily engaged for two days in this battle with the Rebel enemy. The 51st makes a charge up Montgomery Hill and secures that residence, then they attack Brentwood Hill. By the end of the second day of battle the Confederate army is totally routed, almost to the point of disintegration. It is a glorious victory for the Union army. Most of William's regimental brothers have reenlisted and the 51st IVI becomes a veteranized unit. The captain resigns his commission but remains in command of his company during the battle, even though he was "officially" mustered out the night before their engagement. William Wallick has seen enough of war these past three years. Immediately after the battle he begins his journey home to his wife, Mary, and baby daughter, Flora.

DEC 17   William leaves his regiment the day after his regiment's great victory in the Battle of Nashville. He begins his journey home to Peru, IN.

Epilogue - William returned to Peru, Indiana, for a short time after the war and then moved his family to St. Johns, Michigan. He spent three years in St. Johns before going back to Peru, where he continued his carpentry trade. He gave lectures on his escape from Libby Prison for many years. In 1880, he and a fellow escapee felt compelled to defend their commanding officer, Colonel Streight, when the colonel's participation in the escape attempt came into question by some newspaper reporters after the colonel gave a lecture before the Union Veterans Association of Indianapolis. The following excerpt is from *The History of the Fifty-First Indiana Volunteer Infantry*. William Hartpence first gives a brief description of the newspaper editorial that outraged so many veterans, then follows Captain William Wallick's response to the editor of the *Indianapolis News*. Mr. Hartpence writes:

> *...A garbled report of this* [lecture] *was published in a prominent paper in that city* [Indianapolis], *with an accompanying editorial, belittling the accomplishment of the tunneling out; saying, "a rat might have done as well or better;" and it even virtually, if not actually, ridiculed the idea that Colonel Streight had anything to do with originating the tunnel, and saying that he was barely an accidental beneficiary. In reply to this, **Captain Wm. Wallick**, of the Fifty-First, and Major John D. Simpson, of the 10th Indiana, both of whom escaped with Colonel Streight, published the following in the* Indianapolis News.

Only William's letter to the editor is reprinted on the next page. Major Simpson wrote a different response, which is also recorded in the Hartpence regimental history.

Escape of "The Rats"

Letter from William Wallick - To the Editor of the Indianapolis News*:*

If the Union soldiers who, after long and weary months of confinement and misery in Libby Prison, with incredible labor dug out to freedom, are at this distant day to be classed with vermin and moles, it seems to me that it makes little difference who projected the work or who participated in it. I notice with astonishment and mortification, from a publication in the Indianapolis Journal, that "a rat might have done as well or better." I was a Libby prisoner, and I helped dig in two tunnels, one of which was never completed. It seems to me then that we were digging for life, and we hoped we had the prayers and kind wishes of Union-loving friends at home. But if any rat might have done as well or better, as the Indianapolis Journal thinks, what matters who was the head rat? It is a prominence not to be coveted; a leadership not to be envied. When prominent Republican editors revile and burlesque the sufferings of unfortunate Union soldiers, it matters little who was prominent and conspicuous in miseries, or most active and efficient in escaping them. Better be an unknown and obscure Union soldier than a disgraced and defamed rat. I was one of the unfortunate rodents who, under the direction of Gen. Streight, assisted in digging out of Libby Prison. I have carefully read the synopsis of his lecture to the Veteran Club; and I indorse its accuracy in all substantial particulars.

There were two tunnels; I dug in both; one was not completed. Some confusion has no doubt arisen from confounding the operation of the two tunnels. This I know: Gen. Streight was the commander-in-chief in Libby of the Council of Five, the friend and helper of everybody. He was of the Council upon whose discretion, sagacity and secrecy everything depended. We all looked up to him and loved him. So much depended upon secrecy and stillness, our hopes for liberty and life and one more sight of home and friends, that the men who worked and dug were as silent as rats, and as industrious. They dug and worked, or, as the Journal probably would have it, "gnawed" away in the darkness and utter silence. Death was the penalty of failure, and with bated breath, they dug on, rarely whispering and often not knowing who were their helpers, caring or knowing little or nothing as to who was the "head rat," satisfied that it was better to dig on desperately rather than "die like a rat in a hole." I always considered Gen. Streight the projector and superintendent of the last tunnel, through which he escaped; and I, with others, was willing to work under his direction.

One word more: Gen. Streight has never claimed any special merit in the tunnel business, wonderful achievement as it was. He always insisted upon giving to the boys full credit, and disclaimed for himself anything like the prominence he really had. His lecture before the Veteran Association, of which a mere synopsis is printed, has been called for earnestly a thousand times. He has been importuned and earnestly besought to make it by the old soldiers and citizens for years. It is the plain unvarnished narrative of an honest, frank, noble old soldier, of whose achievements the tunnel work and subsequent escape was a very small part. He deserves the thanks, the gratitude and the honors of his countrymen; and the pitiful attempt to defame and defile him merits the scorn, denunciation and contempt of every honorable man believing in justice and fair play.

William Wallick,
Late Captain Co. G, 51st Indiana, Peru, Indiana.

Due to his battlefield and prisoner of war experiences, William suffered chronic health problems for the rest of his life. However, he did receive a disability pension from the government for his sciatica and deafness. He continued his carpentry trade as best he could but his physical impairments made full-time work extremely difficult. William died after a prolonged summer illness on August 31, 1892, at age 59. In 1898 his wife, Mary, had to fight to get her widow's pension increased from a paltry $8 a month to $20 a month (William was receiving $27 a month at the time of his death). But it is through Mary's legal battles that William Wallick's military record is forever emblazoned into the congressional record of the United States House of Representatives. On January 24, 1898, the Committee on Invalid Pensions received and approved a report submitted by Indiana Representative Robert W. Miers, requesting that because of William Wallick's exemplary service to his country, Mary's pension should be increased. What follows is Representative Miers' full report to the committee.

MARY E. WALLICK.

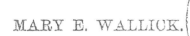

JANUARY 24, 1898.—Committed to the Committee of the Whole House and ordered to be printed.

Mr. MIERS, from the Committee on Invalid Pensions, submitted the following

REPORT.

[To accompany H. R. 1802.]

The Committee on Invalid Pensions, to whom was referred the bill (H. R. 1802) granting a pension to Mary E. Wallick, widow of William Wallick, late captain Company G, Fifty-first Indiana Volunteer Infantry, having carefully examined and considered the facts presented, respectfully report:

This bill proposes to increase from $8 to $20 per month the pension of Mary E. Wallick, of Peru, Ind., widow of William Wallick, late captain Company G, Fifty-first Regiment Indiana Volunteer Infantry.

William Wallick entered the service as a second lieutenant October 8, 1861; was promoted to captain Company G, Fifty-first Indiana Infantry Volunteers, in February, 1863, and served faithfully until honorably discharged, December 16, 1864. He was taken prisoner with Colonel Streight's command at Rome, Ga., on May 3, 1863, and confined in Libby Prison until February 9, 1864, when he and others escaped, and after much hardship and exertion reached the Union lines sick, emaciated, and nearly starved, and suffering from rheumatism, the result of his hardship and exposure. Though he returned to duty and performed his part, the testimony shows clearly that he never recovered from his broken-down and weakened condition.

He was pensioned at $27 per month for sciatic rheumatism of left side and nearly total deafness of both ears, and died at Peru, Ind., August 31, 1892.

Dr. Willis B. Stewart, who treated him during June, July, and August, 1892, testifies that:

He suffered with rheumatism and malassimilation, and as a result was feeble and emaciated somewhat when he took his bed. He had many erratic pains before he took his bed, suffered much with left side and hip and thigh with a chronic form of sciatic rheumatism. After he was bedfast some twenty or more days (as near as I can remember), there developed in his left pleura an asthenic type of pleurisy, which in some eighteen days invaded the lower part of the left lung; this went through a slow process of hepatization and abscess. His nervous system was prostrated and

13

impoverished and he was much weakened and emaciated before his last sickness developed. The pain from the sciatica so enervated his system that it was an easy prey to asthenic inflammation, and I am of the opinion that his last sickness was the result of, and induced by, his impoverished physical condition, as a result of pain and suffering caused by long-standing sciatic rheumatism of the left hip. This condition of enervative emaciation and physical debility superinduced the inveterate inflammatory process in the pleura and rendered the system unable to withstand the drain of a chronic pleurisy of a purulent character, and he died from sheer exhaustion and inanition, as the result of the purulent inflammatory process in left pleura and lung.

The widow, who was married to the soldier March 11, 1860, was pensioned December 6, 1892, at $8 per month, under the act of June 27, 1890, certificate No. 355159. She is now 55 years of age, of frail and delicate physique, is in poor health and in very necessitous financial condition, and unable to perform manual labor. She has no relatives on whom she can depend for assistance.

From the testimony presented, showing clearly that the soldier was a sound, able-bodied man when he entered the service, and an invalid thereafter from causes arising in and due to his hardships and exposures in service, and from no other cause, your committee can and do readily accept his death cause as due to his army service. In fact your committee entertain no doubt on the subject.

This young wife gave her husband to her country soon after their marriage. He was a faithful and a brave soldier, and endured the sufferings of Libby prison when his health was broken and he incurred disabilities which resulted in his death.

The beneficiary of this bill is entitled to the $20 per month given by the general law to the widow of a captain whose death-cause was incurred while he held that rank. She is now in a destitute and suffering condition, and her mistake in applying under the act of June 27, 1890, will not be held to deprive her of her legal and equitable rights. Nor under the circumstances will we compel her to make a new application. The death of many of the important witnesses makes it impossible to obtain their evidence in the form that the Pension Office would require.

The Committee attach a history of his service by Captain Ballou, a comrade, and report the bill with the recommendation that it pass when amended as follows: Amend the title by striking out the words "granting a pension to" and insert in lieu thereof the words "increasing the pension of;" and at the end of line 9 add the following, "in lieu of the pension she is now receiving."

WASHINGTON, D. C., *March 2, 1896.*

SIR: By request of Hon. George W. Steele, I have the honor to state to your committee what I know of the services of Capt. William Wallick, late of Company G, Fifty-first Indiana Infantry, in behalf of whose widow, Mary Wallick, a bill, No. 1802, providing for additional pension, has been referred to you, and trust that brevity, if nothing else, will command attention.

I knew Captain Wallick before the war; we were neighbors and friends; we enlisted at the same time and became officers in the same company, and served as such from October, 1861, to February, 1863, when I resigned, and he became captain of the company.

When I say that he was an ideal soldier, brave and true to all obligations as citizen or soldier, I have said all that the most extended vocabulary can express.

He was captured, as will appear from the records of the War Department, and confined in Libby Prison many months. He was one of the trusted and confidential officers who dug the tunnel, made famous in history, through which many officers of the United States Army made their escape, and he, with one comrade, was the first to reach the Union lines and report the "prison delivery."

Clad only in the clothes he wore when he entered the prison nine months before, begrimed with dirt, half starved and haggard, with face and hands scratched by briers incident to night travel (for daylight and the roads had to be avoided, it was not surprising that General Butler's chief of staff, to whom he first reported, should suspect his sincerity and genuineness. But after an hour's cross-examination the bugle sounded "Boots and saddles," and in fifteen minutes 2,000 cavalry troops were on the gallop to the front to rescue such other of the escaped prisoners as might be making their way to the Union lines.

Many gallant officers were thus restored to the Union Army through the intrepidity and endurance of Captain Wallick.

Captain Wallick was the first of the escaped prisoners to reach Washington. He was a total stranger here, only remembering the late Schuyler Colfax, who was then our Representative and Speaker of the House.

To the House he made his way and sent his card to the Speaker, who had read in the morning papers of the prison delivery.

The Speaker rushed to the corridor, seized the young officer by the hand, and throwing one arm around his neck pulled him in on the floor of the House and announced to Congress the arrival of one of the escaped prisoners.

Instantly the House was in an uproar; Members left their seats and crowded round the officer, plying him with questions, until it become evident that no business could be done and the House took a recess; and the dirty, ragged, disfigured, and extremely modest young officer was forced to take the platform in front of the Speaker's chair and tell the Congress the particulars of his escape.

After thirty days' leave of absence Captain Wallick joined his regiment and served faithfully until mustered out.

He was mustered out the day before the battle of Nashville, in December, 1864, but at the solicitation of the colonel of his regiment the captain remained in command of the company, which he and I had recruited, during the great battle of December 15 and 16, 1864, in front of Nashville, Tenn., thus imperiling his life without the hope of fee or reward in case of a casualty to himself.

I make this statement partly on personal knowledge and partly on the statements of Captain Wallick, Col. A. D. Streight, and Schuyler Colfax, all deceased, made to me at a time when there was no thought of such a bill being introduced as that to which I have referred.

Let me, in conclusion, express the sentiment of hundreds of thousands of surviving soldiers of the late war, that no general's widow is entitled to a higher consideration by you than is Mary E. Wallick.

Very respectfully,

J. Y. BALLOU.

Hon. S. S. KIRKPATRICK,
Chairman Subcommittee on Invalid Pensions, House of Representatives.

An Act Increasing the pension of Mary E. Wallick.

Be it enacted by the Senate and House of Representatives of the United States of America in Congress assembled, That the Secretary of the Interior be, and he is hereby, authorized and directed to place upon the pension roll, subject to the provisions and limitations of the pension laws, the name of Mary E. Wallick, widow of William Wallick, late captain of Company G, Fifty-first Regiment Indiana Volunteer Infantry, and pay to her the sum of twenty dollars per month in lieu of the pension she is now receiving.

Approved, April 11, 1898.

DEPARTMENT OF THE INTERIOR,
April 18, 1898.

The above is a true copy of the original as certified by the Department of State.

Edward M. Dawson

Chief Clerk.

Mary Wallick died May 25, 1906, and was buried in Reyburn Cemetery next to William and their only child, Flora, who in 1876, as a fifteen-year-old girl, died of tuberculosis. It is very appropriate that this volume of Civil War biographies should start with William Wallick. In the Wallick family there is no greater example of personal courage, sacrifice and honor exhibited during the American Civil War than the iconic service of Captain William Wallick.

Captain William Wallick, 51st Indiana Volunteer Infantry.

Craig Dunn Collection

Comrades-in-Arms

Father
Benjamin Jr.   109th IVI

Brothers
Charles F.   87th IVI
John W.   138th & 151st IVI

Uncles
Christopher   109th IVI
Wesley   109th & 151st IVI

Cousins
Benjamin   162nd OVI
Jeremiah   109th IVI
William F.   13th, 109th & 138th IVI
Washington   71st PVI

William Wallick is buried with his wife, Mary, and daughter, Flora, in Reyburn Cemetery, Peru, Indiana.

Enhanced inscription of William's headstone.

Obituary for Captain Wallick.

Died

Captain William Wallick died at his home on West Seventh street. Wednesday Aug. 31st, 1892, at 5:25 a. m. of phthisis pulmonalis or hasty consumption, in the sixtieth year of his age. Captain Wallick was born in Canal Dover, Ohio, on November 4th, 1832 and came to Miami county with his parents in 1840, locating in Peru. He was united in marriage with Mary E. Burns at Canal Dover, Ohio, but one child, a daughter, was born to this union, who died of consumption at fifteen years of age. He enlisted in Co. G 51st Indiana Volunteer Infantry, in August 1861 and on the organization of the company, was chosen second lieutenant. He took part with his regiment in many battles of the late war. He was taken prisoner near Rome, Georgia, in the summer of 1863, and sent together with A. D. Strieght, Colonel of the 51st regiment and number of other officers and members of the regiment, to Libby prison at Richmond, Virginia, where he was confined as a prisoner for more than nine months. Captain Wallick took an active part in the planning and digging of the Libby prison tunnel, made famous in history, through which 109 of the inmates of that institution gained their liberty, some of them only temporarily, as fifty-six of them were re-captured and re-incarcerated, but the deceased was among the fifty-three lucky ones who reached the Union lines. He came home early in 1864, and remained two months, when he went to the front, rejoined his regiment and served until the close of the war. He was successively promoted from the first position to which he was chosen to the First Lieutenancy and Captaincy of his company, the latter honor being conferred upon him while yet confined within the walls of Libby prison. At the close of the war he came home and after a short stay removed with his family to St. Johns, Michigan. After a three years residence at that place they returned to Peru and have resided here since. The Captain's health was broken down by the hardships and exposures incident to soldier life, and he has been far from a strong, healthy man during all these years that have passed since the close of the war. The funeral will occur from the residence, No. 108 West Seventh street, Friday afternoon, Sept. 2d, at 2 o'clock, under the auspices of Wm. B. Reyburn Post, G. A. R., of which the deceased was a member. Services at the house by Rev. S. C. Dickey. Burial in the Reyburn cemetery, 1½ miles west of the city.

Map 3 Journey of Charles F. Wallick with the 87th Indiana Volunteer Infantry.

Charles F. Wallick - 87th Indiana Volunteer Infantry, Co. C

2

Rank: Private, promoted to 4th Corporal

Place of enlistment: Miami County, Peru, Indiana

Mustered into Federal service: August 31, 1862

Service time: 2 years, 10 months, 23 days

Born: August 8, 1843 - Miami County, Indiana

Age at enlistment: 19 years old

Physical description: height - 5' 7", dark hair, blue eyes

Civilian occupation: miller

Family Lineage: Charles, son of "Peru" Benjamin Junior, son of "Peru" Benjamin Senior, son of Johannes, son of Hans Michael Wallick

Charles Fletcher Wallick was one of three brothers from the Benjamin Wallick Jr. family who served in the Federal army during the American Civil War. He was a younger brother to Libby Prison escapee, William Wallick, and twin brother to John Wesley Wallick, another volunteer. All three brothers enlisted in Peru, Indiana, with eldest sibling William being the first to join the army in 1861. He was followed by Charles in 1862 and John Wesley in 1864. Even their father, Benjamin Jr., was mustered into Federal service for a very brief period during the summer of 1863. No other Wallick family unit contributed more manpower to our country's war effort.

Benjamin Wallick Jr. (1804-1884) was born, raised and learned carpentry in Tuscarawas County, Ohio. In 1841 he decided to uproot his young family, taking along his mother and father, to start a new life further west in Miami County, Indiana (brother William was born in Ohio but the twins, Charles and John Wesley, were born in Indiana). Benjamin built and operated a very successful sawmill on Little Pike Creek where all three boys at one time or another worked for their father.

Benjamin Wallick home- Little Pipe Creek, Peru, IN. In this 1879 picture, Charles is far right, holding a rifle (see next page), and an unidentified woman is by the fence. Charles's mother, Eliza, is in the doorway and Charles's twin brother, John Wesley, is in the center holding a rifle. This is the only known picture of the two Wallick brothers.

Charles F. Wallick

Miami County Historical Society

Charles was working at the Wallick sawmill in August of 1862 and by that time the Civil War was well into its second year. There was a strong push by the Federal government to recruit more volunteers that summer and Charles was one of thousands from the Hoosier State to enlist. He joined a unit of Miami County men who eventually became Company C of the 87th Indiana Volunteer Infantry. The regiment was organized in South Bend, Indiana, on August 28, 1862, and was mustered into Federal service on August 31st with 945 men. With the eventual addition of 317 more recruits and replacements, 1,262 soldiers served in the regiment over the course of its three-year history.

The regiment's first major engagement was with General Buell at the Battle of Perryville in October of 1862. Then on September 19 and 20, 1863, the regiment had a true test of its mettle when it fought heroically at the Battle of Chickamauga, where more than 50 percent of its men became casualties (Charles was one of them, with a bullet wound to his left hand). In May 1864, the regiment chased Confederate General Joseph Johnston through the hills of north Georgia and eventually helped capture Atlanta. Charles then took part in General Shermans "March to the Sea," bringing the war to the civilians in the heartland of the South. The regiment stayed in Savannah for two months to resupply and then moved up through South Carolina, where they created more havoc and destruction there than in their march through Georgia.

For a time, Charles and his regiment were attached to General Sherman's Pioneer Corps, which became legendary in their march up through the Carolinas. Comprised of lumbermen from Michigan and rail-splitters from Illinois and Indiana, the Pioneers corduroyed roads, built bridges, and forded rivers. The corps allowed Union forces, with 2,500 wagons and 600 ambulances, to move at the rate of twelve miles a day (the 87th Regiment's responsibility at that time was guarding and helping to move the wagon trains). Such a rapid pace through the Carolina swamps in the middle of winter was thought to be impossible. After South Carolina was thoroughly humbled, Sherman's Army moved into North Carolina where it fought a few small engagements and then moved with the Federals to defeat the Rebel army at the Battle of Bentonville, the last major battle in the east. They proceeded to Richmond, Virginia, and then to Washington, D.C., where they marched in the Grand Review of the Western Army. Finally, on June 21, 1865, and with full military honors, the 87th Indiana Volunteer Infantry was mustered out of Federal service in Indianapolis with only 313 of its original 945 soldiers, Charles F. Wallick being one of them.

We know a great deal about the wartime experiences of Charles and his brother William because both served in famous regiments that documented their adventures in post-war histories and each brother kept a diary for a short time while serving with his unit. Charles' original diary was lost with the passing of time, but a partial transcript has survived at the Miami County Historical Society's Museum in Peru, Indiana. Although the transcript is incomplete, it does contain daily entries about his regiment fighting its way from northern Georgia to Atlanta and its march of destruction from Savannah through the Carolinas. He closes his diary by recording the death of President Lincoln. Unfortunately, Charles' experiences in General Sherman's "March to the Sea" were never transcribed and forever lost. A few excerpts from his diary are included in the narrative of his regiment's activities.

There were two Charles Wallicks who served in the American Civil War, one from Indiana and one from Ohio. The one here, Charles **F.** Wallick, served with the 87th Indiana Volunteer Infantry. The other Charles Wallick (his comrades called him "Charley") served in the 16th Ohio Volunteer Infantry (OVI). To help avoid any confusion, these biographical sketches will refer to the Ohio soldier as "Charley" and the Indiana soldier as "Charles."

Charles F. Wallick with the 87th Indiana Volunteer Infantry

1862

AUG 31 The 87th Indiana Volunteer Infantry is mustered into Federal service and ordered to Louisville, KY.

SEP The regiment pursues Confederate General Bragg in Kentucky and is then posted in the vicinity of Louisville, KY. Here they are called upon to defend that threatened city.

OCT 8   Battle of Perryville Charles and the 87th IVI experience their first taste of battle at Perryville, KY. The regiment is hastily marched onto the battlefield at the close of the day to reinforce the Union army, which is in serious trouble. The 87th is the last regiment in their brigade to arrive on the field and nearly cause a catastrophe in their first major engagement. Darkness is falling and the regiment is anxious as they march through woods to go into battle formation behind the 2nd Minnesota. The 87th is anticipating an encounter with the enemy at any moment and seeing dark silhouettes before them, they cock their muskets, ready to fire. The sounds of the hammers being pulled all at once on a few hundred percussion lock plates alerts the Minnesotans. Colonel Judson Bishop of the 2nd Minnesota later said, *"A prompt and vigorous introduction of the two regiments by name probably saved us from what would have been a sad misfortune."* He added, *"We had no experience in the whole war so startling as the cocking of muskets behind us."*

Once in line, the 87th is ordered to lie down near the edge of the woods on the terraced-like ground and not fire until the enemy is positively identified. The order to fire never needs to be given. Though they fail to be harassed by infantry, three Rebel batteries do locate them and commence fire. The cannon shells are *"deathly music... some sounded like a threshing machine cylinder when they went through the air and the* grape *shot sounded like hail in the trees and leaves,"* wrote a 2nd Minnesota corporal. Amazingly, there are only two men from the 87th Indiana who are wounded. Later that evening the regiment moves forward and becomes the lead unit in the line of battle in anticipation of an early morning attack. The night is chilly and they sleep with their arms on the battlefield. There is good reason for a renewed Confederate attack in the morning, for the Rebels have out fought the Federals, whose army is at least a third larger. Over 7,600 men have fallen in battle, 4,200 Union versus 3,400 Confederate. But General Bragg, commander of the Confederate forces, decides to retreat in the face of being vastly outnumbered. Perryville is a strategic defeat for the Confederates as this engagement forces them to withdraw from the state of Kentucky.

NOV 15 After ten weeks in the field only 400 men are listed "effective for duty," due to illness and the hardships of the soldier's life. This is less than half the regiment's enlistment strength.

DEC 14 Only 200 are present for roll call, most are absent on sick call. The 87th left South Bend, IN, on August 31, with 945 men. Disease caused twice as many deaths as did casualties in battle during the Civil War.

DEC 31   Battle of Stones River Part of Charles' division are at this battle, however, Charles and his brigade are near Gallatin, TN, guarding the Louisville & Nashville Railroad.

1863

JAN - MAR The 87th IVI is on duty in middle-Tennessee.

MAR 5 Charles is involved in a raid to Columbia, TN, against General Nathan Bedford Forrest's cavalry.

JUN 23 The Union army begins their Tullahoma Campaign in middle-Tennessee by starting over the Cumberland Mountains toward Chattanooga, TN.

87th IVI monument on Snodgrass Hill.

JUL - AUG The 87th maneuvers through the Cumberland Mountains to reach Chattanooga. It is slow going through the valleys and dangerous mountain roads.

SEP 12 The regiment arrives at Chickamauga Creek, supposedly an Indian name that means "River of Death."

SEP 19 - 20   Battle of Chickamauga   Chickamauga is the bloodiest battle between the western armies and the worst two-day loss of life in the entire Civil War. On the first morning of battle the 87th turns away three fierce assaults by the Confederates. The regiment is ordered about the battlefield, moving from place to place, and continues to engage the enemy in heavy fighting throughout the day. The regiment bivouacs without fires on the first evening of battle and resumes their stubborn defensive line the next morning at Kelly Field. Distant cousins Isaiah Wallick of the 49th Ohio, and Levi Wallick of the 44th Indiana, also see action on or near Kelly Field on the second day of battle.

By the afternoon of September 20th, the Union army is in serious trouble and in danger of being overwhelmed by the Rebel forces. In order to provide a safe withdrawal of all Union troops from the battlefield the 87th, plus remnants of the 44th Indiana, join forces with other Federal units on Snodgrass Hill and offer a stiff resistance to the attacking Confederates. This hotly contested late-afternoon fight helps avoid a Federal rout and it creates the opportunity for an orderly retreat back to Chattanooga (see page 81 for a more detailed narrative). Major General George Thomas is so successful in organizing this last-ditch effort on Snodgrass Hill that he is awarded the moniker "The Rock of Chickamauga."

The 87th begins the Battle of Chickamauga with 366 officers and men, only one-third of its original strength. By sundown on the second day only 174 men are available to fight in the engagement. One hundred and ninety-two have become casualties in the 36-hour battle. This 52 percent casualty rate inflicted on the 87th is the highest of all 28 Indiana regiments who were present at Chickamauga and the eighth highest rate of all 131 Union infantry regiments engaged. The 87th Indiana and its brigade is one of the last organized units from the Union army to leave the battlefield.

At some point during the battle Charles is wounded in the left hand by a Rebel ball. He will spend a month in a Chattanooga hospital before going home on furlough.

NOV 25 Battle of Missionary Ridge   While Charles is home recuperating from his hand wound, in Chattanooga his regiment is taking part in a spectacular charge up Missionary Ridge, where the Federal army overruns well-entrenched Confederate positions. The 87th is one of the first to plant its colors on the summit of Missionary Ridge. This is also the battle where distant cousin Isaiah Wallick is mortally wounded. Isaiah struggles for two days but eventually succumbs to death on November 27, 1863, the day after Thanksgiving.

DEC 25 Christmas Day   Charles returns from his furlough and rejoins his regimental brothers, who are stationed in Chattanooga, TN.

1864

JAN - APR The 87th IVI is posted in the Chattanooga/Northern Georgia region, preparing for General Sherman's campaign to take Atlanta.

APR 25 Charles F. Wallick writes his first entry into the new diary his friend and comrade, Isaiah Shafer, sent him from the Soldiers Home in Indianapolis (Charles **W**allick **D**iary- **CWD**). He will faithfully make an addition to the diary every day for the next year. His entry pattern is always the same. He will enter a daily weather report, acknowledge any receipt of mail and then give a very brief accounting of the day's activities. Sometimes he will mention sending or receiving letters from brother "Bill" (William Wallick) of the 51st Indiana, who is also posted near Chattanooga, TN. The location of Charles' original diary is unknown. However, a transcript of the diary was typewritten by Walter Reyburn sometime after the war and survives today. Walter was perhaps an uncle or cousin to Charles, for the Reyburns were related by marriage to the Wallicks. Unfortunately, the transcript was not completed and the entries for July 3rd through December 31, 1864, have been lost. A few selections from Charles' diary are presented in the body of his biographical sketch so he can tell, in his own words, about his experiences during the war. The spelling and grammar have been left unedited in these excerpts.[5]

APR 30 CWD *"The night was cold with some rain. The morning was very pleasant...I tried for a pass to go to Chattanooga to see Bill Wallick but failed to get the commanding General to sign it for me. I was very much out of humour all day. My health is very good excepting a very severe cold I caught carelessly. There was a detail sent out of the Division to Nashville after mules for Company and Regimental teams."*

Although Charles does not know it at the time, his pass is denied because all 110,000 men in General Sherman's Army are getting prepared to step-off toward Atlanta in a few days. Charles tries to get another pass May 1, but that one is also denied.

MAY 3 CWD *"... This day one year ago, Captain Wallick was captured near Rome, Ga. He is now at Chattanooga with his regiment."*

MAY 7 The 87th begins its "March to Atlanta" Campaign CWD *"The first thing on docket was to get up at 3 o'clock in the morning and get breakfast, strike tents, pack knapsacks and we moved at seven o'clock. The day was intolerably hot but we marched very steady and rested several times. We camped about one mile southwest from Tunnel Hill. Our troops skirmished here today with the Rebels. Our men fired a shot from the bridge with our cannon. We went into camp about three o'clock a.m. and pitched our tents and took our rest of which we needed."*

Almost daily, for the next four months, there will be skirmishes and engagements with the Confederate army.

Battlefield at Resaca, GA.
Charles F. Wallick and distant cousin Michael Wallick
fought together on this field at the Battle of Resaca.

MAY 14 Battle of Resaca Both Charles F. and "Daviess" Michael are engaged in this battle. In fact, they could have been within a few hundred yards of each other and never have known it. It is also very likely that they didn't know of each other's existence because of the great distance between their family tree branches. Charles' regiment was placed in the center of the Union line with Michael's regiment cattycorner and behind them in support. As the battle progresses, Michael and the 27th are moved to the far left of the Union line and there they are later engaged in combat. Michael is wounded in the left hip by an artillery shell fragment during this battle.

---

[5] The complete Charles F. Wallick diary transcript can be read in Appendix I, page 197.

MAY 14 CWD "...*The skirmishing began about seven o'clock and our division was in the second line. We moved forward till the balls commenced whistling around us. Our rations were out and we drew here in line of battle and about 11 o'clock we moved forward and our men made a charge. It was the most awful musketry I ever heard and in the evening the cannonading was the hardest. The fight has begun sure.*"

MAY 22 CWD "*The morning is very beautiful and the golden sun shines down upon us in all his glory and richness. The mail come this morning but did not bring any news for me. The day past away and we did not move along in the evening. The mail come. The captain received a letter that stated that William was wounded but it was only a report. I do not know whether it is so or not.* [William's complied service record does not mention him being wounded, but not all wounds were recorded]. *Our chaplain preached to us today and received good news from the Potomac.*"

MAY 25 - JUN 5 Battle of New Hope Church and Allatoona Hills CWD "*The morning was clear and the day was warm. Heavy cannonading was heard along the front this morning. We are now about 30 miles from Atlanta. Our front is about six miles ahead of us. We moved out of camp about 12 o'clock and marched about two miles farther to the front and went into camp for the night. There was heavy skirmishing all day, today. The mail come in but I did not receive anything from the north and the day wore away in all its glory.*"

JUN 20 CWD "*The morning is very wet and the rain continues to fall. The roads are almost impassable for our teams. There has been more heavy cannonading today than ever I heard before at one time. Our shells would burst on the very top of the mountain* [Kennesaw Mountain]. *The Rebels shell more today than they have since we left Resaca. They have a very strong position here for the artillery. The mail did not come in today. I had my shirt hit today by a ball from a Reb and the day was noisy.*"

JUN 27 Battle of Kennesaw Mountain In order to break the Confederate line in the hills of northern Georgia, General Sherman makes a disastrous frontal assault at Kennesaw Mountain. There are over 2,000 Union casualties verses 500 Confederate. Sherman accomplishes nothing in the process except getting many of his soldiers killed. He never makes that same mistake again. Fortunately, Charles' brigade is held in reserve.

CWD "*The morning finds us some four miles from where we were yesterday. We moved into position in the rear of the 2nd Division of our Corp. We were hardly in our place when the 2nd Division made a charge on the Rebel works at this point, with what success I am not able to tell yet; but there were several hundred killed and wounded. The day was warm as ever I saw. The majority of our wounded men were only slightly wounded. Our division was not in the engagement today. We were held in reserve.*"

Little Kennesaw Mountain shortly after the battle. This is the sector where Charles and the 87th were deployed during the Battle of Kennesaw Mountain.

JUN 29 CWD "*The morning was pleasant and the day was very hot. There was a cessation of hostilities today until our men could bury our dead. Our men and the Rebels were all together during the time of the flag of truce. When the time was up, a good many of them deserted and ran and jumped into our entrenchments. Our line of battle is in a stone's throw of the Rebel's work. Our works are at the foot of a hill and the Rebels are on the top.*"

JUL 2 CWD *"The morning was pleasant, the day was hot. The mail come in today. The skirmishing is still going on. We are taking it somewhat easy now. The Rebels say they intend to celebrate the Fourth of July by whipping us out of our works. Let them come on. That is what we want them to try. We think that we will be rid of here and that the Rebels will make a permanent stand here. The weather is dry and the roads are full of dust. Every place that you would go that is so."*

Unfortunately, this was the last diary entry transcribed by Walter Reyburn for the year 1864. Why only half of the transcript was copied is a mystery. We will miss hearing Charles' first-hand account of Sherman's "March to the Sea" and his "Siege of Atlanta and Savannah." Charles' diary will continue on Jan 1, 1865.

JUL 19 - 20 Battle of Peach Tree Creek On July 20th Charles and his regiment are under heavy artillery fire all day but are otherwise not engaged.

JUL 22 - SEP 2 Siege of Atlanta and Battle of Jonesboro On August 31st the 87th IVI is posted southwest of Atlanta and held in reserve at the Battle of Jonesboro. Three days later the city is evacuated by the Rebel army.

SEP 29 - NOV 3 The 87th Regiment has operations and small engagements with General Hood's Confederate forces in northern Georgia and Alabama.

NOV 15 - DEC 10 Sherman's March to the Sea. Without exception, all the men in Sherman's army who make the march tell of the wonderful foraging and most of the men say they never ate so well in all their lives. This is, of course, at the expense of the Southern civilian population. Commanders try to keep order as best they can during the march but when the stated objective of their mission is to destroy the South's ability to wage war and make the war come to ALL the southern peoples, not just the armies, things quickly get out of hand. Sherman's own estimate of property destroyed is put at over 100 million 1864 dollars. It is unfortunate that this portion of Charles' diary was not transcribed. He would have given a fine record of this event.

DEC 10 - 21 Siege of Savannah

DEC 25 Christmas Day and Surrender of Savannah. Sherman's Army finally gets new rations, supplies and long-awaited mail after being on the march for six weeks through Georgia.

1865

JAN 8 CWD *"The morning was cold and the day was warm. The mail come in and I received a letter from home.* [The day before, Charles says he had not received any mail since November 14th, almost two months previous. The March to the Sea and Siege of Savannah had put them out of touch with mail and supplies since leaving Atlanta]. *The folks were all well. Bill* [brother William] *was out of the service, his time was out. My health is very good and the diarrhea has come back on me but is not very bad and does not hurt me as it did before. The time goes very slow. My old watch is not running, the matter is it is so dirty it can't run."*

FEB 5 Charles and the 87th begin their march in the Carolinas Campaign. Sherman's Army causes more mayhem and destruction to the "Cradle of the rebellion," South Carolina, than they ever did in Georgia.

FEB 15 CWD *"The morning was cold and wet, the day was cloudy. We march at 7 o'clock and on the way we saw a man that had been accidentally shot. We passed over a very hilly and rugged country. The road was downhill all the day long. We marched all day very hard and went into camp after dark. We drew rations, one day's rations to do three days. The forage is plenty, we live fat off the country."*

FEB 16 CWD *"We are train guards yet. Companies C and I went out a foraging and the rest was put along the trains at various points as guards. We passed through a town by the name of Texington [Lexington, SC]. We laid here long enough to get dinner then took up our line of march for Columbia, the capital of this state. We went into camp at about 7 miles from the city. We had all the potatoes we wanted to eat."*

FEB 17 CWD *"The morning was cold and the day warm. We marched around ten miles and crossed a river by the name of Saluda and passed by Columbia to the right. The roads were very bad. The country is very hilly and is covered with pine, cedar and oak. It is not so sandy here as it was in Georgia. The time passed away very fast with me. I saw more fire since I have been in this state than I ever saw since I have been in the service."*

Columbia, South Carolina. This picture was taken from the State Capitol Building in 1865 after the passing of the Union army.

The last sentence in Charles' diary is not surprising. The Federal army laid waste to the South Carolina capital and many other towns and plantations as they traveled through the Palmetto State.

MAR 19 - 21 Battle of Bentonville, North Carolina The 87th is not engaged in this battle but is ordered to the rear to guard the wagon trains. Charles states, *"There has been some hard fighting, but we were so far off that we could not hear it from where the train was."* Hewit Wallick, son of veteran "Daviess" Michael and distant cousin to Charles, is with the 38th Indiana Infantry and in the front lines at the beginning of the battle. His regiment is eventually forced to retreat and is chased off the field by the Rebel army. Charles and Hewit have been in the same army corps since the beginning of the Carolinas Campaign.

MAR 31 CWD *"I witnessed a sight today I never wish to see again, that was the shooting of a soldier for inhuman conduct. The court sentenced him to be shot for the third offence. There were a great many lookers on and there was one brigade of infantry formed three sides and he was shot in the center. The boys did not like to see it, although it may be for the best. It is not for me to decide."*

APR 12 CWD *"We received a dispatch from Grant that Lee had surrendered his whole force to him* [the surrender happened April 9th]. *We marched about 14 miles and went into camp for the night. We're within 13 miles of Raleigh* [North Carolina]. *The time goes fast."*

APR 18 CWD *"We laid in camp. Company C went out foraging. They brought in all the sweet potatoes we wanted to use and sorghum molasses also and other things. We received the orders that President Lincoln had been assassinated in a theater and other officials had been fixed upon for the same."*

This is the last entry of any significance that Charles wrote in his diary.

APR 26 Surrender of the Confederate Army Confederate General Joseph Johnston surrenders to General Sherman at the Bennett House in Durham, NC. Two weeks earlier General Lee had surrendered the Army of Northern Virginia to General Grant. This Confederate Army of the Carolinas, Georgia, and Florida is the largest Rebel force in the field and Johnston surrenders over 89,000 soldiers. It is the largest surrender of soldiers from either side during the Civil War.[6] Charles and the 87th Regiment are with General Sherman's army during this event.

APR 29 - MAY 19   The 87th Indiana Volunteer Infantry marches to Washington, D.C., via Richmond, VA.

MAY 24   Grand Review of General Sherman's 65,000 men Army of the West in Washington, D.C.

Excerpt from *A Stupendous Effort, The 87th Indiana in The War of the Rebellion* by Jack K. Overmyer:

> *Marching 12 abreast* [down Pennsylvania Ave.], *it took more than six hours for them to pass the White House reviewing stand before President Johnson, Lt. General Ulysses S. Grant and other dignitaries. The 87th Indiana's turn came about noon and its Hoosiers never forgot the magnificence and the thrill of the sight that greeted them as they wheeled about the Capital and looked down the long, broad avenue, endless troops, marching curb-to-curb to the rhythm of the martial music, their bright uniforms and muskets glistening in the sunshine. It was a moment to savor for the rest of their lives.*

JUN 10   Charles is mustered out of Federal service at a formal military ceremony on the State Capitol grounds in Indianapolis, IN.

Epilogue - Charles F. Wallick returned home to Peru, Indiana, and began working for the railroad. On November 10, 1876, he married Lucy A. Search and the couple had three children. He became an invalid late in life and was moved in mid-December, 1903, to the Soldiers Home in Lafayette, Indiana. He struggled with multiple health issues there until he died on March 3, 1904, with Lucy at his side.

Grand Review of the Armies, Washington D.C. May 24, 1865.
Both Charles and distant cousin Hewit Wallick were in this parade.

---

[6] There was a great amount of respect between the combatants both during and after the Civil War. General Johnston was a pallbearer at General Sherman's funeral. It was a blustery, cold and rainy February day and during the procession a friend of General Johnston pleaded with the General to wear his hat. Johnston replied, "If I were in his place and he standing in mine, he would not put on his hat." General Johnston caught a cold that day, which turned into pneumonia and within a month the General was dead.

Obituary for Charles Fletcher Wallick.

Obituary.

The deceased, Charles F. Wallick, was born in Peru, Ind., August 8th, 1843, and has resided here continuously until his removal to the Soldiers' Home at Lafayette on December 16, 1903, where he remained until the grim reaper claimed him, March 3, 1904, at the age of sixty years, seven months and twenty-four days.

He has been a long and patient sufferer, conscious most of the time during his illness, and conscious when the Almighty called him and gave him relief from his suffering. He prayed to be allowed his mental faculties at the last and seemingly his prayers were granted, as when dying he bid his wife good-bye, telling her not to worry, as he was leaving a world of suffering and was not afraid of death, so he would just step on the old ship and all would be over.

He was a member of the Jasper Packard Post, No. 589, having been reinstated since he went to the home. He leaves a wife, Lucy A. Wallick, two sons, Charles Milo and William Custer Wallick, and one daughter, Mrs. John E. Miles, and one sister, Mrs. Emma Ewing, of Rochester, to mourn his loss.

Mr. Wallick served in the civil war, enlisting in Company C, Eighty-seventh Indiana infantry August 31st, 1862, and was mustered out June 10th, 1865. He was with his company continually except for a period of two months when he had a furlough because of a gunshot wound.

The remains will arrive at 3:25 tomorrow and be taken to the Methodist church where the funeral services will be held by Rev. Cain. Burial in Reyburn cemetery. *.*

Courtesy of the Miami County Historical Society

Comrades-in-Arms

Father
Benjamin Jr.   109 IVI

Brothers
William   51st IVI
John Wesley   138th IVI, 151st IVI

Uncles
Christopher   109th IVI
Wesley   109th IVI, 138th IVI

Cousins
Benjamin   162nd OVI
Jeremiah   109th IVI
Washington   71st PVI
William F.   13th, 109th, 138th IVI

This modest headstone reads:

**Corp'l
C. F. Wallick
Co. C
87th IND. INF.**

Charles F. Wallick's grave can be found
in Reyburn Cemetery, Peru, Indiana.
He is buried near his parents, Benjamin Jr. and
Elizabeth, and brothers William and John Wesley.

John Wesley Wallick - 138th Indiana Volunteer Infantry, Co. A
151st Indiana, Volunteer Infantry, Co. D

3

Rank: 138th IVI - Private, promoted to 3rd Corporal
151st IVI - Private

Place of enlistment: 138th IVI - Peru, Indiana
151st IVI - La Porte, Indiana

Mustered into Federal service: 138th IVI - May 27, 1864
151st IVI - January 28, 1865

Service time: 138th IVI - 100 Days
151st IVI - 7 months

Born: January, 1843/44 - Miami County, Indiana

Age at first enlistment: 20 years old

Physical description: height - 5' 10", brown hair, hazel eyes

Civilian occupation: miller

Family Lineage: John Wesley, son of "Peru" Benjamin Junior, son of "Peru" Benjamin Senior, son of Johannes, son of Hans Michael Wallick

It appears that there were two men living in Peru, Indiana, in 1864 who would answer to the name Wesley Wallick and both men served for 100 days in the same regiment and company of the Union army (138th Indiana Volunteer Infantry, Company A). These facts, compounded by the errors written in family histories and in government documents, required hours of research to reconcile in order to discover the truth concerning the two Wesley Wallicks. However, once the soldiers' service records were obtained the truth became obvious: the two men named Wesley were a generation apart and were related as uncle and nephew. One Wesley was a forty-five-year-old first lieutenant and the other was a twenty-year-old private. Fortunately, and unlike their civilian records, different given names were used by the military: Wesley Wallick for the uncle and John W. Wallick for the nephew.[7]

In civilian life Uncle Wesley Wallick, "the Elder" (1819-1890), was simply called Wesley in most documents. But nephew John Wesley Wallick, "the Younger" (1844-1889), answered to both John and Wesley throughout his life, hence the source of confusion in unraveling both soldiers' narratives. To help clarify these biographies, the given names "John" or "John W." will be used when referring to nephew John Wesley Wallick and the name "Wesley" will be used for his uncle.

John was a younger brother to William Wallick, who served with the 51st Indiana Volunteer Infantry (IVI), and twin brother to Charles F., who served with the 87th IVI. William joined the army in 1861 and Charles enlisted in 1862. Both brothers fought against the Confederacy for three years. Their two regiments became famous after the war due to where they had fought and their distinguished service records. In the spring of 1863, William took part in Colonel Abel Streight's "Raid to Rome, Georgia," with the "Mule Brigade". This was a spectacular disaster which ended in William being captured by the legendary and brilliant southern cavalryman, General Nathan Bedford Forrest, who

---

[7] There was confusion late in Uncle Wesley's life when he entered the Soldiers and Sailors Home in Dayton, Ohio. He is buried in the Dayton National Cemetery under his nephew's name, J.W. Wallick. See Wesley Wallick's biography for details.

unceremoniously sent William and his comrades to Libby Federal Prison in Richmond, Virginia. After a nine-month incarceration, William and 108 other prisoners of war, tunneled out of Libby Prison. He eventually did make it back to his regiment. Brother Charles was wounded in the left hand at the Battle of Chickamauga and took part in General Sherman's "March to the Sea" and Carolinas Campaign. At the close of the war Charles and his regiment paraded down Pennsylvania Ave, in Washington, D.C., in the Grand Review of the Union armies.

The Wallick homestead, Peru, Indiana, 1879.
John Wallick is left with a rifle, his mother, Eliza, is in the doorway, an unidentified woman is by the fence and twin brother, Charles, far right.

This is the only known photograph of John Wallick.

In the spring of 1864, thousands of men enlisted for 100 days to help support the Union army's grand offensive. General Grant wanted to mobilize as many troops as possible so they could attack the Confederate armies on multiple fronts. Tens of thousands of fresh troops and state militias were called into Federal service to strike one mighty blow against the Confederacy. Simultaneous attacks in the eastern and western theatres of the war were coordinated so the North could take advantage of its superior numbers in manpower. For the most part, these new recruits were given rear echelon assignments so the more experienced veteran soldiers could be made available for combat operations. Unfortunately, the Federal troops were outmaneuvered by General Lee at Petersburg, Virginia, and forced into a siege of that city, which negated the numerical advantage of the North and prolonged the war for yet another year. It was during this final year of the war that John Wallick enlisted twice in the Union army, always joining with a relative.

John's first enlistment was with the 138th Indiana Volunteer Infantry. Here he served as a private for three weeks, and was then promoted to 3rd Corporal. His uncle, Wesley Wallick, was a 1st lieutenant in his company. The two immediately went south with their regiment to the state of Tennessee where their primary responsibility was security for the southern Tennessee and northern Alabama railroads. There appears to have been no heavy combat action during their 100 days of service.

Three months after his discharge from the 138th Infantry, John enlisted for a second time in the 151st Indiana Volunteer Infantry. The war was drawing to a close but there was still a great need for new recruits, since three-year veteran enlistments were beginning to expire. A one-hundred-dollar bounty was paid by the U. S. Government to each recruit for one year's service. John enlisted at the same time as his cousin, William F. Wallick, although they served in two different companies of the regiment. For some very complicated reasons that are not thoroughly understood, William F. enlisted in the 151st as William H. Wallick. His interesting but confusing service record is detailed in the William F. Wallick biography on page 33.

John W. Wallick with the 138th Indiana Volunteer Infantry

1864

MAY 11   Private Wallick reports to Camp Morton in Indianapolis, IN.

MAY 27   The 138th Indiana Volunteer Infantry is mustered into Federal service and John Wallick is promoted to 3rd Corporal.

MAY - SEP   John and the 138th travel south to Tennessee and Alabama, where their primary responsibilities are railroad guard duty. No hostile action is reported but there is always the threat of confronting Rebel guerrillas.

SEP 22   John Wallick is mustered out of Federal service in Indianapolis, IN. The regiment has lost 8 soldiers to disease.

John W. Wallick with the 151st Indiana Volunteer Infantry

1865

John W. Wallick's volunteer enlistment paper.

JAN 28   John Wallick enlists in the Union army for one year at La Porte, IN. He is assigned to Company D of the 151st IVI. He will soon be joined by his cousin William F. Wallick (known as William H. Wallick in the 151st Infantry). William H. begins as a private but will soon make an astonishing leap in one promotion to the rank of sergeant-major. William and John each receive one-third of their $100 dollar bounty upon enlistment.

MAR 3   John and the 151st Indiana Infantry are mustered into Federal service at La Porte, IN.

MAR 6   Private Wallick and his regiment leave for Nashville, TN.

MAR 14 - JUN 14   The 151st has duty at Tullahoma, TN, guarding Union supplies and railroads. Tullahoma is an important railroad terminus in the mid-South.

MAY 15 - JUN   John Wallick is assigned to cattle guard duty. Cousin William F. Wallick (alias William H. Wallick) is promoted by Special Order #13, Regimental Headquarters, from private to sergeant-major.

JUL - AUG Private Wallick is detached from his regiment and detailed a teamster at post headquarters. An interesting note is placed in his record: "stoppage, one canteen." This probably means he had stoppage of an undisclosed amount of pay withheld to replace one canteen.

AUG - SEP 19 The regiment moves back to Nashville, TN, and has garrison duty there until they are mustered out on September 19, 1865. John receives $33.66 as a final payment from his enlistment bounty. Although the regiment has seen little action in what one might consider light duty, in seven months the regiment has lost 66 men to disease. John Wallick returns home to Miami County, IN, where he continues to help his father at the mill.

Epilogue - In 1874 John Wallick married Rebecca A. Buskirk, a lady with a strong sense of family history. Before her passing in 1943 she had donated to the Miami County Historical Society Museum pictures, letters and household possessions once owned by the Benjamin Wallick Jr. pioneer family. Among those items donated were Benjamin's trundle bed, a few dishes that belonged to John's mother Eliza, some personal letters and the only surviving photograph of Charles F. and John W. Wallick, which is found at the beginning of this biography. A few of these items are currently on public display at the museum and others may be viewed by appointment.

On March 22, 1889, John W. Wallick passed away at the young age of forty-five years old. He was survived by his wife, Rebecca, and his twelve-year-old son, Rutherford. Rebecca eventually remarried, thus explaining why most of the Wallick family heirlooms donated to the Miami County Historical Society were donated in the name of either Rebecca Wallick Berry or Rebecca Buskirk Berry.

Comrades-in-Arms

Father
Benjamin Jr.   109th IVI

Brothers
Charles F.   87th IVI
William   51st IVI

Uncles
Christopher   109th IVI
Wesley   109th, 138th IVI

Cousins
Washington   71st PVI
Benjamin   162nd OVI
Jeremiah   109th IVI
William F.   13th, 109th, 151st IVI

John W. Wallick and his wife, Rebecca, are buried in Reyburn Cemetery, Peru, Indiana.

William F. Wallick - 13th Indiana Volunteer Infantry, Co. B
109th Indiana Volunteer Infantry, Co. F

William H. (alias) - 151st Indiana Volunteer Infantry, Co. C

Rank: 13th IVI - 2nd Lt. to 1st Lt. Dismissed from service June 15, 1863
    109th IVI - 2nd Lt. (Seven Days Soldiers Regiment)
    151st IVI - Private, skipped in rank to Sergeant-Major

Service time: 13th IVI - 2 years, 2months: April 19, 1861 to June 15, 1863
    109th IVI - one week: July 10 - 17, 1863
    151st IVI - 7 months: February 2 to September 19, 1865

Born: January 28, 1841 - Tuscarawas County, Ohio

Age at enlistment: 13th IVI - 20 years old
    109th IVI - 22 years old
    151st IVI - 24 years old

Physical description: height - 5' 9", brown hair, gray eyes

Occupation: carpenter

Family Lineage: William F., son of Christopher, son of "Peru" Benjamin Senior, son of Johannes, son of Hans Michael Wallick

By just reading the summary above to William F. Wallick's biography one can immediately sense a complicated story, rich with mysteries. No other Wallick soldier's Civil War service prompts so many unanswered questions. Even his name is inconsistent in war records: sometimes he is William F, sometimes William F. M., and this author believes he is the alias William H. Wallick. William F. was a complicated man and that is reflected in his muddled service record. His story is very opaque, with many contradictory facts and sometimes it becomes necessary to "read between the lines" to reconstruct his past. We can assume he was a proud patriot, for when war was declared he was the first of all the Wallick soldiers to volunteer. He enlisted on April, 19, 1861, one week after the attack on Ft. Sumter.

The subject throughout this biography will be referred to as William F. Wallick, to help distinguish him from his famous cousin, William Wallick of the 51st Indiana Volunteer Infantry, who escaped from Libby Prison. The compiled military service records from the National Archives sometimes give two middle initials- William F.M. It is unknown what the two initials stood for and this biography will only use the first initial of his two middle names. William F. was eight years junior to "Libby Prison" William. Both men were born in Ohio but raised in Indiana and both men were carpenters when war broke out in the spring of 1861. Their grandfather was "Peru" Benjamin Wallick Senior, who came from Tuscarawas County, Ohio, to Peru, Indiana, in the winter of 1840. Christopher Wallick, father of William F, followed the family migration to Peru sometime in the 1850s. On April 12, 1861, the first shots were fired on Ft. Sumter and within a week William F. helped organize a company of soldiers from Peru who, in turn, elected him 2nd Lieutenant. William F. was known to be a brash and daring youth. He died young, only thirty-one years old, and his obituary states: "He knew no fear, acknowledged no danger and was frequently rash in acting upon the impulse of the moment." It appears that the same characteristics that made him a brave officer more than once got him into trouble with the army.

A portion of William F. Wallick's compiled military service record.

W | 13 | Ind.

William F. M. Wallick

2 Lt., Co. B, 13 Reg't Indiana Infantry.

Appears on **Returns** as follows:

Sept. to Dec. 1861 - Present.

Apl. 1862 - Present. In arrest by order of Lt. Col. Foster, since Apl. 26/62.

May 1862 - Present.

June + July 1862 - 1 Lt. - Present.

Aug. 1862 - Absent. Absent without leave.

Sept. 1862 - Present. In arrest by order Lt. Col. C. J. Dobbs.

Oct. 1862 to Jan. 1863 - Present.

Feb. 1863 - Present. In arrest by order Lt. Col. C. J. Dobbs.

Mch. 1863 - Present.

Apl. + May 1863 - Present. In arrest order of Lt. Col. C. J. Dobbs since Apl. 25/63.

June 1863 - Dismissed by order of G. C. M. June 15/63.

Book mark

(546) King, Copyist.

William F. Wallick was mustered into Federal service with the 13th Indiana Volunteer Infantry on June 19, 1861, in Indianapolis, Indiana. The regiment was involved in some early successful skirmishes in West Virginia. By March of 1862 they had moved into northern Virginia and fought against General Stonewall Jackson in the first engagement of his Shenandoah Valley Campaign, the First Battle of Kernstown. It was here that General Jackson had the first and only defeat of his vaunted Valley campaign, and it was here that William F. and distant cousin Henry M. Wallick, of the 67 OVI, fought together. At the close of this engagement the regiments of William F. and Henry M. were both on the battlefield and in the same line of battle. But the First Battle of Kernstown was a minor setback for General Jackson and a brief but fleeting victory for the Federal forces. William F. and Henry M. continued to chase General Jackson all over the Shenandoah Valley for the next few months, with the General frustrating all Federal efforts to destroy him.

William's service begins to get a bit murky and confused at this point in his record. One of his service index cards states he was placed under arrest (or in this particular case "in arrest") for the first time April 25, 1862. Another record for the month of April lists him present for duty and promoted to 1st. Lieutenant just weeks later, making no mention of the arrest.

By the summer of 1862 the 13th Indiana had moved to Fortress Monroe, located at the mouth of the James River, and they began to advance into Virginia. A special roll call was conducted on August 18, 1862, and William F. was found to be absent without leave (AWOL). He was placed under arrest and detailed to Alexandria, Virginia, by order of General McClellan. No explanation is given for this temporary assignment but it could have been a disciplinary matter due to his being AWOL. William F. did not return to duty with the 13th Indiana until October 1st. The records state that William F. was again placed under arrest in February and April of 1863. It is not clear if these arrests were connected to the AWOL incident of August, 1862 or whether they were new charges. *War of the Rebellion: Official Records of the Union and Confederate Armies* includes a report by Colonel Foster (commander of the 13th IVI) that mentions William F. Wallick by name in regards to a patrol and skirmish in which he took part on April 16, 1863, near Suffolk, Virginia. There is only praise for all the soldiers in this report. But one week later on April 25, it is recorded that William F. was again placed under arrest.

Being charged AWOL is a very serious offense with the army. This author also speculates that perhaps intoxication could have led to some arrests (see William's obituary at the conclusion of his biography). Since there were numerous breaches of military regulations or discipline, it is no wonder he was court-martialed and finally dismissed from service on June 15, 1863.

If his story ended here this would be a sad account of a young man's military career cut short by court-martial and dismissal. But William F. believed himself wronged in the events that led to his dismissal and the military justice system eventually did restore William's rank and honor, albeit sometime after the war. William F. may have perhaps lacked self-discipline, but he was no quitter. He served with two more regiments before his military career ended.

William F. Wallick with the 13th Indiana Volunteer Infantry

1861

APR 19   Only six days after the Confederates attacked Ft. Sumter, William F. Wallick is the first of all Wallick soldiers to answer President Lincoln's call for 75,000 volunteers to put down the Southern Rebellion. William F. helps organize a company of men from Peru, IN, and is elected a 2nd Lieutenant in Company B of the 13th Indiana Volunteer Infantry.

MAY 1   The 13th IVI is organized in Indianapolis, IN, for one year's service

JUN 19   After only six weeks the 13th Indiana is reorganized for three years Federal service.

JUL 11 Battle of Rich Mountain   William F. is under the command of future heavy-weight Generals George B. McClellan and William S. Rosecrans in this battle at Rich Mountain, just west of Beverly, WV.[8]   The Confederate forces are atop Rich Mountain and in a strong defensive position, but they are badly outnumbered by the 2,000 Federals. A local boy, named David Hart, helps lead the Union forces up the mountain and through heavy brush to outflank the Rebels. The 13th Indiana takes part in a brisk two-hour fight that ends with a successful bayonet charge that dislodges the enemy. That night the Union forces camp on the battlefield and the next morning find that the Confederates have left their mountaintop position. Two days later most of the Confederates who were engaged surrender to the Union forces. This battle, plus a few other minor engagements in West Virginia, helps secure the reputation of General McClellan as a winner and is a factor in his later being promoted to General-in-Chief of all the Union armies.

JUL 13   The 13th Indiana moves to Beverly, WV, then on to Cheat Mountain.

SEP 11 - 17   William F. is at the foot of Cheat Mountain, ten miles from the summit. In his first major campaign since coming to West Virginia, Robert E. Lee is moving against the Union forces in this region. There is much maneuvering between the opposing forces with marching and countermarching around Cheat Mountain and Elkwater. Some feeble attempts are made by the Confederates to engage the Federals but eventually Robert E. Lee and his forces retire.

OCT 3   William F. and the 13th Indiana leave Cheat Mountain and make a reconnaissance of the enemy's position at Greenbrier River, twelve miles distant. There is some minor skirmishing as they approach the Rebel camp and then clear a space for federal artillery to open fire. After a complete examination of the ground to their front, by sundown they have returned to Cheat Mountain.

OCT - NOV 7   The regiment is on a scouting expedition through the Kanawha District of West Virginia.

---

[8] At that time, Beverly was still part of Virginia. The state of West Virginia was created in 1863.

DEC 13 Action at Camp Allegheny   The Confederates have established a camp on the summit of Allegheny Mountain in Pocahontas County, WV. The 13th Indiana and four other regiments are ordered to advance up the mountain and attack the enemy camp. The 1,900 Federals assault the 1,200 Confederates for seven hours but all attacks are ineffective in dislodging the Rebels. By sunset many of the Federal troops have become exhausted and straggle to the rear. The attack is called off and the Union soldiers return to their own camp on Cheat Mountain.

DEC 18   William F. and his regiment move to Green Springs Run, WV, twenty miles south of Cumberland, MD.

1862

JAN 1 - 4   Skirmishes at Bath, Hancock & Great Cacapon Bridge   The 13th Indiana is involved in skirmishing that is to help keep the Rebels from interfering with railroad traffic on the West Virginia-Maryland border. The B&O Railroad dips down into northern West Virginia and is vulnerable to Confederate attack. Control of the railway is vital for communication and transportation between the western and eastern states of the Union. The skirmishes at Bath, Hancock, Great Cacapon Bridge, Alpine Station and Sir John's Run are all an effort to drive the Confederate forces from the threatened area.

MAR 5 - 15   William F. and his regiment advance to Winchester, VA. The Shenandoah Valley will become a battleground over the next three years and as a result will be savaged and plundered by both armies. Winchester will change hands seventy-two times before the end of the war. The 13th Indiana has moved to the region in response to the threat posed by General Stonewall Jackson, who is moving down the valley.

MAR 22 - 23   First Battle of Kernstown   The Confederates under Stonewall Jackson have advanced down the Shenandoah Valley (meaning they advanced north) and encounter General James Shields' Division at Kernstown, just south of Winchester, VA. In Shields' division Henry M. Wallick is in the first brigade and William F. is in the second. At the beginning of the battle Henry is on Pritchard's Hill, west of the Valley Pike (today US 11) and William F. and his brigade have formed on the east side of the Valley Pike. As the battle unfolds, both brigades have moved laterally to a ridge west of Middle Road. By 4:00 PM Henry is on the Federal right flank, over the ridge, and William and his brigade anchor the Federal left. Fighting continues for about two hours and just before nightfall the center of the Confederate line folds, causing the entire line to collapse.

First Kernstown Battlefield.

Two Wallick Soldiers fought here at the First Battle of Kernstown. Henry M. Wallick of the 67th Ohio Infantry was deployed on the far-left ridge at the beginning of the battle. William F. Wallick advanced through this field, from right to left, halfway through the engagement with the 13th Indiana Volunteer Infantry.

APR 17 Occupation of Mt. Jackson   After the First Battle of Kernstown the Union forces pursue the Confederates up the Shenandoah Valley. There are small skirmishes throughout the chase. William F. and the 13th IVI move to Mt. Jackson, which is 45 miles south of Winchester, VA.

APR 26   1st Arrest   William F. is placed under arrest by order of his commanding officer, Colonel Robert S. Foster. Unfortunately, this is just the beginning of multiple arrests for William F. Wallick.

MAY 12 - 21 March to Fredericksburg, VA   The Union high command is trying to balance the need for troops in the Shenandoah Valley and its ability to support General McClellan's Peninsula Campaign. William F. and his regiment are on their way to support General McClellan but suddenly must return to the Shenandoah Valley because of another threat made by Stonewall Jackson.

MAY 25 - 30 March to Front Royal   The 13th Indiana is marched back to Front Royal in response to General Jackson's continued harassment in the Shenandoah Valley. There is an engagement at Front Royal but William F. and his regiment do not return soon enough to be see any action. Distant cousin Michael Wallick, of the 27th Indiana, is wounded and captured at Buckton Station in action related to this engagement (see pages 55-57).

JUN 9   Battle of Port Republic   The regiment helps cover the retreat of the Federal forces in this last battle of Jackson's Shenandoah Valley Campaign. They are not engaged during the battle.

JUN 29 - JUL 2   13th Indiana is moved to the Virginia Peninsula   General McClellan is moving through the Virginia Peninsula in an effort to take the capital city of the Confederacy, Richmond, VA. The 13th Indiana is moved down to the tip of the peninsula, between the James and York Rivers.

JUL 3 - AUG 16   Posting at Harrison's Landing, VA   This is the Headquarters for General McClellan, on the north bank of the James River near Charles City, VA.

AUG 17 - 30 Moved to Fortress Monroe and then to Suffolk, VA   Fortress Monroe is **THE** major Federal military installation on the Virginia coast. It controls all traffic from the Atlantic Ocean into the James River. Richmond is located about 80 miles up the James River, so the fort is vital to all operations in central Virginia.

AUG 18   A special roll call is taken and William F. is found to be absent without leave (AWOL).

SEP 1 - 30   2nd Arrest   William F. is again placed under arrest, this time by Lt. Colonel Dobbs. He is then detailed (temporarily assigned) to Alexandria, VA, by order of General McClellan. It is unknown for what purpose he is detailed or if it is a consequence of his being AWOL August 18th.

OCT 3   Reconnaissance to Franklin on the Blackwater River   The Federals begin to move into the interior of Virginia and control the tributaries of the James River.

DEC 12   The 13th IVI makes a movement toward the Blackwater River at Zuni Ford, VA.

1863

JAN 8 - 10   William and the 13th Indiana participate in an expedition with skirmishing at Blackwater River.

JAN 30   Action at Deserted House   The 13th Indiana gets involved in a small skirmish at a deserted house north of McClenna's Station.

FEB   3rd Arrest   William F. is placed under arrest by Lt. Colonel Dobbs and this time he is to be court-martialed. As in previous incidents, the nature of the arrest is not recorded in his compiled military service record. A thorough reading of William's obituary reveals that he had a drinking problem, which led to illness and an early death. Perhaps William's multiple arrests could have been related to a dependence on alcohol.

APR 11 Siege of Suffolk, VA   The Union army has occupied Suffolk, VA, for some time now and has established a strong defensive ring of earthworks and forts around the town. William F. and the 13th IVI are in the middle of an entrenched arc on the south side of Suffolk, near Ft. McClellan. The Confederates have learned that great supplies of food and forage exist inside the Union lines in eastern Virginia. Robert E. Lee sends two divisions of his army to keep Federal units in their fortified positions while Confederate troops collect food stuffs and supplies from the surrounding countryside. The siege begins on April 11th and will go on for twenty-two days. There are some demonstrations, skirmishes and probing attacks during the siege, but the Rebels realize the strength of the Union defensive line and make no major assaults.

APR 13   Advance on Edenton, Providence Church and Somerton Roads   These three roads are major arteries into and out of Suffolk, VA. No serious fighting occurs, but William F. is involved in some of these probing attacks.

APR 16   There are only three references to anyone named Wallick in the mammoth government archive, *War of the Rebellion: Official Records of the Union and Confederate Armies* (1880-1901). This publication has 128 books in 70 volumes with 138,579 pages. One report concerns "Libby William" upon his return to headquarters at Fortress Monroe, just five days after his escape from Libby Prison. Another is the reporting of Henry M. Wallick being killed in action at the Battle of Chester Station. And the third is William F. Wallick being mentioned by his commanding officer, Col. Robert S. Foster, in regards to a skirmish on April 16, 1863. It is a two-page report that gives an accounting of four days' activities and included in the report is this statement:

> On Thursday, April 16, a party of skirmishers, under Lieutenants Wallick and Conron, of the Thirteenth Indiana, were sent out. They exchanged a few shots with the enemy, but found them too strong to make any advance.

The next day Lt. Conron goes out on patrol without William and is involved in a "sharp engagement," where he is mortally wounded and dies a few days later.

APR 25   4th Arrest   William F. is again placed under arrest by Lt. Colonel Dobbs.

MAY 4   Siege of Suffolk Raised   Confederate General George E. Pickett's division has been the Rebel force opposing William F. Wallick and the Federals on the south side of the Suffolk's defensive ring.   After three weeks of siege operations the Confederate high-command decides to withdraw. The 13th IVI pursues the Rebels down the Sumerton Road. but there is little resistance.

MAY 9   William's commanding officer, Colonel Robert S. Foster, writes a report about the patrol William F. helped lead against the Rebels on April 16th. In the report the Colonel makes no criticism of anyone and has only praise for all soldiers involved. However, six weeks after this glowing report is written William F. is dismissed from the service.

JUN 15   William is dismissed from the army   "*Dismissed* [from] *the service of the United States with a forfeiture of all pay and allowances by order of general court-martial, June 15, 1863.*"   With these words, William F. Wallick is drummed out of the 13th Indiana Volunteer Infantry in disgrace. He returns home to Peru, IN.

William F. Wallick and the 109th Indiana Infantry
(The Seven Days Soldiers)

JUL 10 - 17   William F. has come home after being dismissed from the 13th Indiana and is immediately called back into his country's service because of a cavalry raid in southern Indiana by Confederate General John Hunt Morgan. Five Wallick soldiers from Peru serve in the 109th Indiana Volunteer Infantry from July 10-17, 1863.

These "Seven Days Soldiers" include William F., his father Christopher and three of his uncles- Jeremiah, Wesley and 59-year-old Benjamin Jr. William is a 2nd Lieutenant in this regiment and it is unknown why he is given this rank or even allowed to serve for three weeks prior he had been dismissed from the service. The Confederate raiders make a quick but destructive exit from Indiana and move into southern Ohio, where the alarm soon passes for the Hoosiers. After only seven days in Federal service, the 109th is disbanded.[9]

William F. Wallick in the 151st Indiana Volunteer Infantry
and
The case for William H. Wallick being an alias for William F. Wallick

William H. Wallick enlisted as a private on February 5, 1864, and in ten weeks made a meteoric rise in rank to sergeant-major, with only one promotion. Genealogical evidence records no such person as William H. Wallick living in Peru, Indiana, before, during, or after the Civil War. The only two Wallicks named William from Peru were "Libby Prison" William of the 51st Indiana Volunteers, and William F. Wallick of the 13th IVI. Both were born in Tuscarawas County, Ohio, moved to Peru, Indiana, when they were boys and grew up to become carpenters. One major difference between the two was that "Libby Prison" William, as far as we know, had no middle initial and was at least eight years older than William F. According to the enlistment papers for William H. Wallick, he also was born in Tuscarawas County, Ohio, lived in Peru Indiana, became a carpenter and was twenty-four years old, exactly the same age as William F. "Libby" William would have been thirty-two years old in February of 1865.

Given these facts, there seems to be no question as to the real identity of William H. Wallick. William H. must have been William F. Wallick with an alias as middle initial. The evidence seems conclusive, except for one thing: the records of internments at the Reyburn Cemetery, where "Libby" William and William F. are both buried, lists "Libby" William as being in the 51st *and* 151st Indiana Regiments. However, this author believes that to be an error in the records of the cemetery for these reasons:

1. "Libby" William had been a captain and company commander in the 51st Indiana Volunteer Infantry. It is doubtful that he would reenlist as a private in a new regiment, knowing the status and privileges he would forfeit as an enlisted man. If "Libby" William wanted to stay in the army, he had the opportunity to extend his commission with the 51st Regiment as a veteran volunteer and as an officer. He did not.

2. "Libby" William had been married for ten years, had a 4 year-old daughter and knew he was extremely lucky to have survived in and escaped from Libby Prison. As bad as conditions were in Libby (which was an officers only prison), he knew the enlisted men just down the river on Belle Island had it much worse.

3. There is a diary of "Libby" William, written in his own hand, and we have enlistment papers filled out and signed by William H. Wallick. The handwriting of the two Williams is quite different. William H. could not possibly be "Libby" William.

4. It seems more plausible that William F. might be the one to reenlist since he left the army twenty months earlier in a dishonorable condition; perhaps he wanted to redeem himself. Accepting the rank of second lieutenant in the 109th, just weeks after being dismissed, shows a willingness to still serve his country and command men. His cousin, John W. Wallick, also from Peru, enlisted in the 151st at the same time as William F. and perhaps the prospect of serving together was a motivating factor in his reenlistment.

5. When William H. enlisted in the 151st, he had to sign a statement swearing that he had never been court-martialed or dismissed from service. Maybe William F. thought it best to use an alias middle initial to help keep his records separate.

---

[9] For more information on General Morgan's raid, see Chapter Six, titled "The Seven Days Soldiers."

6. The strongest argument for William H. being William F. is that they have the same place of birth (Tuscarawas County, Ohio), the same residence (Peru, Indiana), the same occupation (carpenter) **and** are exactly the same age in all the official records for both regiments. There is no historical evidence of a third William Wallick, who was of military age and living in Peru, Indiana, in the 1860s. It is difficult to believe that there is an "undiscovered" William Wallick with exactly the same age, hometown, background and experiences as William F.

7. It is likely the copyist of the cemetery records made the error. It is not known exactly when the internment records were copied but it was definitely sometime after 1943, long after the deaths of both Williams and their immediate family members.

This volunteer enlistment application was completed and signed by William H. Wallick. In no way does it resemble the handwriting in "Libby" William's prison diary. To compare the two handwritings, see page 9 in the William Wallick biography.

Signature for William H. Wallick

This statement, filled out and signed by William H. Wallick, declares that the new recruit is 24 years old and had never been court-martialed or dismissed from previous military service. If William H. is indeed an alias for William F, he lied on this form in order to enlist in the 151st IVI.

One of the great curiosities about William H. Wallick's service is his leap from private to sergeant-major in one promotion. This was not an incremental rise but he actually catapulted from the lowest rank to the highest non-commissioned officer rank after serving only three months in his regiment. This suggests a person with special circumstances and past military experience and William F. had both. Perhaps he was able to explain to his commanding officer that he had been unjustly court-martialed while in the 13th Indiana. If William F. was able to distinguish himself as a soldier in the 151st, maybe his commanding officer took the unusual step of jumping him from private to sergeant-major. This promotion is just one of many oddities in the record of William F. Wallick.

William F. Wallick (alias William H. Wallick) with the 151st Indiana Infantry

1865

FEB 2 William F. Wallick enlists as William H. Wallick at La Porte, IN. He has joined with his cousin, John Wesley Wallick, who is a private in Company D. William begins as a private in Company C but makes an astonishing leap in rank to sergeant-major after ten weeks. He receives one-third of his $100 dollar bounty upon enlistment.

MAR 3 William H. and the 151st Indiana Volunteer Infantry are mustered into Federal service.

MAR 6 The 151st Regiment leaves for Nashville, TN.

MAR 14 - JUN 14 William H. has duty at Tullahoma, TN, guarding Union supplies and railroads. Tullahoma is an important railroad terminal in the mid-South.

MAY 15 William H. is promoted by Special Order #13, Regimental Headquarters, from private to sergeant-major.

JUN 15 - SEP 19 The regiment moves back to Nashville, TN, and has garrison duty there until they are mustered out on September 19, 1865. William H. travels to Indianapolis, then returns home to Peru.

Epilogue - William F. (alias William H.) returned home after the war and married Elizabeth Hagee on June 28, 1868. They stayed in Peru, IN, and had two children, Maude, born the spring of 1870, and Pearle, born the summer of 1872. Unfortunately, William F. did not see these daughters grow past childhood, for he died on January 16, 1873, just 12 days shy of his thirty-second birthday. The account of William F. Wallick's service in the Civil War is extremely complex and leaves many unanswered questions for the reader. From his obituary, he appeared to have been a very complicated man, both as a soldier and as a civilian. It is difficult to know what the long-term effects of his military service had upon him. He may have struggled with issues of post-traumatic stress disorder (PTSD) for years. There certainly was no diagnosis, let alone treatment, for the disorder 150 years ago. We learn from his obituary that he apparently had problems with alcohol. But through his tangled story we can still see a patriot to the Union's cause and be thankful to him for his sacrifice and service when our nation confronted its greatest crisis.

Obituary for William F. Wallick.

Death of Captain Wallick.

Wm. F. Wallick was born in Tuscorawas county, Ohio, January 28, 1842, died, in Peru, Jan. 16, 1873. Funeral services at the residence, by Rev. W. L. Huffman.

The deceased came to this city, with his parents, in early youth and spent the remainder of his life here. He entered the volunteer service, soon after the rebellion broke out and was a member of the first company that went from Peru, of which he was elected Second Lieutenant. He was a brave soldier and served with honorable distinction; although, after promotion to the first lieutenancy of his company, he was dismissed and remained for a little time under a cloud. The facts coming to the knowledge of the War Department, he was afterwards restored to his rank, honorably discharged, and brevetted a captain. He knew no fear, acknowledged no danger, and was frequently rash in acting upon the impulse of the moment. In 1867 he married the daughter of Wm. Hagee, Esq., who, with two little children, survives him.

For several years the deceased had been considerably dissipated in his habits. While he had many noble qualities, his friends had to regret this indulgence. Intemperance is a stronger enemy than a hostile army; it blights the life of a young man and destroys his power for usefulness.

William F. Wallick is buried in Reyburn Cemetery, Peru, Indiana.

Enhanced inscription.

Comrades-in-Arms

Father
Christopher   109th IVI

Uncles
Benjamin Jr. 109th IVI
Wesley   109th & 138th IVI

Cousins
William   51st IVI
Charles F.   87th IVI
John W.   138th & 151st IVI
Benjamin   162nd OVI
Jeremiah   109th IVI
Washington   71st PVI

Wesley Wallick - 109th Indiana Volunteer Infantry, Co. F
138th Indiana Volunteer Infantry, Co. A

5

Rank: 109th IVI - Private
          138th IVI - 1st Lieutenant

Place of enlistment: 109th IVI - Peru, Indiana
                        138th IVI - Miami County, Indiana

Mustered into Federal service: 109th IVI - July 10, 1863
                                  138th IVI - May 27, 1864

Service time: 109th IVI - 7 days
                 138th IVI - 100 Days

Born: February 4, 1819 - Tuscarawas County, Ohio

Age at enlistment in the 138th IVI: 45 years old

Family Lineage: Wesley, son of "Peru" Benjamin Senior, son of Johannes, son of Hans Michael Wallick

Benjamin Wallick (AKA "Peru" Benjamin Sr.), had nine sons and grandsons who fought in the American Civil War. Born in Pennsylvania in 1772, he and his wife Mary migrated to Tuscarawas County, Ohio, in 1801, becoming some of the first Wallicks to settle in the Old Northwest Territory. Their son, Benjamin Jr., was born three years later in 1804, one year after the Ohio Country became a state. Both Benjamin Sr. and Benjamin Jr. eventually had sons called Wesley, and both of them served in the American Civil War. Wesley "the Elder" was Benjamin Jr.'s brother. Wesley "the Younger" (whose full given name was John Wesley, but he answered to both) was Benjamin Jr.'s son. Having a son named after one's brother is not unusual and is found quite often in families. But what makes this situation extraordinary is that both Wesleys, the uncle and the nephew, served together at the same time and in the same regiment and company during the American Civil War - Company A, 138th Indiana Volunteer Infantry. As one can imagine, these facts led to a great deal of confusion when researching these soldiers. All civilian documents record Wesley Wallick "the Elder" with his correct given name, but not so with his nephew, John Wesley. His first and middle names were used interchangeably in historical documents. Sometimes he is called John, sometimes Wesley and sometimes both, even in Federal census records. Thankfully, the military records for the two soldiers are consistent in calling Uncle Wesley Wallick just "Wesley Wallick" and his nephew just "John W. Wallick", with one big exception. Uncle Wesley is buried in Dayton National Cemetery under his nephew's name - John W. Wallick. To keep the two separated for the reader, the subject of this biography will just be called "Wesley," uncle and commanding officer to his nephew, Private John W. Wallick.

Uncle Wesley was one of thirteen Wallick Civil War soldiers who were born in Tuscarawas County, Ohio, yet by 1861 only one soldier of the twelve still resided in the county; such was the magnitude of the Wallicks' western migration in the mid-1800s. The one remaining soldier, Elias Wallick, did not survive the war, dying at the Battle of Opequon Creek (also called Third Winchester) in the fall of 1864. All the other soldiers who claimed nativity in Tuscarawas County were scattered across the Midwest by the time Fort Sumter was attacked. Wesley's family had moved to Miami County, Indiana, in the early 1840s.

The Wallicks of Miami County were primarily carpenters and millers by trade and by 1861 they had well-established businesses. Wesley, too, was a carpenter but pursued other interests as well, both before and after the war. In 1852 he traveled to California, apparently with his wife Mary Ann and two young daughters. He, along with many of his friends and neighbors from Peru, made the long journey, hoping to strike it rich in the California Gold Rush.

It is unknown how much success Wesley achieved as a prospector, panning for gold. But by November 1857, he was back in Indiana operating the Western House Hotel in downtown Peru. Three years later, in 1860, Wesley made another career move and was elected to his first two-year term as sheriff of Miami County.

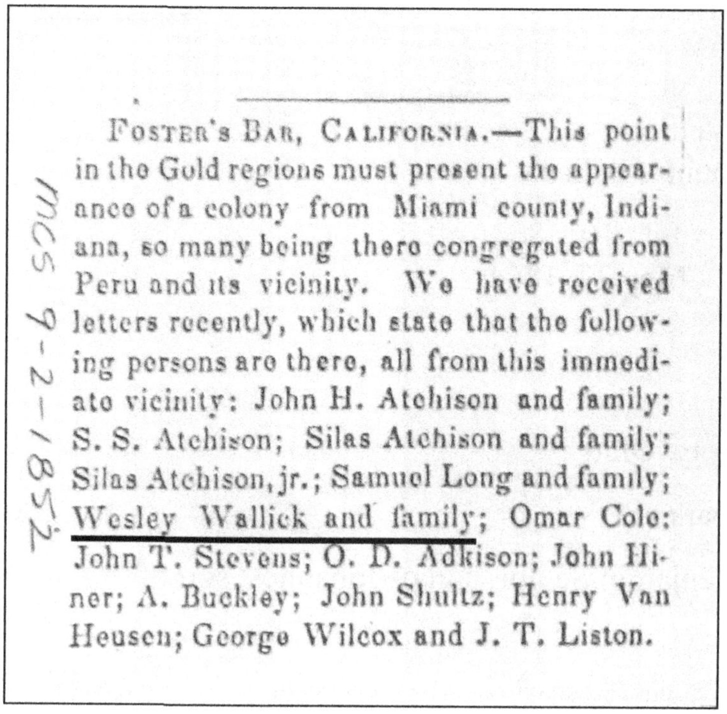

FOSTER'S BAR, CALIFORNIA.—This point in the Gold regions must present the appearance of a colony from Miami county, Indiana, so many being there congregated from Peru and its vicinity. We have received letters recently, which state that the following persons are there, all from this immediate vicinity: John H. Atchison and family; S. S. Atchison; Silas Atchison and family; Silas Atchison, jr.; Samuel Long and family; Wesley Wallick and family; Omar Cole; John T. Stevens; O. D. Adkison; John Hiner; A. Buckley; John Shultz; Henry Van Heusen; George Wilcox and J. T. Liston.

(handwritten margin: MCHS 9-2-1852)

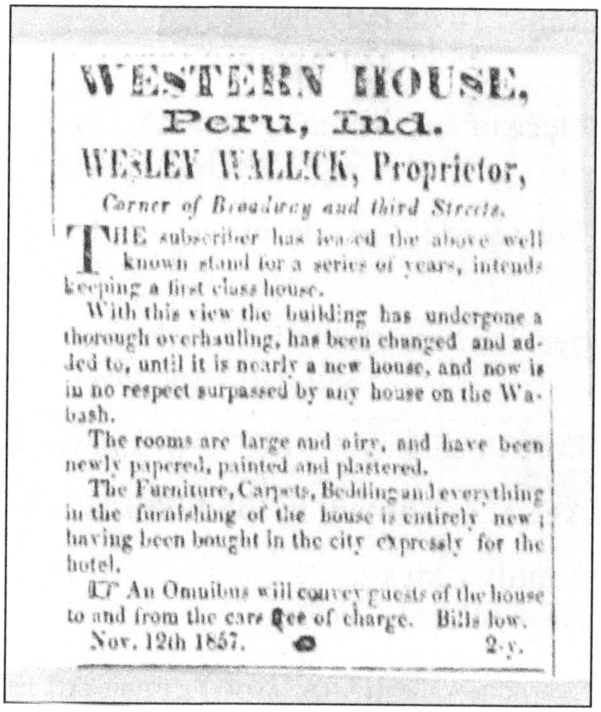

WESTERN HOUSE,
Peru, Ind.
WESLEY WALLICK, Proprietor,
Corner of Broadway and Third Streets.

THE subscriber has leased the above well known stand for a series of years, intends keeping a first class house.

With this view the building has undergone a thorough overhauling, has been changed and added to, until it is nearly a new house, and now is in no respect surpassed by any house on the Wabash.

The rooms are large and airy, and have been newly papered, painted and plastered.

The Furniture, Carpets, Bedding and everything in the furnishing of the house is entirely new; having been bought in the city expressly for the hotel.

☞ An Omnibus will convey guests of the house to and from the cars free of charge. Bills low.

Nov. 12th 1857.   2-y.

Miami County newspaper dated September 2, 1852, reporting that Wesley Wallick and family are in the California Gold Rush.   Miami County Historical Society

Advertisement for the Western House Hotel - dated November 12, 1857.
Miami County Historical Society

Wesley was 42 years old when our nation's worst sectional strife exploded into a full-scale war. While many younger members of his family quickly enlisted, he waited to enlist until he had completed his term as Miami County Sheriff.[10] It wasn't until late May of 1864 that both he and his nephew John W. Wallick enlisted in the 138th IVI. His experience as a sheriff served him well, for he became a lieutenant in Company A; nephew John was a private. The 138th Indiana was a Hundred-Days Regiment that was created to help supplement the manpower needs of the Union army for General Grant's Overland Offensive in the spring of 1864. Most of the regiment's responsibilities were in railroad and supply depot security, seeing little or no hostile action.

Wesley Wallick with the 109th Indiana Volunteer Infantry

1863

JUL 10 - 17   The invasion of southern Indiana by Confederate General John Hunt Morgan causes a panic throughout the state and Governor Morton calls up the militia to defend the Hoosier homeland. All able-bodied males were asked to grab their rifles, mount up and proceed to Indianapolis to be mustered into Federal service as a Minute Men Regiment. Five Wallick soldiers from Miami County respond to the call. They are Wesley, his two brothers, Benjamin Jr. and Christopher, and two nephews, Jeremiah and William F. Wallick. The regiment is only activated for one week before the invaders move far enough into Ohio that the emergency expires. For more information about the Confederate invasion and the Wallicks of the 109th Indiana Volunteer Infantry, see chapter six, The Seven Days Soldiers.

---

[10] Wesley did serve with the "Seven Days Soldiers" in July of 1863 while sheriff, but that regiment was more an ad hoc Indiana militia unit than a long-term federalized regiment.

Wesley Wallick with the 138th Indiana Volunteer Infantry

1864

MAY 7 Wesley is commissioned a 1st Lieutenant in the 138th Indiana Volunteer Infantry.

MAY 11 Lieutenant Wallick reports to Camp Morton at Indianapolis, IN.

MAY 27 The 138th IVI is mustered into Federal service.

MAY - SEP Wesley and the 138th travel south to Tennessee and Alabama where their primary responsibility is guarding the railroads. No hostile action is reported but there is always the threat of confronting Confederate cavalry and guerrillas.

SEP 22 The 138th Infantry is mustered out of Federal service. In a little over three months the regiment has lost eight soldiers to disease.

Epilogue - After Wesley was discharged from the army he returned to Miami County to run again for county sheriff. He was elected to a second term and served his community in that office from 1865 to 1867. For the next twenty-four years he worked in retail as a feed store clerk and did other odd jobs. Hard times fell on Wesley in his "golden years" for he concluded his life as a patient at the National Home for Disabled Volunteer Soldiers in Dayton, Ohio (also called the Soldiers and Sailors Home). This facility was primarily used as a refuge for three types of veterans: the very sick, the very destitute and those who wanted to escape their wives and live off the government dole. Wesley certainly belonged to the former, and not the latter.

We know little about the circumstances that brought Wesley to the Dayton hospital other than he was ill, destitute and admitted by his daughter, Myra (Wallick) Houser, on May 15, 1890. It was not a lengthy stay, for after seven weeks he died of a bladder infection and was then buried in the Dayton National Cemetery, Dayton, Ohio. His wife of forty-one years, Mary Ann (Fisher), had preceded him in death, passing away on October 17, 1884. She is buried in Mt. Hope Cemetery, Miami County, Indiana, 160 miles away from her husband.

Wesley's muster-in and muster-out cards from the National Archives.

Wesley Wallick was admitted to the Soldiers and Sailors Home in Dayton, Ohio, on May 15, 1890, Here, Wesley's rank is recorded as a first lieutenant in the 138th IVI, which is correct.

Below is another record of Wesley's from the Soldiers and Sailors Home. Here, Wesley is mistakenly ranked a private, his nephew's rank in the 138th IVI. Wesley was a first lieutenant.

The contradictory hospital records led to confusion at the time of his burial. All his life he was called "Wesley" by friends, family and himself. Yet on his headstone application from the Veterans Administration the name John W. Wallick is written instead of Wesley Wallick. Could the soldier buried in the Dayton National Cemetery be Private John Wesley "the Younger" and not Lieutenant Wesley Wallick "the Elder"? That is impossible. John Wesley "the Younger" died in 1889, the year before Wesley, and he is buried next to his wife Rebecca (Buskirk) in Reyburn Cemetery in Peru, Indiana. This John W. Wallick who is buried in Dayton, Ohio, is without question Uncle Wesley Wallick. One possible explanation for the error is that the person who filled out the headstone application was not a family member and didn't realize there were two Wallicks in Company A of the 138th Indiana Volunteer Infantry, one a lieutenant, and one a private. In the 1869 publication, *Report of the Adjutant General of the State of Indiana 1861-1865* (an official roster of all soldiers who served in the war from the State of Indiana), the officers and enlisted men are recorded in two separate books. First Lieutenant Wesley Wallick is recorded in the book of officers, whereas Private John W. Wallick is recorded in the book of enlisted men. It is theorized that whoever filled out the headstone application looked in the wrong book, the result being a mistaken name on Wesley Wallick's headstone.

Bottom left – An index card showing Wesley's headstone application with the incorrect rank and name. Wesley's nephew John W. Wallick is buried in Reyburn Cemetery, Peru, Indiana.

Bottom right - Wesley Wallick is buried in the National Cemetery in Dayton, Ohio. His grave is located in Section H, Plot #141, and he is interred as J. W. Wallick, his nephew's name.

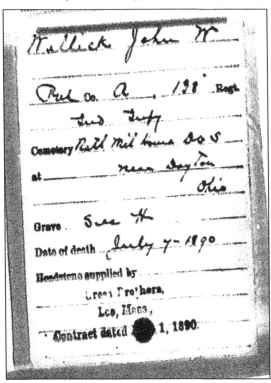

Comrades-in-Arms

Wesley Wallick, 1819-1890

Brothers
Benjamin   109th IVI
Christopher   109th IVI

Nephews
John W.	38th & 151st IVI	William F.	13th, 109th & 151st IVI
Charles F.	87th IVI	Washington	71st PVI
William	51st IVI	Benjamin	162nd OVI
Jeremiah	109th IVI		

The Seven Days Soldiers - 109th Indiana Volunteer Infantry, Co. F

6

Benjamin Wallick Jr. - age 59, Private

Christopher Wallick - age 58, Private

Wesley Wallick - age 44, Private

Jeremiah Wallick - age 33, Corporal

William F. Wallick - age 22, 2nd Lieutenant

Place of enlistment - Miami County, Peru, Indiana

Service time: seven days, July 10 - 17, 1863

Born in Tuscarawas County, Ohio - Benjamin Jr, Christopher, Wesley and William

Born in Miami County, Indiana - Jeremiah

Mustered into Federal service: July 10, 1863

Family Lineage: All soldiers are sons and grandsons of "Peru" Benjamin Senior, son of Johannes, son of Hans Michael Wallick

This is an unusual story of how five Wallick men from Peru, Indiana, became soldiers for only seven days in the summer of 1863.

General John Hunt Morgan

The story begins with a very brilliant and cunning Rebel cavalry commander, General John Hunt Morgan, and the need for a diversionary cavalry raid into Kentucky. General Morgan was born in Alabama, raised in Kentucky and was everything one would expect to find in a southern-gentleman cavalry officer. He was intelligent, handsome, daring, self-confident and impetuous to a fault, which sometimes got him into serious trouble. Once, while a student at Transylvania College in Lexington, KY, he was suspended for dueling. He fought bravely in the Mexican War and afterwards became a successful businessman. At the beginning of the sectional crisis he did not support secession. But when the Civil War exploded and Kentucky proclaimed itself neutral, he declared himself loyal to the Confederacy and organized a cavalry regiment for the Confederate States of America. He entered the militia as a captain but quickly rose to the rank of colonel in the 2nd Kentucky Cavalry. The regiment fought at the Battle of Shiloh and executed brilliant raids in Kentucky against General Buell and his Federal army. By December, 1862, Morgan had achieved the rank of brigadier general and was famous throughout the South.

The Five Wallicks of the 109th Indiana Volunteer Infantry

JUL 10 - 17 The summer of 1863 sees one of the most spectacular cavalry raids of the entire Civil War. Confederate General Braxton Bragg orders General Morgan to conduct a raid from Tennessee into Kentucky and to become a distraction to the Union forces moving against Vicksburg, Gettysburg and east Tennessee. Bragg orders that under no circumstances are General Morgan and his cavalry to cross the Ohio River. After raiding numerous towns, attacking Union supply depots and destroying thousands of dollars' worth of Kentucky civilian and government property, General Morgan exceeds Bragg's orders, crosses the Ohio River and begins to march toward Croydon, IN. He does this believing that bringing the war to the northern people will help encourage the Copperheads (peace democrats in the north) and rally them to the cause of the Confederacy. On the evening of July 8th, Indianapolis receives word of the Confederate invaders moving toward Croydon, and the citizens of Indiana are called upon to organize for defense. By July 10th, thousands of men from across the state have volunteered for service. From these "Indiana Minute Men" thirteen regiments are formed, the 109th Indiana Volunteer Infantry being one of them. Five Wallicks from Peru are soldiers in this home guard and are mustered into Federal service on July 10th. These five "Seven-Days Soldiers" are, from eldest to youngest, Benjamin Jr.- age 59, Christopher- age 48, Wesley- age 44, Jeremiah- age 31 and William F.- age 22. All are assigned to company F. Although he is the youngest of the five, William F. Wallick (recently dismissed from the service) is the only officer in the group. He is a 2nd Lieutenant, Jeremiah is a corporal and Wesley, Christopher and Benjamin are privates.

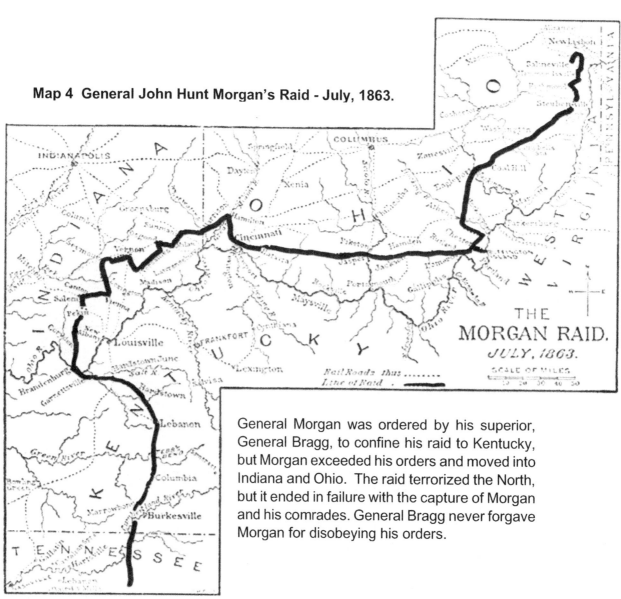

Map 4 General John Hunt Morgan's Raid - July, 1863.

General Morgan was ordered by his superior, General Bragg, to confine his raid to Kentucky, but Morgan exceeded his orders and moved into Indiana and Ohio. The raid terrorized the North, but it ended in failure with the capture of Morgan and his comrades. General Bragg never forgave Morgan for disobeying his orders.

JUL 13 The 109th departs Indianapolis on July 13th for Hamilton, Ohio, then moves south towards Cincinnati. By the time the regiment nears Cincinnati General Morgan has galloped out of the region and the 109th IVI returns to Indianapolis.

JUL 17 With the Confederate threat to Indiana ended, the 109th is mustered out of Federal service.[11]

Epilogue - General Morgan moved through central and southern Ohio destroying bridges, railroads and government stores. He and his raiders were finally captured on July 26, 1863, near Salineville, Ohio. His men had ridden over a thousand miles in 46 days, from Tennessee to northern Ohio. After Morgan's capture he was sent to the Ohio Penitentiary in Columbus. Within weeks he and six others made a dramatic escape by tunneling from his cell into the prison yard and scaling the penitentiary walls. He returned home to the Confederacy, honored as a great war hero by all except General Bragg, who was still very angry at Morgan for defying his orders. William Wallick of the 51st Indiana wrote in his Libby Prison diary on January 8, 1864, that General Morgan had come to see the prisoners (it is well documented that General Morgan did go to Libby Prison and visit the prisoners that day). There is a bit of irony in this, for William and his comrades were at that moment digging their own escape tunnel when William wrote, "We get through the wall" (basement wall of the prison) and "Morgan comes to see us." Just as General Morgan escaped through tunneling out of the Ohio Penitentiary, so William and his cohorts will escape from Libby Prison.

General Morgan and his raiders riding through Old Washington, Ohio.

Harper's Weekly, August 15, 1863

---

[11] Twenty-five Wallicks from the Hans Michael lineage were mustered into Federal service during the American Civil War but only twenty-two soldiers have biographies in this volume. Benjamin, Christopher and Jeremiah Wallick do not have individual biographies because they were mustered into Federal service for only seven days. The material in this chapter covers the enlistments for all three soldiers.

Map 5 Journey of Michael Wallick with the 27th Indiana Volunteer Infantry.

Michael Wallick was a prisoner of war in Richmond, VA, while the 27th Indiana Volunteer Infantry fought at the battles of Cedar Mountain and Antietam Creek.

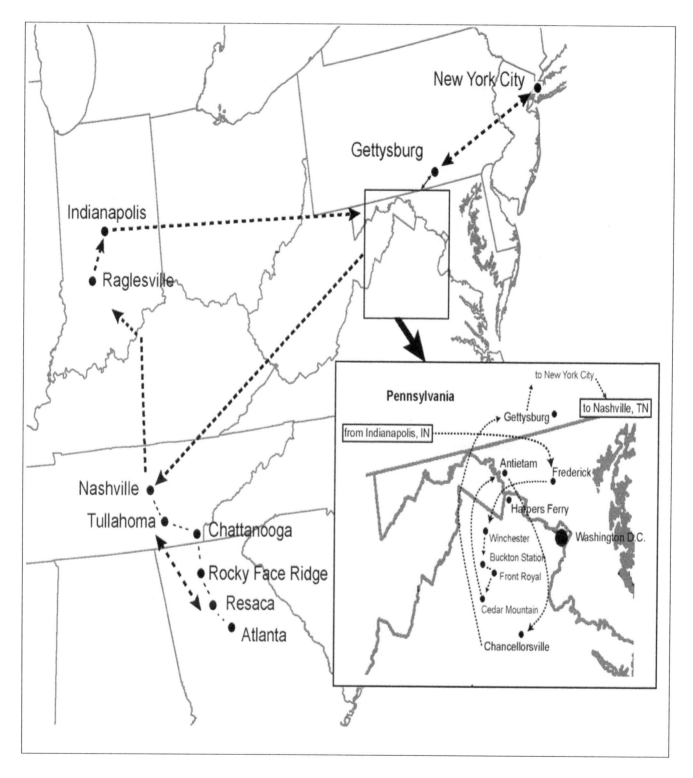

Michael Wallick - 27th Indiana Volunteer Infantry, Co. B & F

7

Rank: Corporal, promoted to 4th Sergeant

Place of enlistment: Daviess County, Indiana - August 10, 1861

Mustered into Federal service: September 12, 1861

Service time: 3 years

Born: March 6, 1817 - Bedford County, Pennsylvania

Age at enlistment: 44 years old

Physical description: height - 5' 8", black hair, gray eyes

Civilian occupation: farmer

Family Lineage: Michael, son of "Bunker Hill" Michael, son of "Bedford"" Michael, son of Hans Michael Wallick

On a warm August afternoon in 1861, Michael Wallick, age 44, left his wife, his five children (ages 6 to 18) and his farm to go into the little village of Raglesville, Indiana, and enlist in the Union army. There he joined friends and neighbors from Daviess County and they all quickly marched off to Camp Morton, Indianapolis, to help quell the southern rebellion. This group of men was to become Company B of the 27th Indiana Volunteer Infantry and Michael was, at the time, old enough to be a father to most of them. It is not too surprising that he joined to fight against the Confederate secession, given his staunch Republican sentiments and patriotic ideals. Also, as a young boy he undoubtedly heard his family tell of the adventures and hardships his grandfather, "Bedford" Michael, had endured while fighting in the Pennsylvania Militia during the American Revolution. "Daviess" Michael (1817-1905) now joined a regiment that was destined to make a name for itself during the Civil War and fight in some of its most famous battles.

He was born in Bedford County, Pennsylvania, on March 6, 1817, and by his lineage he could rightfully be called Michael IV. His great-grandfather Hans Michael (1707-67) came to the New World from the Baden-Württemberg region of Germany in 1732 and settled in York, Pennsylvania. His grandfather "Bedford" Michael (1740-1823) helped settle the Upper Juniata Valley on the Pennsylvania frontier (near

Michael Wallick, 87 years old.
Photo courtesy of James Wallick, Yreka, Ca.

present day Altoona) and fought in our country's War of Independence. His father "Bunker Hill" Michael (1775-1845) moved the family west in 1822 to Tuscarawas County, Ohio, where "Daviess" Michael was raised and spent most of his young adulthood. There he became a farmer and in 1847 laid out 12 tracks of land that comprise the present-day village of Dundee, Ohio. In 1851 he moved his young family west to Daviess County, Indiana, and settled on a farm in Madison Township.

The 1850s saw an explosion in regional conflicts between the North and South. Slavery was an open sore that had festered for many years in the United States and it aggravated all other points of disagreement between the two sections. With the passage of the Fugitive Slave Law, the Kansas-Nebraska Act, and John Brown's raid on Harper's Ferry, southern Indiana quickly became a battleground of ideologies between those with pro-southern sympathies and the Unionists. Many of the Daviess County residents still had family members living in the South. Michael and his companions were firmly committed to the preservation of the Union and served in the army for three years to prevent the splintering of our country.

In this titanic national struggle, "Uncle Mike" (as he was called by his comrades) saw action in both the western and eastern theaters of the war. In the spring of 1862, he and his regiment were part of the Union's effort to defeat Stonewall Jackson in the Shenandoah Valley. In the process, Michael was wounded and captured during an engagement at Buckton Station. He then experienced the hell of a Confederate prison for three months. While in prison his regimental brothers took part in the bloodiest day of battle in American history, the Battle of Antietam. There his regiment sustained heavy casualties in what has become known as "The Cornfield." Michael was paroled on September 13, 1862, and exchanged five days later (the day after the Battle of Antietam). In the spring of 1863, his regiment gave a good accounting of itself when they helped the Union army avoid a disastrous rout at the Battle of Chancellorsville. But perhaps the most glorious day for the regiment was when they made their ill-fated charge in "The Swale" at Spangler's Spring during the Battle of Gettysburg. Many men were needlessly slaughtered in the suicide attack. Michael was then moved to the western theater of the war where his regiment helped chase the Confederate army out of northern Georgia and fought their way to Atlanta. During this campaign he was wounded at the Battle of Resaca. After the fall of Atlanta, Michael and the men of Company B were mustered out of service and returned to Daviess County.

Michael Wallick with the 27th Indiana Volunteer Infantry

<u>1861</u>

AUG 10 Michael enlists as a corporal in what becomes Company B of the 27th Indiana Volunteer Infantry.

Michael and the Daviess County boys assembled on this field in August of 1861 before marching to Camp Morton in Indianapolis. This community park is located on Co. Rd. 1000 N. in Raglesville.

SEP 12 - DEC Company B is mustered into Federal service on September 12th and departs from Camp Morton for operations around Camp Frederick, MD, and the upper Potomac River.

1862

JAN - FEB The regiment continues to be active in northern Virginia and Maryland. They also help guard the Baltimore & Ohio Railroad and its junctions.

MAR - JUN Stonewall Jackson's Shenandoah Valley Campaign The 27th Indiana is part of the Union force that pursues General Stonewall Jackson's Corps in the Shenandoah Valley. General Jackson is outnumbered by the Federals but he continually confounds the Union army by quick maneuvers up and down the Shenandoah Valley and by fighting when the Federal force has divided itself. Jackson's strategy is to keep as many Union soldiers as possible occupied in the valley, thus relieving the pressure of Federal operations being conducted toward Richmond, VA. He is tremendously successful. On March 23, 1862, Michael and the 27th Indiana are near the hamlet of Kernstown, VA, where the opening battle of the campaign is fought. In this first engagement the 27th IVI is near but not part of the action. Distant cousins Henry M. Wallick of the 67th Ohio and William F. Wallick of the 13th Indiana are actually in combat at the First Battle of Kernstown and at one point in the engagement they are in the same line of battle. For the next ten weeks all three Wallick regiments will be chasing General Jackson and his small army of Confederate volunteers.

MAY 23   Engagement at Buckton Station, Michael is wounded then captured Michael's company, plus one company from the 3rd Wisconsin Infantry, is sent to Buckton Station to prevent the Confederates from destroying the railroad and telegraph communications between Front Royal and Strasburg, VA. At 2:00 PM the Confederates make their first of two unsuccessful attacks on the railroad station at Buckton. They are easily repulsed. However, in the course of Michael's first engagement of the war he is wounded and taken prisoner by the Rebels. On June 1st, one of Michael's comrades from Raglesville, Private Thoms Wirts, writes a letter to Michael's wife, Jane, saying that her husband is missing and thought a prisoner of war.

Buckton Station as it appears today.

Michael was captured near here while fighting against the Rebels on May 23, 1862. This station was a stop on the Manassas Gap Railroad and Company B was sent here to help secure the communication lines between Front Royal and Strasburg, Virginia.

One week after Michael Wallick was captured at Buckton Station, Virginia, Private Thomas Wirts wrote a letter to Michael's wife, Jane, to inform her that Michael was missing and thought a prisoner of war. To aid the reader, some spelling corrections and puntuation marks have been added to this transcription. However, throughout the letter Thomas Wirts spells Michael's name, Micle, and that spelling has been retained. Errors in grammer have also been uncorrected. Private Wirts was in the same company as Michael and enlisted at the same time and place, Raglesville, Indiana. The opening salutation, "Dear friend," would indicate that Thomas Wirts was quite familiar with Jane.

Page 1

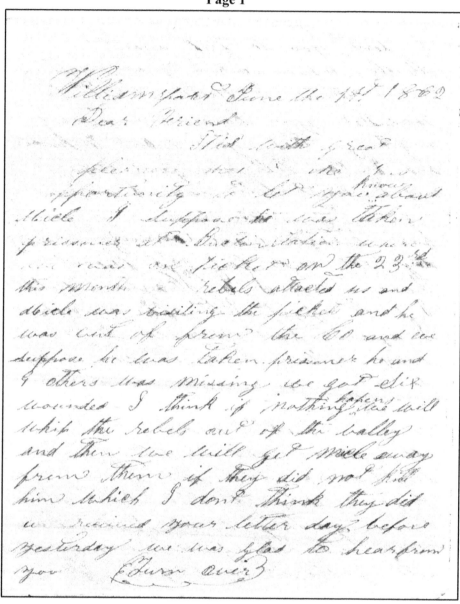

Williamsport, [MD] June 1st 1862

Dear Friend
It is with great pleasure that I have an opportunity to let you know about Micle. I suppose he was taken prisoner at Buckton Station where he was on picket on the 23rd [May] this month as Rebels attacked us and Micle was visiting the pickets and he was cut off from the Company and we suppose he was taken prisoner; he and 9 others was missing. We got six wounded, I think. If nothing happens, we will whip the Rebels out of the Valley and then we will get Micle away from them, if they did not kill him, which I don't think they did. We received your letter day before yesterday, we was glad to hear from you.

PAGE 2- I don't want you to fret about Micle. Whenever I hear anything from him I will write to you and let you know. If there is anything that you want to know and I can tell you, just write and I will tell you. I am in hopes that Micle will come up, for stragglers are coming in every day that was cut off from the Company. J.E. Hayes* is well. I will quit till after dinner…. I again seat myself to finish my letter. I will now try to give you a small history of the fight we was in the ____. Micle was missing, we was all sitting about the camp and the first we knew about the Rebels coming they was right there and shooting at us. We all gathered our guns…

*J.E.Hayes was a private also from Raglesville,
Indiana.

Page 3- …and run a meeting them. We fired at them a few times and we found there was so many of them that they was about to surround us and cut us off from the Wisconsin Company. We retired about 200 yards and crossed the bridge and there we held our position against 700 cavalry and there was only about 100 of us and we fought them about 2 hours and drove them. Our boys took one of them prisoner and said we killed 2 captains, one lieutenant and 13 privates, and wounded about 40 and they killed one man, wounded about 10 and took prisoners, or we suppose so as they was missing. I will now bring my letter to a close by signing my name.

{To Jane Wallick}   {Thomas S. Wirts}

MAY 24 - SEP 12   Michael becomes a prisoner of war and is first taken to Lynchburg, VA. He is then transferred to Libby Prison, then moved to the enlisted man's prison on Belle Island. This facility is located in the middle of the James River at Richmond, VA. Michael will remain imprisoned on Belle Island for the next three months. His oldest daughter, Sarah, gets married on July 31st while he is still a prisoner of war. One of the commanding officers during Michael's incarceration at Libby Prison is Henry Wirz, the infamous commandant of the future Andersonville Prison. At the conclusion of the war, Wirz will be the only soldier from the Confederate army executed for war crimes.

The following account is from Wilbur D. Jones's book *Giants in the Cornfield*:

> **Corporal Michael Wallick**, *sliced in the shoulder by a saber at Buckton, was never treated. He had 'a sponge and much cold water applications and kept down the pus and it healed all right.' Wallick, one of the few Hoosiers imprisoned at Lynchburg, Libby and Belle Isle, [all in Virginia] also contracted rheumatism, sore eyes and a cataract which went untreated. Private Jones Davis remembered Wallick: 'We were badly exposed then and had insufficient food, great deal of sickness among the prisoners.'*

Another account of his capture is recorded in James E. Garten's book *Clarksburg and Early Odon, Indiana.*

> *In one skirmish,* **Mike Wallick**, *Andrew J. Vest, and Bob Shears of the 27th regiment were captured* [at Buckton Station]. *The Rebels wanted to shoot Wallick because they said he had killed their general.*[12] *His fellow prisoners knew that he did it, for 'Uncle Mike' was a fine shot. After a long and heated argument, they finally made the Rebels believe that the man who did the killing had escaped. The three were imprisoned at Belle Isle. The food was bad, as in all other Rebel prisons. Wallick and Vest said that while they sickened on the food, Bob Shears, who had been reared in the slums of Cincinnati, got fat. It was better than he had been accustomed to at home.*

SEP 13   Michael is paroled at Aikens Landing, Virginia. On that same day, three regimental comrades from Company F find a copy of General Robert E. Lee's "Special Orders #191" wrapped around three cigars in an abandoned field outside of Frederick, MD. These lost orders are from General Lee to his top corps commanders and tell of the movements to be carried out by the Army of Northern Virginia for the next four days. General McClellan, commander of the Union army, is slow to act on this treasure of information. This episode is considered the most grievous breach of security during the Civil War. Near the end of his enlistment, Michael will be transferred to Company F.

SEP 17 Battle of Antietam   Michael is waiting to be exchanged while his regiment sees action in "The Cornfield" during the early morning hours at the Battle of Antietam. This engagement nearly destroys some companies in his regiment. Michael is fortunate to miss this battle. There are 440 men engaged from his regiment and by the end of the day 209 are killed or wounded.

SEP 18   Michael is exchanged as a prisoner of war and begins his return trip to his regiment.

OCT - DEC   The 27th Regiment has guard duty from Harper's Ferry to Fredericksburg, VA.

1863

JAN 20 - 24 "The Mud March"   The 27th Indiana participates in General Burnside's disastrous "Mud March". In December the general had been humiliated by his defeat at Fredericksburg, VA. To right the reversal, General Burnside plans a winter offensive (against the wishes of his subordinates) and will attack the rear of General Lee's army in order to destroy his supply line. Two days of unseasonably warm weather with heavy rains turn the Virginia dirt roads into a quagmire. The Army of the Potomac becomes paralyzed in knee-deep mud, making movement impossible. This is the last straw for President Lincoln and the bungling Burnside is relieved of command.

---

[12] No general was involved in this engagement. However, two Confederate captains were killed during the skirmish. Michael may have killed one of them.

MAR 13 Michael is promoted to 4th Sergeant.

MAY 2 - 3 Battle of Chancellorsville General Robert E. Lee is at his best and boldest in this battle in the wilderness of Virginia. He breaks all the conventional rules by splitting his army before a superior force not only once, but twice. He sends Stonewall Jackson on an end-run rear attack that takes the Union commanding general, "Fighting Joe Hooker", totally by surprise. General Hooker is known for his aggressive spirit in battle, but for some reason his nerve leaves him when he becomes the supreme commander at Chancellorsville.

Michael and the 27th Indiana bravely withstand the crushing evening attack made by General Jackson's Corps at the end of the first day of battle. This helps forestall a Federal panic and collapse. The repulse of this late day charge, together with the next morning's counterattack at Fairview, helps avoid a general rout of the Union army.   The counterattack on the second day is with fixed bayonets and Colonel Silas Colgrove, commanding officer of the 27th Regiment, reports, *"the Rebels fled before us like sheep."* The regiment is then engaged in hand-to-hand combat with soldiers from North Carolina and pushes them back into a tangled abatis (a network of field fortifications lying on the ground, usually with sharpened tree branches pointing outward to slow charging infantrymen). Colonel Colgrove reports that the Rebels, *"became mixed up in a perfect jam, our men all the time pouring in the most deadly fire. I can safely say that I have never witnessed on any other occasion so perfect a slaughter."*

For the next three hours the 27th Indiana's brigade counters numerous Confederate attacks and only withdraws after they have exhausted their supply of ammunition. The brigade is then moved to the rear and off the front line of battle. By midday, the whole Federal army has to retreat due to the poor decisions made by the Union high-command. The numbers alone tell the story of the fierce fighting Michael's regiment sees at the Battle of Chancellorsville. On May 1st there are 300 men present for duty. Two days later 36 men have been killed and 114 wounded, a casualty rate of fifty percent.

This monument to the 27th Indiana is located between the battlefields of Hazel Grove and Fairview, on Berry-Paxton Road. The regiment fought here on the night of May 2nd and morning of May 3rd. During this battle fifty percent of those engaged were killed or wounded.

Monument inscription:

The 27th INDIANA INFANTRY
3rd BRIGADE, 12th CORPS
HELD THIS POSITION FROM 7 PM
MAY 2nd TO 9 AM MAY 3rd 1863

PRESENT FOR DUTY 300
KILLED 36, WOUNDED 114

MUSTERED IN AUG. 1861
MUSTERED OUT SEPT. 1864

TOTAL ENROLLED 1,101
KILLED 172, WOUNDED 505
DIED OF DISEASE, 120

Looking from Fairview to Hazel Grove, where Michael and the 27th Indiana were deployed at Chancellorsville. Hazel Grove is approximately one mile in the distance, at the end of the open ground.

Battle of Gettysburg   The 27th Indiana is involved in a controversial early morning attack at Gettysburg. Most people are familiar with General Pickett's tragic charge that was made on the last afternoon of the three-day battle. Michael's regiment will also make a futile and disastrous charge on the third day of battle and will suffer the same result as General Pickett's division. Many men of the 27th will be needlessly butchered due to a misunderstanding of orders and an aggressive colonel demonstrating his fighting spirit.

JUL 1 First Day of Battle   The 27th Indiana has been marching all day from Littlestown and arrives at Gettysburg at about 4:00 PM. Michael spends the night near Wolf Hill and receives orders to form and entrench the next day at the base of Culp's Hill.

JUL 2 Second Day of Battle - 8:00 AM   Michael and his regiment march to Spangler's Spring at the base of Culp's Hill and they become the extreme right of the Union army at Gettysburg. In the morning, skirmishers from the 27th have a long-range duel with the famed Stonewall Brigade. The regiment spends the day entrenching at their new position near Rock Creek. At 6:00 PM the regiment is ordered south toward Little Round Top to help bolster that position, which has been under heavy attack all day. As they march toward their assigned position near the Wheatfield they are exposed to artillery fire. There are only a few casualties. After 45 minutes they are ordered to counter-march back to their original position at Culp's Hill. When they return they find that the Confederates have taken their old position and occupy the breastworks. The men are furious that the Rebels now benefit from their hard day's labor and want to retake the works immediately, but they must wait until the next morning.

JUL 3 Third Day of Battle - 5:00 AM. The 27th Indiana's brigade and regimental commander, Colonel Colgrove, receives orders to advance two regiments across the swale (or meadow) and retake the Union position that was lost the preceding day. What was actually ordered has been disputed and a controversy about the orders arose immediately after the battle.

Monument to the 27th Indiana at the foot of Culp's Hill.

Colonel Colgrove insisted that the officer from headquarters who communicated the orders to him demanded that two regiments from his brigade cross the swale and retake the entrenched position. General Ruger, the commanding officer at headquarters, remembers Colonel Colgrove being ordered to *"advance skirmishers at that point* [the swale] *and, if not found in too great a force, to take two regiments and dislodge the Confederates from the breastworks."* By not advancing skirmishers first (to test the strength of the Rebel works) the 27th Indiana and 2nd Massachusetts march into an enemy meat grinder. Colonel Colgrove writes:

> *The enemy was entirely sheltered by the breastworks and ledges of rock. It was impossible to send forward skirmishers. The enemy's advantages were such that a line of skirmishers would be cut down before they could fairly gain the open ground that intervened. The only possible chance I had to advance was to carry the position by storming it.*

Confederates fired at the 27th Indiana from behind breastworks (represented by the stone wall) which the Indianans had constructed the previous day to use against the very enemy that now possessed them. The 27th Indiana and 2nd Massachusetts charged across the open ground pictured below. Three Indiana monuments are placed in the swale.

Below is "The Swale", where the 27th Indiana and 2nd Massachusetts charged at Confederate breast-works on the morning of July 3, 1863. This picture is taken from the Confederate perspective. The Hoosiers advanced out of the left woods and charged toward the well-entrenched Rebels.

The Confederates outnumber the Federals two to one in this hopeless attack. Lt. Colonel Charles Mudge of the 2nd Massachusetts Infantry, upon receiving his orders asks, *"Are you sure that is the order?"* The orderly answers in the affirmative. Lt. Colonel Mudge then says, *"Well, it is murder, but that's the order."* He does not survive the charge. It is said that Colonel Colgrove, upon receiving his orders, is dismayed but cool. He pulls on his nose, which he does when pondering a difficult problem, and repeats, *"It cannot be done; it cannot be done."* Pausing and looking upward he then says, *"If it can be done, the 2nd Massachusetts and the 27th Indiana can do it."*

Michael's regiment first has to make a complex marching movement to begin the charge. In the first 100 yards the 27th maneuvers down a slope that is thickly covered with oak and hickory saplings. They then pick up the pace as they enter the clearing of the swale. Confederate volleys decimate the men of the 27th but the survivors merely close ranks and continue. The fire grows more intense and the two regiments have to fall back and retreat to their own breastworks. Immediately the Rebels mount an ill-conceived counterattack that is easily beaten back by the 27th Indiana and 2nd Massachusetts. For the rest of the day the troops must remain under a boiling hot sun amidst the groans of the wounded and decaying bodies of the dead.

This monument, pictured to the left and below, marks the farthest advance made by the 27th Indiana in its attack at The Swale. The Rebels fired from behind the breastworks at the bottom of the tree line. Four color bearers were killed and four more wounded in the attack.

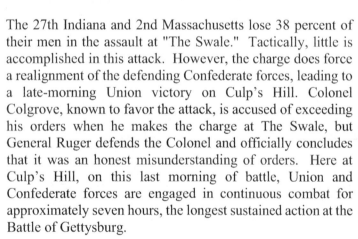

The 27th Indiana and 2nd Massachusetts lose 38 percent of their men in the assault at "The Swale." Tactically, little is accomplished in this attack. However, the charge does force a realignment of the defending Confederate forces, leading to a late-morning Union victory on Culp's Hill. Colonel Colgrove, known to favor the attack, is accused of exceeding his orders when he makes the charge at The Swale, but General Ruger defends the Colonel and officially concludes that it was an honest misunderstanding of orders. Here at Culp's Hill, on this last morning of battle, Union and Confederate forces are engaged in continuous combat for approximately seven hours, the longest sustained action at the Battle of Gettysburg.

AUG 15 - SEP 5   The 27th Indiana is posted in New York City during the summer draft riots of 1863. It is the worst civil insurrection in American history, excluding the Civil War itself. Michael and distant cousin, Elias Wallick, travel on the same steamship, The Merrimac, from Alexandria, VA, to New York City and both bivouac in Battery Park.

OCT 3 - 30   Michael is home on furlough most of the month and returns to duty November 1st.

NOV - DEC   The 27th is moved to the western theater of the war and guards the Nashville & Chattanooga Railroad at Tullahoma, TN. On November 20th, Michael pens a letter to his wife, Jane. It is Michael's only letter that survived the war.

Below is a letter written by Michael Wallick to his wife, Jane, on November 20, 1863, from Tullahoma, Tennessee. Unfortunately, with the passage of time, the ink has bled through to the other side of the page making it extremely difficult to read. It is believed that the severe bleeding was caused by Michael using ink made from blackberry juice, which was commonly done at that time. To the right of the missive is a transcription of the letter. During the months of November and December, 1863, Michael's regiment provided security for this very important Federal railroad terminus. After returning to his regiment from a month-long furlough at home, Michael wrote the following letter to his wife.

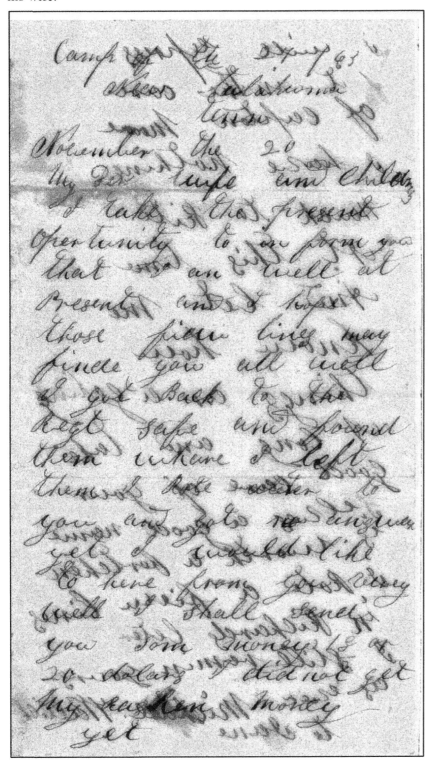

Camp of the 27

Near Tullahoma,

    Tennessee,

November the 20,

My dear wife and children,

I take the present

opportunity to inform you

that I am well at

present and I hope

these few lines may

fine you all well.

I got back to the

regiment safe and found

them where I left

them. I wrote a letter to

you and got no answer

yet I would like

to hear from you very

well. I shall send

you some money, 18 or

20 dollars. I did not get

my regular money

yet.

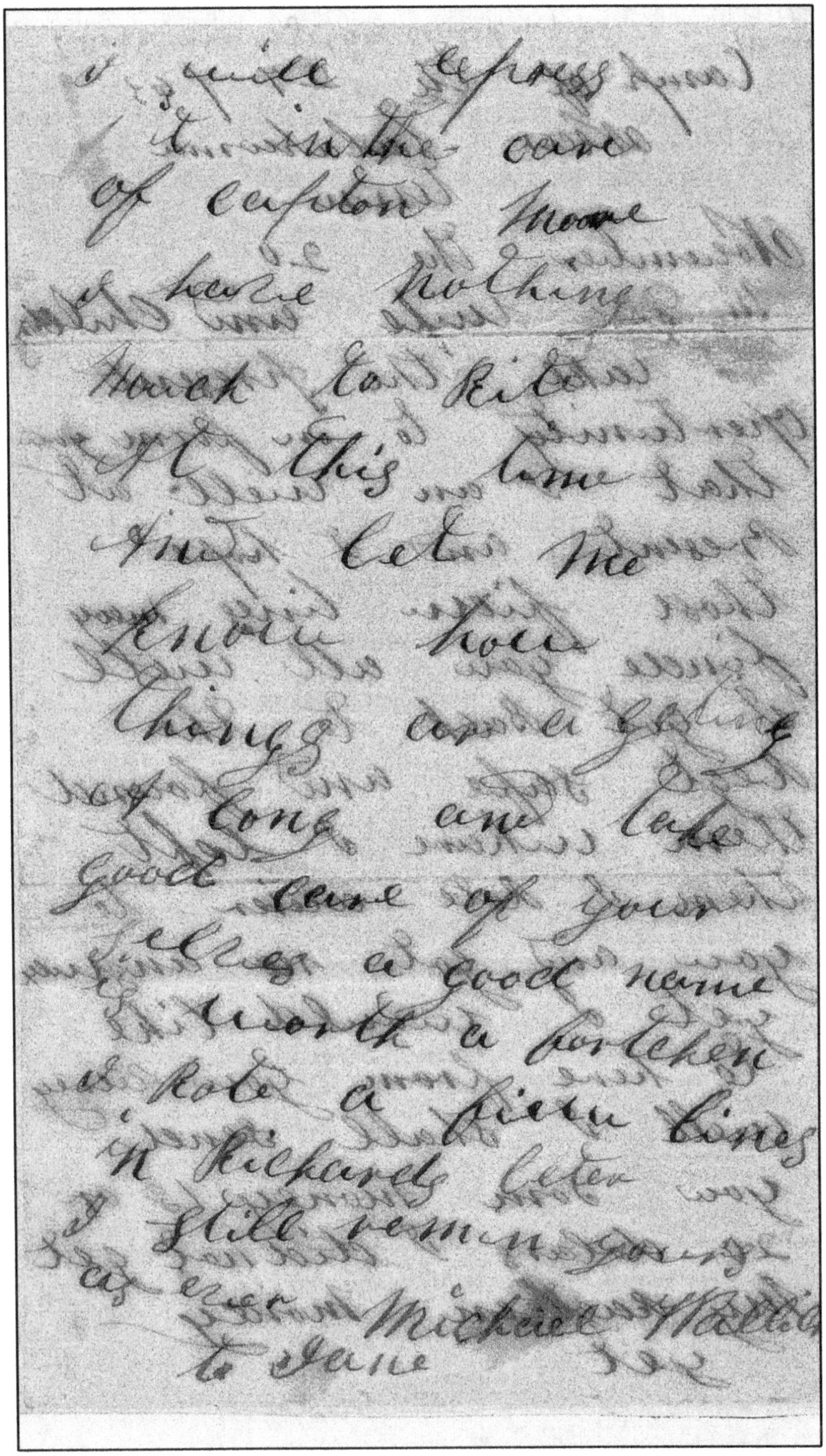

I will express

it in the care

of Captain Moore.

I have nothing

much to write

at this time.

And let me

know how

things are getting

along and take

good care of your

self. A good name

is worth a fortune.

I wrote a few lines

in Richard's* letter.

I still remain yours

as ever. Michael Wallick
To Jane

*This is probably Richard Trueblood. He was the only Richard in the regiment from Raglesville, Indiana.

1864

JAN - APR Preparations for the Atlanta Campaign On February 13, Michael is transferred from Co. B to Co. F by order of the colonel. Those wishing to reenlist do so at this time. Michael refuses a second enlistment and will be discharged the beginning of September 1864.

MAY 4 The Atlanta Campaign Begins The 27th steps out of camp near Chattanooga, TN, to begin its march to Atlanta, GA. They are in a skirmish at Rocky Face Ridge, GA.

MAY 14 - 15 Battle of Resaca, GA. Both "Daviess" Michael and Charles F. Wallick (a distant cousin from Peru, IN, who is in the 87th Indiana Infantry) are engaged in this battle. They are within a few hundred yards of each other and never know it. It is also very likely that they don't know of each other's existence due to the great distance in the branches of the family tree. Charles' regiment, the 87th Indiana, is placed at the center of the Union line with Michael's regiment cattycorner and behind them in support. However, as the battle progresses, Michael and the 27th are moved to the far left of the Union line where they are engaged in combat and achieve a great victory. At 4:00 PM that afternoon, Michael and his regiment are ordered by their colonel to lie on the backside of a knoll that is in the path of a Confederate advance. Being hidden from the oncoming enemy, the trap is set. When the Confederates are within 35 yards, the colonel gives his signal and the men of the 27th Indiana rise up to deliver a massive volley into the ranks of the 38th Alabama. The 27th Indiana captures not only the Alabamians' battle flag (a feat of great honor in the war), but also their colonel along with 35 prisoners. In this battle Michael receives his second wound of the war when a Confederate artillery shell fragment creates a contusion, or slight bruise, on his left hip.[13] He is first taken to Jefferson General Hospital in Jeffersonville, IN, then Madison, IN, for treatment.

Both Michael and Charles F. Wallick fought on the field below at the beginning of the Battle of Resaca. Later, the 27th Indiana was moved north to check a Rebel advance. During the battle Michael is slightly wounded in the left hip by a shell fragment, forcing a three-month recuperation.

MAY 27 Michael is admitted to Jefferson General Hospital in Jeffersonville, IN, for treatment of the wound he received at the Battle of Resaca.

JUN 28 - AUG Sergeant Wallick is transferred to Madison Medical Hospital in Madison, IN, for recuperation from his hip injury.

---

[13] In Michael's compiled military service records it says he is "slightly wounded in the left hip." On his pension applications the "slightly wounded in the left hip" is transformed into a "gunshot wound to the left hip," making the injury sound far more serious.

SEP 1 Michael reports back for duty in the field.   He has missed the final push to and siege of Atlanta, but will be with his regiment when they conclude their service.

SEP 12 Michael is mustered out of Federal service at Camp Morton, Indianapolis, and returns to Daviess County, IN. Veterans who chose to reenlist are transferred to the 70th Indiana Volunteer Infantry.

Epilogue - Michael returned to Daviess County after being discharged from the 27th Indiana and two months later his eighteen-year-old son, William Hewit, enlisted in the army. .

The war had broken Michael's health. He has an exhaustive pension file that reveals what diseases and injuries he incurred during the war. They include: a shell (gunshot) wound to his left hip, a saber wound to his right shoulder, pleurisy, chronic diarrhea resulting in disease of the rectum (severe hemorrhoids) and various eye diseases. The effects of these ailments continued to plague him for the rest of his life. For all of this sacrifice to his health, by 1896, he was receiving a $12 a month pension. By 1900 Michael had retired from farming and was living in Odon, Indiana. There he died on February 13, 1905, and was buried next to his wife, Jane, in Raglesville Cemetery.

Michael Wallick, 27th Indiana Infantry.

From Odon Journal, February, 1905

Michael Wallick Dead
Aged Soldier Answers The Last Roll Call

After many long weeks of illness, Michael Wallick died Monday, aged 87, 11 months, 7 days.

Mr. Wallick was born March 6, 1817, in Bedford County. Pennsylvania. When quite young he moved with his parents to Ohio. He lived there until 1855, when he came to Indiana. While in Ohio, on August 29, 1833, he married Jane Booth. To the union five children were born. A son died during the Civil War and a daughter died in 1886. The living are W.H. Wallick, Mrs. George Correll and Mrs. J.W. Whitlock. His wife died in May of 1899, and a few years later he married Mary Perkins, who survives him.

When he first came to Indiana, he settled on a farm near Raglesville, but later moved on a farm on First Creek. He lived there until after the war, where he moved to Odon. He served three years in the Civil War, enlisted in Co. B, 27th Indiana Volunteers. For five months he was a prisoner of war. He was a member of the Methodist Episcopal Church and in politics was a republican. The funeral services were conducted by Rev. J. Broder Tuesday at the home of his daughter, J.W. Whitlock, where he died. At Raglesville Rev. S.D. Dorsey preached the funeral discourse. Burial is the cemetery at that place. His six grandchildren, Oscar, Ray and Henry Wallick, Les, Richard and Belden Correll were pall bearers.

Comrades-in-Arms

Son
Hewit	38th IVI

Cousins
Daniel	20th OVI
David	139th OVI
Elijah	102nd OVI
Henry M.	67th OVI
David H.	102nd OVI

Nephews
Isaiah	49th OVI
Edward	34th & 36th OVI

William "Hewit" Wallick - 38th Indiana Volunteer Infantry, Co. D

Rank: Private

Place of enlistment: Vanderburgh County, Evansville, Indiana

Mustered into Federal service: November 11, 1864

Service time: 8 Months, 4 days

Born: May 10, 1845 - Tuscarawas County, Ohio

Age at enlistment: 18 years old

Physical description: height - 5' 9", black hair, black eyes

Civilian occupation: farmer

Family Lineage: William, son of "Daviess" Michael, son of "Bunker Hill" Michael, son of "Bedford" Michael, son of Hans Michael Wallick

8

In the American Civil War it was possible for a man who was drafted to escape his military obligation by hiring a substitute in his place. A draftee at the beginning of the war could pay a three-hundred-dollar commutation fee to the United States Government and be excused from service. However, as the war dragged on, the government grew weary of trying to find men to replace those who bought their service time and the draftee had to find his own replacement and negotiate a mutually agreed upon fee with the substitute. Commutation fees skyrocketed in price as more men were required for the war and fewer men volunteered. This fusion of military obligation to free market economics meant that by the war's end the "substitute soldier" could demand double, triple or even quadruple the original $300 dollar fee. The controversial policy gave rise to the slogan in both the North and South, "Rich man's war, poor man's fight."

William Hewit Wallick was a substitute soldier and he is the only Wallick who served as such during the war. His family called him by his middle name, "Hewit", and that is how we will refer to him in this biographical sketch. There were actually four William Wallicks from the Hans Michael lineage who served during the war, three from Indiana and one from Ohio. The use of their middle names or initials is essential to help distinguish one soldier from another.

Hewit was the first-born son of "Daviess" Michael and would have been about sixteen years old when he saw his father march off to war. At this young age, Hewit found himself the "man of the house" and was left to tend the family farm and help his mother, Jane, raise four siblings. One can imagine the anticipation and excitement every time the family opened a letter from their father. However, the horrors of war were quickly realized when Papa Michael, in his first engagement, was wounded in the shoulder, captured by the Confederates and became a prisoner of war for five months. By the end of his service Michael had been wounded twice in battle and knew well the hardships of a soldier's life. What influences he brought to bear on Hewit's decision to become a soldier we will never know. Michael certainly had no romanticized notion of soldiering, so it could have been Hewit's strong sense of patriotism that motivated him to join the ranks. Or, the enticement of good money for one year's military service may have helped Hewit decide to become a soldier. It was probably a combination of both, as it is today, when young men and women join the military. Hewit enlisted in the army just two

William "Hewit" Wallick

James Wallick Collection

67

months after his father's discharge. Michael and Hewit are the only father and son duo from the Wallick clan to have served during the war.[14]

There was a mistake by the state of Indiana when it compiled its reference, *Report of the Adjutant General of the State of Indiana on soldiers who served in the Civil War*. Hewit's name is recorded as William **H Walker,** from Scotland, instead of William H **Wallick**. It was an error that caused a little difficulty when researching this biography and must have created problems at the time for Hewit, since the disability and widow's pension applications for Hewit and his wife always include the alias name, Walker. In Hewit's compiled military service record they use his correct given and surnames. And we know the "H" stand for Hewit, because of letters his father, Michael, sent home during the war.

William Hewit Wallick with the 38th Indiana Volunteer Infantry

1864

NOV 11 Hewit is mustered into Federal service in Evansville, IN. He enlists as a substitute for draftee Taylor A. Pensinger of Daviess County, IN. The amount of the commutation fee is unknown. Hewit is obligated to serve one year for Mr. Pensinger.

Opposite - Hewit Wallick's enlistment paper stating he is a substitute for Taylor A. Pensinger.

Hewit's signature

---

[14] "The Seven Days Soldiers" of the 109th Indiana had father/son combinations, but they were federalized for only seven days. For more details read chapter six, page 49.

1865

JAN Hewit is posted with the 38th Indiana in Savannah, GA, and prepares for General Sherman's advance into the Carolinas. Life in the army could have been difficult at first for Hewit, for he joined an outfit that had been together since September of 1861 and the veterans had reenlisted the previous fall. Replacements were not always welcomed by veteran soldiers.

FEB 5 Sherman's Carolina Campaign The 38th Indiana marches out of Savannah, GA, to begin the "Campaign of the Carolinas" with General William Tecumseh Sherman. Earlier, "Uncle Billy," as his troops called General Sherman, declared that his campaign through Georgia would be so harsh that he would "make Georgia howl." If he made Georgia "howl" then he must have made South Carolina *"scream,"* for the destruction and ruin he brought upon that state exceeded the devastation of Georgia. General Sherman always considered South Carolina the cradle of the rebellion and, as such, it should be punished. The 38th Regiment participates in one of the most remarkable troop movements in history. Military historians have marveled at the ability of that army to travel twelve miles a day in the swamps of South Carolina during the middle of winter. Many of the logistic and engineering lessons learned during Civil War campaigns were utilized a few years later in building our transcontinental railroad.

Ruins of Columbia, South Carolina - February 1865.

The 38th Indiana was a participant in the destruction of the Palmetto State.

MAR 16 Battle of Averysboro, NC. The 38th is held in reserve and sees no action.

MAR 19 - 21 Battle of Bentonville Hewit and the 38th Indiana make a probing attack at the beginning of the battle but are repulsed by a veteran Confederate brigade. Although the attack fails, it causes the Rebels to make a tactical blunder. Confederate reinforcements are diverted from their original deployment and this weakens a Rebel counterattack. It is considered the biggest mistake the Rebels make during the battle. Distant cousin Charles F. Wallick of the 87th Indiana is also at Bentonville and is guarding the wagon trains.

The 38th Indiana was deployed on this field, just in front of the trees at the opening of the Battle of Bentonville. Their corps attacked but was thoroughly routed and had to retreat before the enemy in what became mockingly known as "The Battle of Acorn Run." The title ridiculed Hewit's XIV Army Corps performance, for their corps insignia was the acorn.

MAR 24   The Regiment occupies Goldsboro, NC.

APR 10 - 14   Hewit and the 38th Indiana advance on Raleigh, NC.

APR 26   Surrender of General Johnston's Confederate Army at Bennett House, Durham, NC.

Hewit's regiment was in the vicinity when the Confederate terms of surrender are discussed and signed here, at Bennett House, April 26, 1865. Over 89,000 Rebel troops are ordered to stack arms. It is the largest surrender of forces during the war. One can argue that it is here, and not at Appomattox, that the final defeat of the southern armies in the War of the Rebellion was achieved.

APR 29 - May 20   The 38th IVI march to Richmond, VA, and then on to Washington, D.C.

MAY 24   Grand Review of General Sherman's Western Army.   At the conclusion of the war both Hewit and Charles F. Wallick march past this Presidential Reviewing Stand during the Grand Review of the Western Army in Washington, D.C. General Grant, President Johnson and his Cabinet, plus other important political and military dignitaries are present. There are 65,000 men in the parade and it takes six hours to pass by the grandstand.

Presidential Reviewing Stand on Pennsylvania Ave. May 24, 1865.

JUN   The 38th Indiana travels to Louisville, KY.

JUL 15   Hewit and the men of the 38th Indiana Infantry are mustered out of Federal service at Louisville. Hewit is discharged after serving only eight months of his one-year commitment.

William Hewit Wallick is buried in the Mount Olive Cemetery, just east of Odon, Indiana.

<u>**Comrades-in-Arms**</u>

Father
Michael   27th IVI

Cousins
Isaiah   49th OVI
Edward   34th & 36th OVI

71

Levi Wallick - 44th Indiana Volunteer Infantry, Company K

9

Rank: Private

Place of first enlistment: De Kalb County, November 17, 1861

Mustered into Federal service: November 22, 1861

Reenlisted as a veteran in Chattanooga, Tennessee: January 1, 1864

Mustered into Federal service for a second time: January 9, 1864

Combined service time: 3 years, 10 months

Born: c.1826 (discrepancy in records)

Age at first enlistment: 34 or 35 years old

Physical description: height - 5' 7", dark eyes, dark hair

Civilian occupation: laborer

Proposed Family Lineage: Levi, son of "Coshocton" Philip, son of "Bedford" Michael, son of Hans Michael Wallick

Levi Wallick is a soldier with a mysterious life and lineage. We know nothing about Levi until he enlists in the Union army during the American Civil War. This biography gives a proposed family lineage because, at this point, there is no documentation that definitively connects this Levi to any descendants of Hans Michael Wallick (1707-1767). Nevertheless, circumstantial evidence gleaned from Levi's war record, together with the work of genealogist Jeffrey Wallick, makes a strong enough case to warrant his inclusion in these Civil War biographies. Below are two scenarios that could possibly link Levi to the Hans Michael Wallick family.

When Levi Wallick enlisted in the Union army in late 1861, he was living in DeKalb County, Indiana, a region where Wallick families were known to have lived for over a decade. One of the families was the clan of "Kansas" Benjamin Wallick, who moved his family from Tuscarawas County, Ohio, to DeKalb County, Indiana, in 1850. By 1860 Benjamin's family was living in the little village of Butler, Indiana, a mere eight miles from the settlement of Waterloo, where Levi was living at the time of his enlistment. There is no specific information to link Levi with Benjamin's family, but it could be more than coincidental that the two lived within a short buggy ride of each other. Perhaps Levi was living in the area because he was possibly related to Benjamin.

Another possible affiliation that deserves serious consideration is that Levi may have been one of the sons of Philip Wallick (1783-1841). Philip first came to Tuscarawas County in 1813, where he married his wife Elizabeth Showalter, then quickly moved on to settle in northern Coshocton County. Only one descendent from Hans Michael Wallick, out of the hundreds that were born in the nineteenth century, had the given name Levi and that person was the first born of Philip. Jeff Wallick states that Levi was born in Coshocton County sometime between 1819-1823 and died after August, 1866. That is all we know about that son of Philip. What we know about the personal history of Levi Wallick, the soldier, is what he states about himself in his enlistment papers: he was born in Tuscarawas County, he was 35 years old when he first enlisted in 1861, and his occupation was that of a laborer. Nothing more is known about the background of this soldier. Given that it is very common to find errors in Civil War military records and that men would sometimes lie or not even know their true age upon enlistment, it is possible that Levi Wallick of the 44th Indiana could have been the son of "Coshocton" Philip Wallick. Levi claimed himself to be a laborer. If he worked for others, he may have never owned any property of his own. If he were a bachelor, there would be no marriage documents and possibly no record of home ownership, a likely explanation for the very sparse paper trail. Jeff Wallick's materials also state that the son of Philip was born in Coshocton County between 1819 and

1823, a broad range for a birth date. The age for Levi the soldier is reasonably close to that of Philip's son, given that dates were notoriously inaccurate in the early nineteenth century. There is documentation that Philip and Elizabeth were married in Tuscarawas County in February 1819 and that their first-born was named Levi. Perhaps he was born in Tuscarawas County before they moved to Coshocton County. The entire period is indefinite.

Whether Levi was related to Philip or "Kansas" Benjamin is secondary to the question of whether Levi is a descendent of Hans Michael Wallick. There is one piece of evidence, albeit circumstantial, that gives us good reason to believe he descended from Hans Michael. When Levi enlisted for the second time as a veteran, he listed his place of birth as Tuscarawas County, Ohio. That in itself may seem insignificant. However, for the past two hundred years every Wallick who was born in Tuscarawas County has descended from Hans Michael, without exception. This fact alone is cause enough to have Levi included in this account of Wallick soldiers from the American Civil War. This author also believes that it is most likely that this soldier is indeed the son of Philip Wallick.

Levi Wallick's second enlistment papers are dated January 1,1864, and states that he is 37 years old and born in Tuscarawas County, Ohio. For the past two hundred years every Wallick born in Tuscarawas County has been related to Hans Michael Wallick.

Born in Tuscarawas County, Ohio

Levi Wallick's signature

All that being said, the only historical evidence that exists for Levi Wallick concerns his war years and his post-war migration to Missouri. He served in the Union army longer than any other Wallick soldier, serving from November 22, 1861 until September 14, 1865. When Levi left the service, he moved to Missouri and it has been discovered that he made two applications for United States land grants, both located in the Ozark Mountains, forty acres in 1868 and eighty acres in 1875. There are no census or court records uncovered as yet to indicate what he did with the property, where he died or where he was eventually buried. Apparently, he never married and he left no heirs, so Levi's final years and resting place are as mysterious as his family lineage.

Levi Wallick with the 44th Indiana Volunteer Infantry

<u>1861</u>

NOV 17   Levi Wallick enlists in the Union army at Auburn, IN. He is owed a $100 enlistment bounty.

NOV 22   The 44th Indiana Infantry is mustered into Federal service at Ft. Wayne, IN, then moves south into Kentucky.

DEC   The regiment is posted at Henderson, KY. Levi's Company K along with Company G stays in Henderson while the remainder of his regiment march off to Calhoun, KY. There they help bolster its defenses against Rebel intrusion. Levi will stay at Henderson until March 11, then he will rejoin his regimental brothers at Savanah, TN.

<u>1862</u>

FEB 8   The eight remaining companies of the 44th leave Calhoun, KY, and arrive as reinforcements at Ft. Henry, on the Tennessee River, for General Grant's attack on that Confederate installation.

FEB 12   Attack and Investments of Forts Henry & Donelson   Admiral Foote's flotilla of six gunboats bombard the Confederate forces at Ft. Henry and force the Rebels to withdraw twelve miles north to Ft. Donelson. These two forts on the Tennessee and Cumberland Rivers are built to guard the two river passages that flow into the heartland of the Confederacy. With the surrender of Ft. Henry, central Tennessee and northern Alabama are open to Union conquest by way of the Tennessee River. General Ulysses S. Grant leaves the 44th Indiana at Ft. Henry while he moves the rest of his army to Ft. Donelson.

FEB 13   General Grant is in need of the forces he left at Ft. Henry for his attack on Ft. Donelson. The 44th Indiana is called up and placed at the center of the Union line that surrounds the Confederate forces at Ft. Donelson. The Confederates also occupy the town of Dover, TN. The 44th Regiment's brigade commander is General Lew Wallace, who after the war will write the epic novel "Ben Hur."

Battery on the Cumberland River at Ft. Donelson.

Admiral Foote's gunboats fired from the distant downriver horizon but were driven back by the Confederate defenders. The use of river gunboats alone was unsuccessful in reducing the fort.

FEB 14 Admiral Foote's gunboats attack Ft. Donelson but this time they are not successful in driving the Rebels from their fortifications. The Confederate forces return accurate fire from their large siege guns, driving the admiral's flotilla back with heavy casualties. During the engagement Admiral Foote is wounded in the foot.

FEB 15 The Confederates realize the seriousness of their situation and try a breakout on the far right of the Union line. At first, they succeed. But then for some inexplicable reason they move back into their earthworks and do not exploit their advantage. Only Nathan Bedford Forrest and his cavalry troops escape capture.[15] Levi's regiment is ordered to attack and close the Confederate breakthrough, which has taken place at the Cumberland River on the Union right. There is heavy fighting throughout the contest. At 2:00 PM the Union army assembles a large force to close the Rebel escape route and pin the Confederate army in their earthworks. The 44th Indiana tips the balance of the engagement with an uphill charge near Forge Road. Thirteen thousand Confederates are forced to capitulate and their commanding officer, General Simon Buckner, asks General Grant for his terms of surrender. Buckner and Grant had been classmates at West Point and Buckner even loaned Grant some money in the old days when Grant was quite destitute. The Confederate general is anticipating generous terms. Grant responds, "No terms except an unconditional and immediate surrender can be accepted. I propose to move immediately upon your works." Buckner found these terms both "ungenerous and unchivalrous." This first major victory of the war for the Federals gives the North its first real hero, U. S. Grant. His name is now recognized in every Northern household. Grant's response to Buckner also creates for him a life-long moniker: **"Unconditional Surrender"** Grant.[16]

Dover House, site of General Buckner's surrender to Ulysses S. Grant.

MAR 11 Levi Wallick and those who were left behind at Henderson, KY, last December, now rejoin their regiment at Savanah, TN. The 44th Indiana has been reorganized into General Hurlbut's Division of Grant's Army of the Tennessee and arrive at Pittsburg Landing by steamboat. Hurlbut's Division makes camp south of the intersection of the Main Corinth Road and the Hamburg-Savanna Road. It has been determined by Generals Sherman and Grant that the plateau at Pittsburg Landing will be an ideal place to train the vast numbers of raw recruits that comprise the Union's western army. At this point in the war the Federal army is just as inexperienced at soldiering as the Rebels.

---

[15] General Forrest and his men will be a constant source of aggravation to Union commanders throughout the war and will capture two Wallick soldiers, William Wallick of the 51st Indiana and Elijah Wallick of the 102nd Ohio Infantry.

[16] The quality of men who fought in the American Civil War was unique. To illustrate the point, both Confederate Generals Simon Buckner and Joseph E. Johnston served as pallbearers to President Grant at his funeral.

Background to the Battle of Shiloh (or Pittsburg Landing)

The Federal army in Tennessee is divided; half of its men are with General Grant and the other half are with General Don Carlos Buell and his Army of the Ohio. It is early April and the two are scheduled to rendezvous, but have yet to do so. Most of Grant's troops have never experienced battle and some soldiers have never even fired their new muskets. These raw recruits are surprised by a Confederate attack on the morning of April 6, 1862. The Rebels want to take advantage of the divided Union forces and destroy Grant before he can unite with General Buell. The Army of the Ohio is making its way to Pittsburg Landing, but has yet to arrive. Grant's outnumbered troops must withstand a fierce Rebel assault and hold on until Buell arrives.

APR 6   The Battle of Shiloh: First Day - 7:30 AM   It is Sunday morning and Levi Wallick's regiment is in a relaxed mode with no expectations of battle. They are positioned far to the rear of General Sherman's frontline troops when they hear the sounds of musket fire and artillery. General Sherman has made his headquarters at Shiloh Methodist Church, a log cabin for worship.[17] It is here that the battle begins and the 44th Indiana is quickly moved to a position north of the Peach Orchard and west of the Hamburg-Savannah Road. They wait for orders to engage the enemy. At 10:00 AM General Hurlbut positions the 44th along a wagon road that runs between the Main Corinth Road, and the Hamburg-Savannah Road. This slightly depressed lane that runs through wooded terrain becomes known as the Sunken Road. Levi's unit is on the Union left and north of the Peach Orchard. Here the fighting is fierce and the Federal army must repulse repeated Rebel attacks. The bullets fly so thickly that the Confederate soldiers refer to this sector as "The Hornets Nest." The fighting rages from late morning to mid-afternoon and there are heavy casualties on both sides. At 2:30 PM General Hurlbut is forced to withdraw his troops before he is surrounded by the enemy and captured in "The Hornets Nest. The brigade to Hurlbut's right is under the command of General Prentiss. He and all of his troops are forced to surrender.

Battlefield between The Peach Orchard and The Hornets Nest. Here the 44th Indiana endured some of the worst fighting of the day.

The Sunken Road at Shiloh Military Park.

---

[17] One of the many ironies of the Civil War is that the word "shiloh" in Hebrew means *place of peace.*

The 44th Indiana monument is on a secluded path off the Sunken Road.

Monument inscription reads: *This regiment formed in this line Sunday, April 6, 1862, at 8:30 A.M. it repulsed several charges made by the enemy, including four terrific charges by right of Gibson's Brigade which, under orders of General Bragg, was attempting to force this line back. During these engagements the woods caught fire. At 2:30 P.M. regiment fell back to a line with 1st Brigade, then to rear and left of Bloody Pond, where it charged on enemy's infantry and artillery. Here seven flag-bearers were shot down. At 4:30 P.M. slowly fell back and supported siege guns. On Monday, April 7, regiment fought the enemy till 3:00 P.M. Number of men in action 478. Casualties: Killed 1 officer and 33 men. Wounded 6 officers and 171 men. Missing 1 man: Total 212*

First Day - 2:30 to 4:30 PM The 44th Indiana is moved again, this time to Wicker Field, just north of a small pond that is still on the battlefield today. Wounded men from both sides crawl to the pond to nurse their wounds and quench their thirst. Many die there. Soldiers begin calling the water source "Bloody Pond" because of the death that surrounds its banks and the crimson color of the water. By 3:30 PM General Hurlbut has realized that he is being outflanked by Confederates on his left and he orders the 44th Indiana along with everyone else in his division back to Pittsburg Landing. When they arrive at the landing, they learn that all of the Union artillery has been ordered to the rear to establish one last line of defense along Pittsburg Landing Road. Here the Federals will make one last attempt to stop the Confederate army before they are overrun. General Hurlbut is in command of this position, which has become known as "Grant's Last Line." It is late in the day and about this time the vanguard of General Buell's army begins to arrive, but they can make little impact on the battlefield today. The intensity of the day's battle has exhausted and scattered the Confederate forces so they are not only tired but very unorganized. They wait until the next day to attack and defeat the Union army. Levi and the 44th Indiana are moved to bivouac where they started the day, at the intersection of the Main Corinth Road. and the Hamburg-Savannah Road.

Bloody Pond at Shiloh National Military Park. Even today the water has a reddish hue due to the red clay soil of south Tennessee.

APR 7   Second Day of Battle   The 44th Indiana remains in camp until 11:00 AM when they are summoned to advance not far from their old bivouac and plug a gap in the Union line. About 3:00 PM Levi's brigade commander, General Jacob Lauman, is sent an urgent message that they are to move up the Hamburg-Purdy Road. south of the review field to assist General Gibson's Brigade of General McCook's Division. Isaiah Wallick, of the 49th Ohio, is fighting in Gibson's Brigade. It is very possible that both Isaiah and Levi are fighting on the same field at the same time here at Shiloh. When the Rebels see the reinforcements advance, they begin to withdraw from the field and the 44th will fight the rest of the day here and hold the position until nightfall. The entire Rebel line retreats and the two-day battle ends with the opposing forces basically in the same position as where they started. Combined Union and Confederate casualties are 5,000 dead and 12,000 wounded, more American battle casualties than in all its previous wars combined. The 44th Indiana throws 478 men into the two-day melee. Of that number, 33 are killed and 177 are wounded. It is a hollow victory for Grant. Although winner of the contest, his future is in doubt as a Union commander because of the number of casualties he sustained in the battle and because he was so badly surprised by the Confederate army.

APR 29 - MAY 30   The 44th Indiana is part of an advance to Corinth, MS, driving the Confederates out of that vital railroad junction.

MAY 31 - JUN 12   The regiment pursues the Confederates to Booneville, KY.

JUN - AUG   Levi is part of General Buell's Northern Alabama and Middle Tennessee Campaign.

AUG 21 - SEP 26   The 44th Indiana marches north to Louisville in response to General Bragg's invasion of Kentucky.

OCT 1 - 7   The 44th regiment continues to chase General Bragg and his Confederate forces through Loudon and central Kentucky.

OCT 8   Battle of Perryville   Levi and William Wallick are in the same corps and arrive in the early afternoon on the day of battle. Confederate forces under General Bragg begin their attack about 2:00 PM, hours behind schedule. The commander of the Union army, General Don Carlos Buell, can hear very little of the cannon fire at the opening of the engagement due to an acoustical shadow.[18] General Buell does not realize that he is in a major engagement until 4:00 PM. He fails to engage over half his available force, which includes Levi's and William's regiments. Charles F. Wallick and the 87th Indiana are in the northern portion of the battlefield where they have their first taste of battle; also a terrible scare with friendly fire. It is near dark and due to poor visibility Charles and the 87th Indiana nearly fire their muskets into the 2nd Minnesota Regiment, which is in front of them. General Buell is relieved of command after the battle because he lets the Confederates army escape his grasp, even though he has an overwhelming advantage in troops.

OCT 22 - NOV 7   The 44th IVI marches to Nashville, TN, a major installation in the south for the Union army.

NOV 8 - DEC 26   Levi and his regiment have duty at Nashville guarding railroads and Union supplies.

---

[18] An acoustical shadow is a mysterious phenomenon caused by terrain and other factors where loud noises cannot be heard close by but can be heard very clearly miles away.

DEC 26 - 29 The 44th advances southeast to Murfreesboro, TN.

DEC 31 Battle of Stones River: First Day The 44th Indiana is moved to the rear in reserve at the outset of the battle. The Confederates attack early in the morning and quickly rout the far right of the Union army. Distant cousin Isaiah Wallick is in one of the first brigades engaged in the battle. Isaiah's brigade is totally surprised by the Rebel attack, many still eating their breakfast. At mid-morning Levi's division is moved to the Nashville Pike Road and will become part of a strong defensive line established by the Federals. William Wallick is also at Stones River and his brigade (under General Harker) is deployed adjacent to Levi's (under General Fyffe). Levi's and William's brigades will fight next to each other until William's brigade is out-flanked and driven from the field. Levi's brigade remains on the Nashville Pike Road until sundown, concluding the first day of battle.

1863

JAN 1 The Federal and Confederate armies wait for each other to move or attack. The previous day's battle has exhausted the troops on both sides. Neither side initiates any action and the first day of 1863 is a day of rest for the two armies at Stones River. There is no major change in either army's position on the field.

JAN 2 Second Day of Battle The stillness continues into the next morning but at 2:00 PM the Confederates begin an attack on the Union left, next to Levi's brigade. About 4:00 PM the Rebel army is advancing past the 44th Indiana and the Hoosiers deliver a withering fire into the flank to the passing Confederate brigade. Artillery is then fired into the advancing Rebel troops. The 44th Indiana then joins in a counterattack that drives the Confederate forces from the field. Levi's regiment has 8 men killed, 52 wounded and 25 missing. The Rebels eventually retreat from Murfreesboro, in effect, leaving the Union army in control of middle Tennessee.

McFadden's Farm at Stones River National Military Park. It was near this spot where Levi and the 44th Indiana poured a most devastating crossfire into the Rebel Army in the late afternoon of January 2, 1863.

JAN - JUN Duty at Murfreesboro and construction at Ft. Rosecrans, a major supply base for the Federal army.

JUN 23 - AUG 16 The 44th Indiana is part of General Roscrans' Tullahoma Campaign. This almost bloodless maneuver drives the Confederate army out of middle Tennessee and into Chattanooga in east Tennessee.

AUG 17 - SEP Levi marches over the Cumberland Mountains and moves into northern Georgia with the 44th Indiana.

SEP 19 Battle of Chickamauga: First Day Three Wallicks will fight in this biggest battle of the western theater of the Civil War. Levi Wallick will be joined by distant cousins Charles F. Wallick of the 87th Indiana and Isaiah Wallick of the 49th Ohio. It is the largest two-day battle of the war and is only eclipsed by Gettysburg in the number of casualties and troops engaged. It is the Confederacy's greatest victory in the west. Levi and the 44th Indiana begin the day south of the battlefield at Lee & Gordon's Mills. Early in the morning Charles F. Wallick will engage in the opening volleys of the battle at the north end of the battlefield. The battle will rage all morning and at 1:00 PM Levi (who is in Colonel George Dick's brigade) will be moved up from Lee & Gordon's Mills, form a line of battle east of Brotherton Field, and aid in checking a strong Confederate attack. There is heavy fighting all afternoon along the Union front and Dick's brigade is finally pushed back. Charles F. Wallick is in Colonel Ferdinand Van Deveer's brigade and they are moved from the Union left, down to the Union center, where Levi has been driven back by the Rebels. Around 3:15 PM the 44th is in savage fighting in Brotherton Field and are driven back beyond Glenn-Kelly Road. They bivouac west of Dry Valley Road (present day Lytle Road in Chickamauga National Military Park).

**Monument to the 44th Indiana Infantry
Brotherton Field, Chickamauga Battlefield.**

SEP 20 Second Day of Battle At 10:00 AM Levi and the 44th Indiana are ordered to take a position west of Kelly Field. About an hour later they advance north and drive the Confederates up to McDonald House, where the Visitor's Center is today. All three Wallick soldiers' regiments will fight in and around Kelly Field in the early afternoon of September 20th. The Union army is maintaining their position, in spite of the repeated Rebel assaults, when one of the biggest battlefield blunders of the war is ordered by the Federal high command. An aide to General Rosecrans is passing behind the center of the Union line when he sees what appears to be a large gap between two brigades of the Union battle line. This is a wooded area of the battlefield and the aide fails to see the division where Charles F. Wallick is deployed (Brannan's Division), which has been concealed by the abundant underbrush. This erroneous information is relayed to General Rosecrans, who orders two brigades moved out of the Federal line to plug a non-existent gap. In effect, he creates a gap in his own line to plug a gap that is not there. By chance the Confederates are determined to strike the Union line at that precise sector where the new gap has been created by the Federal high command. There are no Union troops to resist the Rebels' assault and the Confederate army carves a huge hole into the Federal line. This late morning breakthrough enables the Confederates to collapse the Union defenses and force a retreat back towards Chattanooga. Charles F. Wallick's corps commander, General George Thomas, has throughout the day been rallying his men (including remnants of the 44th Indiana) to make a stand on a small ridge southwest of Snodgrass House. In Federal records it is called Snodgrass Hill and in Confederate records it is called Horseshoe Ridge but, by whatever name, it is agreed that General Thomas makes a stand there that saves the Union army from destruction. It is from this action that he earns his moniker, "The Rock of Chickamauga." Fragments of the 44th Indiana are to the far left of the Union position on Snodgrass Hill and the 87th Indiana helps fill the center of the Federal line. Whether Charles is still active on the field at this time is uncertain, for at some point in the battle he is wounded in his left hand and he must retire. At 4:30 PM the Confederates make an all-out attack against the Federal's position. They fight for about an hour and the Confederates sustain heavy losses during their uphill attack against Union artillery and massed infantry. Levi's regimental commander, Lieutenant Colonel Simeon C. Aldrich, in his post-battle official report states: "*Placing our flag on the brink of the hill, our men nobly rallied and fought like veterans. We repulsed the enemy three times with great slaughter. They finally abandoned the ground.*" This delaying action, orchestrated by General Thomas and his subordinates, helps give the Union army time for an orderly retreat. Without this action, the Union army will be routed and destroyed. Levi and the 44th Indiana arrive in Chattanooga in the early morning hours of September 21.

Snodgrass House on Snodgrass Hill (Horseshoe Ridge) - On this ridge Levi and the 44th Indiana battled the surging Confederate forces long enough to help cover the Union army's orderly retreat. Charles F. Wallick's regiment, the 87th Indiana, were also part of the heroic delaying action on Snodgrass Hill.

SEP 21 - NOV 7 The 44th Indiana is trapped in Chattanooga, TN, with the Confederate army occupying the hills that encircle the town. Supplies are very low with soldiers on half, even quarter rations at times. It is from this period, when the Union army is nearly starving, that a little vignette concerning Levi appears in their regimental history, *The Forty-Fourth Indiana Volunteer Infantry - History of its service in the War of the Rebellion*, written in 1880 by Dr. John Rerick. The account reads:

> **Levi Wallack**, *Co.K, an eccentric and well-known character, was noted for the size of his haversack, it being about three times as large as others' and always well filled. But he was not partial, and balanced it by carrying on the other side a triple supply of ammunition, which he dealt out fearlessly to the enemy whenever opportunity offered. He did not know fear, and as little of discipline, unless he was inclined that way at the time. In the skirmish on Missionary Ridge he fired thirty-one rounds, and at every shot was heard to mutter, "There, dem you, take that." One night while on picket, he ascertained that there were some cattle within the Rebel picket lines. The old haversack was sadly depleted then, so down he dropped on the ground and stealthily stole his way to the cattle, faced them for the Union lines, and started them on the run. The Rebels sent the bullets whizzing after him, but when they ascertained that he had escaped, and come out with fifteen head of cattle, they joined the Union boys in a cheer over the exploit.* **Wallack** *was granted the privilege of killing three of the cattle for the benefit of himself and his regiment.*

General Grant is called from his very successful Vicksburg Campaign to help break the Confederate siege about Chattanooga. Grant's arrival brings immediate changes to the Federals' morale and strategy. The supply problem is solved when the Federals capture Brown's Ferry. The taking of this landing allows food and ordnance to cross the Tennessee River into Chattanooga. The supply route is called the "Cracker Line" by the troops and is the lifeline for the Union army. Within weeks the men are well-supplied and mount an offensive against the Rebels.

NOV 8 The 44th is assigned to provost duty (military police) in and around the town of Chattanooga, TN. This duty takes them out of their previous brigade. The regiments from their old brigade will be involved in the famous charge up Missionary Ridge on November 25, 1863. If the regiment had not been given provost duty, Levi would have been alongside Isaiah Wallick's brigade when they charged up Missionary Ridge. During that attack Isaiah was mortally wounded and he died two days later in a Chattanooga army hospital. Charles F. Wallick's regiment, the 87th Indiana, was also in the assault on Missionary Ridge, but he was on furlough, at home in Peru, IN, recovering from a gunshot wound he received at the Battle of Chickamauga.

DEC Levi decides to reenlist as a veteran volunteer soldier with the 44th Indiana. The U.S. Government is desperate for men to join the ranks because the war has taken much longer than anticipated. The commanders running the war also foresee a problem with the next fighting season. In the coming year all 1861 three-year regiments will have completed their terms of service and exit the army. This will create a severe manpower shortage. The government's solution is to offer an incentive to the men who will volunteer for three more years. If three-fourths of a regiment re-enlists, the men can stay together as a veteran unit, an important feature to the soldiers. If too few recommit, those who do reenlist will be assigned to other units as replacements, something very undesirable to the veterans. All men who reenlist are promised a $400 bounty (payable at the whim of the government) and a thirty-day furlough. Levi and the required amount of men take the government's offer and the 44th now becomes a veteran volunteer regiment. They are obligated to serve for three more years or until the conclusion of the war, whichever comes first.

1864

JAN 1 Levi officially signs his reenlistment papers as a veteran soldier. He will spend much of the war in the vicinity of Chattanooga, TN. This southeast Tennessee town is a vital Union supply center and a lifeline to General Sherman's Army for the next year as it marches through Georgia. Levi is the only Wallick soldier to reenlist in a veteranized regiment during the Civil War.

JAN 9 It is recorded in the company books that Levi is owed $340 by the U.S. Government (see the compiled military service record cards on the next page). For reenlisting, he is paid $60 of a $400 bounty (this is four times the amount of his first enlistment bounty). Some of Levi's pay is to be withheld as reimbursement for passage home on his furlough; the cost for transportation from Nashville to Louisville, KY, is $3.80. Levi and all the regiment's veteran volunteers are mustered back into Federal service on this date.

FEB 23 – MAR 24 Levi and all others who reenlisted begin their 30-day furlough while those who did not recommit stay in camp and continue provost duty at Chattanooga, TN.

SEP 28 – OCT 14 Levi and the 44th are sent to Tullahoma, TN, for unspecified service. Tullahoma is an important railroad junction in south-central Tennessee. The regiment is then attached to Colonel Grosvenor's expedition into southern Tennessee and northern Alabama.

OCT 15 The regiment returns to Chattanooga and continues with its provost duty and provides railroad security.

NOV 22 The soldiers who did not reenlist are mustered out of Federal service, free to return home. Levi and the others who did extend their enlistments as veteran volunteers go on furlough.

DEC 6 Levi returns to the 44th Indiana but is either sick or immediately gets sick   Within ten days of his return Levi is admitted to a Nashville hospital for unstated reasons. The record does not show when he is discharged from the hospital.

1865

JAN - SEP Little is documented about the activities of Levi and his regiment during their last nine months of duty in Chattanooga. As exciting and eventful as their first enlistment was, their second enlistment appears to be quite routine with no major incidents or engagements, to the great delight of the veterans, to be sure. The 44th Indiana travels to Nashville, TN, and ends their second enlistment with little fanfare or drama.

SEP 14 Levi and the 44th Indiana are mustered out of Federal service in Nashville, TN. There is a notation in the company record concerning Levi that states, "Retained under General Order 101, one Enfield rifled musket and accoutrements: price, $6.00." In almost four years of service the 44th Indiana has 4 officers and 76 enlisted men killed or mortally wounded. An additional 9 officers and 220 enlisted men have died of disease.

Below are two of Levi Wallick's compiled military service records. The muster card to the left states his place of birth as Tuscarawas County, Ohio, and that he was paid a 400-dollar bounty. He leaves the service with his Enfield rifle and its accoutrements, all purchased for six dollars.

Epilogue - For a time it was unknown what happened to Levi Wallick after he mustered out of service in Chattanooga, Tennessee. However, an examination of Dr. John H. Rerick's regimental history reveals that by 1880 Levi was residing in Missouri. A document search for that state found that in 1868 Levi was granted government lands under the Homestead Act and was awarded 40 acres in Camden County. He again applied for lands in 1875 and was awarded 80 more acres in the same township. With the discovery of these grants, Levi's trail runs cold and it is unknown where he died or where he is buried. It appears from his record that he was never married and had no heirs. A search of cemeteries in Camden and its surrounding counties has revealed nothing. It is hoped that in the future, Levi's final resting place may be discovered, granting closure to this man's life and service.

Comrades-in-Arms

Cousins

Michael	27th IVI
David	139th OVI
Daniel	20th OVI
Elijah	102nd OVI
David H.	102nd OVI
Henry	67th OVI

Levi's regimental brothers from Company H, 44th IVI.
This picture was taken at Chattanooga, Tennessee.

Levi Wallick's 1875 land grant certificate. This certificate from the Federal Land Grant Office in Booneville awards Levi 80 acres in Camden County, Missouri. Levi's property was located in what is called today, "The Heart of the Ozarks."

From Ohio

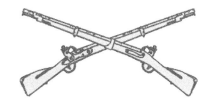

Elias B. Wallick - 126th Ohio Volunteer Infantry, Co. E

10

Rank: Private

Place of enlistment: Tuscarawas County, Strasburg, Ohio

Mustered into Federal service: September 4, 1862

Service time: 2 years, 1 month, 2 days

Born: Aug 13, 1838 - Tuscarawas County, Ohio

Age at enlistment: 24 years old

Physical description: height - 5' 7", light hair, dark eyes

Civilian occupation: farmer

Family Lineage: Elias, son of George Jr, son of "Strasburg" George, son of Johannes, son of Hans Michael Wallick

There is little known about Elias B. Wallick's all-too-short life except for his service record during the Civil War and a bit of family history. Elias' grandfather, George Sr, came to Ohio in 1816 from Cumberland County, Pennsylvania, and it was said at the time he was a cousin to "Bunker Hill" Michael. The genealogical evidence does strongly suggest that Elias' great-grandfather, Johannes, and "Bedford" Michael were brothers.

Elias' father, George Jr, was a farmer living near Strasburg, Ohio, in 1862. We can assume that Elias, at age 24, saw the war as a great opportunity not only to demonstrate his patriotism but also escape from his farming responsibilities for three years and embark on an adventure of a lifetime, at the government's expense. Such feelings were not uncommon with Elias' generation. Also, the $100 bounty offered to new recruits could have been a motivating factor in Elias' decision to leave home and march with his new comrades-in-arms. Whatever the reasons, Elias enlisted on August 21, 1862, and became a member of a regiment that saw some of the ugliest fighting of the Civil War. There are some Wallick soldiers who never did "see the elephant" at any time during their service (the elephant being a euphemism for seeing battle, or taking part in "the big show"). However, there are others, like Elias, who we know were in savage battle because their regimental histories tell of many violent engagements. Elias himself was mortally wounded in the fields of northern Virginia.

The 126th Regiment was part of General Grant's spring of 1864 Overland Campaign which fought four major battles within six weeks. The battles of the Wilderness, Spotsylvania Courthouse (where the 126th participated in the assault at the "The Bloody Angle"), North Anna River and Cold Harbor were all part of the bloodiest campaign of the Civil War. Their summer engagements, especially the Battle at Monocacy, created numerous casualties in Elias' regiment and all the soldiers were by then feeling the awful strain of continuous combat. Elias was fortunate to have survived those horrific events of the late spring and early summer, 1864. However, his good fortune came to a tragic end on September 19th at the Battle of Opequon Creek where he was severely wounded, dying four days later.

**Monument to Elias Wallick in
Grandview Cemetery, Strasburg, OH.**

There is a small monument to Elias next to his father's grave in Strasburg, Ohio, but Elias is not buried there. The army only paid to have officers' remains shipped home during the war and Private Elias' family probably could not afford to pay to have his body returned. It is obvious from the cemetery monument that the family would have wished Elias to be buried in his hometown of Strasburg, Ohio. The truth is that Elias lies in northern Virginia at Winchester National Cemetery - a fitting place of honor for his ultimate sacrifice in the service of his country.

Elias Wallick with the 126th Ohio Volunteer Infantry

1862

AUG 21 Elias enlists at Strasburg, OH, and joins men from Tuscarawas County who become Company E of the 126th Ohio Volunteer Infantry Regiment.

SEP 4 The 126th Infantry is organized at Camp Steubenville, OH, and mustered into Federal service.

OCT 17 The regiment moves to Parkersburg WV, then on to Cumberland, MD.

DEC - JUN 1863 Elias and his comrades perform guard duty on the Baltimore & Ohio Railroad at Martinsburg, VA. Typhoid fever and smallpox wreak havoc in the ranks over the winter of 1863, killing an average of six men in every company. Many of the men who partially recover are rendered unfit for further service and are discharged.

1863

JUL The 126th OVI pursues General Lee to Manassas Gap and sees action at Wapping Heights.

JUL 4 Elias is hospitalized with chronic rheumatism; he returns to duty July 15th.

AUG - SEP 15 Elias and his regiment patrol New York City streets when martial law is declared as a result of the summer draft riots. Over one hundred civilians are killed in the rioting, which is to this day considered the greatest civil unrest in our nation's history. Elias and distant cousin, Michael Wallick of the 27th Indiana, travel on the same steamship, The Merrimac, from Alexandria, VA, to New York City and both bivouac in Battery Park.

OCT - NOV The regiment sees limited action in the Bristoe Campaign and at Brandy Station on Nov 8th. They advance to Rappahannock River line.

DEC - APR, 1864 The 126th is in winter quarters in preparation for General Grant's spring offensive.

1864

MAY 5 - 6 Battle of the Wilderness The 126th is engaged with the enemy at the extreme right flank of the Union line near the end of the first day's battle. On the second day, May 6, they are forced to retreat when Confederate General John B. Gordon initiates a fierce counterattack late in the afternoon. The 126th is cast into the melee where they sustain a great many casualties. The following is an account written by Francis Cordrey of Company E (Elias' company) and what he saw at "The Battle of the Wilderness":

> *The sun had veiled his face beneath the horizon as if refusing to longer witness the bloody scene. Darkness had gathered around us and the Rebels in our midst. Flames issued from guns like many flashes of lightning and the roar of musketry was like that of thunder. Shrieks and groans of the wounded and dying at our feet told that the destruction of the line was appalling. Blue and gray lay side by side and their blood flowed into the same pool while blue and gray stood over them with ball and bayonet, adding more crimson to the pool and often mistaking friend for foe in the dark. Our regiment, consisting of about four hundred men on the field that day, lost 230 killed and wounded.*

Rifle pits at The Wilderness Battlefield.

These rifle pits survive today and were dug where Elias and his regiment were positioned during the Battle of the Wilderness. The 126th OVI fought here, at the extreme right of the Union army. This section of the battlefield has an interpretive walk and the trail is where Confederate General Gordon made his late day attack, which almost destroyed the Federal army.

MAY 10 - 12   Battle of Spotsylvania Courthouse and the Assault at "The Bloody Angle" This battle will witness the longest and most grotesque sustained hand to hand combat of the entire Civil War. For twenty hours, at times in a driving rain, the Federal forces attack the Rebels, where they slaughter one another with sword, rifle-butt and bayonet. In some places slain soldiers are stacked five and six men deep in the mud before the Rebel breastworks. The 126th Ohio is within 100 yards of the Confederate works before it has to withdraw with heavy losses. The following is a detailed description of what Elias must have witnessed during that awful day. Captain John E. Peck of the 126th, from Jewett, OH, describes the carnage:

Monument to the 126th Ohio Infantry at "The Bloody Angle".

On the 12th, desperate fighting began on the left of the line at 5 o'clock in the morning by General Hancock, who had transferred his corps from the right to the left the evening before. The struggle was fierce and terrific all day in order to get possession of an elevated position held by the Rebels for the purpose of using artillery. The roar of the musketry was awful as volley after volley was hurled back and forth and the terrific noise of the artillery was beyond anything before experienced. All day long and far into the night the struggle raged with unceasing fury. If there was a lull in the storm of battle it only proved to be a breathing spell, preparatory to a more desperate onset. At about 11 o'clock that day the 126th Ohio with its division was ordered to the left of the line where both armies appeared to be concentrating. After arriving and forming a line of battle, the regiment was detached from its brigade and sent past several lines of battle to the front line, within 100 yards of the enemy breastworks at what was known as "The Bloody Angle"- so called from the sanguinary struggle that took place at the salient in the Rebel works - and formed a line of battle while the Rebels were pouring volley after volley and thinning the ranks. Having no protection save a few pines, six or eight inches in diameter, the men lay down. They loaded lying; then rising to their knees, took deliberate aim at the heads of the Rebels above the parapet and fired. Although the men were being stricken down at a fearful rate, they were cool and calm and kept up such a constant fire on the Rebels as to nearly stop theirs at times, as it was almost sure death for them to show their heads. There was no standing up and cheering or yelling, except by a few individuals and they were soon hushed in death, as they were targets for the enemy. The men were inspired with more than usual fearlessness and firmly held their position until each man had exhausted fifty rounds of ammunition and then he took cartridges from the boxes of their slain comrades in order to keep up the fire. This was continued for nearly two hours and when the Rebels discovered that the firing had ceased, they came out of their rifle pits and began advancing toward the regiment. The men of the 126th fixed bayonets and held the ground for a short time and only fell back in the rear of the next line of battle when in imminent danger of being annihilated. Now the regiment was very small, only a remnant, not enough for a company of minimum size...

MAY 23 - 26 North Anna River The regiment sees little, if any, action here.

JUN 1 - 3 The Assaults at Cold Harbor The 126th Ohio Infantry makes two assaults at Cold Harbor over a three-day period. In its last assault, June 3rd, General Grant orders what he later described as one of the biggest mistakes he ever made during the war. He orders a frontal attack on the entrenched Confederate positions at Cold Harbor, resulting in 7,000 Union casualties in less than an hour (some estimates have put the casualty figure occurring within the first fifteen minutes). General Grant says of this battle in his memoirs, *"I have always regretted that the last assault at Cold Harbor was ever made. At Cold Harbor no advantage whatever was gained to compensate for the heavy loss we sustained."* Elias is able to survive Grant's Overland Campaign. National Archive records show Elias present for duty and list no wounds received, however, not all wounds were recorded. This series of battles has the worst casualty rates for any single campaign of the war.

Union Casualties Only

Wilderness	May 5-7	18,791
Spotsylvania	May 10 -12	18,000
North Anna	May 23-26	2,100
Cold Harbor	June 1-3	12,737

Rifle pits at Cold Harbor National Military Park.

These rifle pits were constructed by Confederate troops. On the morning of June 3, 1864, Union soldiers charged out of the trees, across what was then open ground and into a hail of bullets. Within minutes, thousands were slaughtered in the attack. This sector is where Elias and his brigade were deployed during the disastrous assault.

JUN 18 - JUL 6   Attack at Petersburg   The Union army attacks and begins its nine-month siege at Petersburg, VA. Elias is at the extreme northern flank of the Union trenches at the beginning of the siege.

JUL 9   Battle of Monocacy   Elias is detached from Petersburg and quickly moved up to Maryland to help thwart the planned attack on Washington, D.C., by Confederate General Jubal Early. The opposing Union commander is General Lew Wallace, future author of the biblical epic novel, *Ben Hur*. The day is stifling hot. The regiment is in the center of the Union lines, near Thomas House, and counters two vicious Confederate attacks before they must retreat; their courage being unable to offset the superior numbers of the Rebels. The 126th has again taken heavy casualties this day.

Battlefield at Monocacy.

Elias Wallick and the 126th Ohio charged toward the top of the hill at the Battle of Monocacy. Elias' regiment was part of the first Federal reinforcements to arrive from Petersburg, VA, to stop the advance of General Early. They were unloaded from the troop trains and immediately sent into battle.

Although a tactical defeat, it is a strategic victory. This battle delays the Confederates long enough to allow Federal reinforcements to mobilize and come to the aid of Washington, D.C. On July 12th, General Early's attack on Washington is easily repulsed. This is the only serious threat to our nation's capital during the war.

AUG 1   The 126th is attached to General Sheridan's Shenandoah Valley Campaign.

SEP 19   Battle of Opequon Creek - Elias is mortally wounded

Excerpt from the *National Parks Service Study Team of the Shenandoah Valley Campaign*:

> **Overview of the Battle**   *Opequon Creek, or Third Winchester, is the largest and most desperately contested battle of the Civil War in the Shenandoah Valley, resulting in more than 9,000 casualties. The battle is the turning point of the war in the Valley, marking the rise of Sheridan and the decline of Confederate power. Sheridan defeats the Confederate army again three days later at Fisher's Hill [September 22], forcing it to retreat up the Valley to near Waynesboro, VA. The Confederate Army of Lt. Gen. Jubal A. Early suffers about a 23 percent casualty rate. Casualties for the larger Union army under Maj. Gen. Philip Sheridan exceeded 5,000, nearly 20 percent.*
>
> **Mistakes are made at the Battle of Opequon**
> *At 1 a.m. on September 19, the morning call rang throughout the Army of the Shenandoah. By 4:30 a.m., the Union army encountered its first major hurdle of the day. After crossing Opequon Creek, the Berryville Road passes through the two-mile narrow Berryville Canyon. General Horatio Wright's Sixth Corps [Elias's Corps] encounters heavy resistance when it finally exits the canyon. Additionally, Wright has ordered the slow-moving wagon trains and ambulances to accompany the soldiers into the canyon. Soon, the narrow canyon becomes clogged with men*

pushing forward, wagon trains laden with supplies, and the wounded filtering back to makeshift hospitals. General William Emory, leading the Nineteenth Corp, incensed by Wright's incompetence, ignores Wright's orders and directs his men to circumvent the wagons. Soldiers of the Nineteenth Corps climb along the sides of the hills and trample over the wounded, seriously affecting their morale before even seeing the enemy and delaying their arrival on the field. Confederate General Early later wrote about the battle, "When I look back to the battle, I can but attribute my escape from utter annihilation to the incompetence of my opponent." General Sheridan's attempt to squeeze 20,000 troops through the narrow canyon is a tactical blunder that eliminates any possibility of destroying General Early's troops in detail. General Wright's Corps of three divisions- Getty, Ricketts [Elias' division] and Russell- emerge from the canyon in order. Getty's division is deployed south of the Berryville pike with its left flank resting on Abrams Creek. Rickett's division is formed north of the pike on Getty's right and is extended to Redbud Run. Russell's division is held in reserve.

As Elias and the 126th emerge from Berryville Canyon they form a line of battle and become painfully aware of the daunting task before them. The regiment must charge across open ground, then march uphill into the face of Confederate guns that are placed on the crest of the ridge. The casualty rate is very high and this may be when Elias is mortally wounded.

In tandem with the charge of the Nineteenth Corps, the Sixth Corps advances, but the left flank of the Nineteenth crumbles under the pressure. During the Union advance however, a gap develops between the two corps. Confederate General Rodes launches a counterattack into the gap. After shouting, "Charge them boys! Charge them!" Gen. Rodes is killed instantly from an exploding shell. A valiant countercharge by Union General Upton brakes Rodes' division. General Wright would later refer to Upton's charge as "the turning point of the conflict."[19]

This ridge east of Winchester, VA, and north of US Route 7 (Berryville Pike) could be the site of Elias B. Wallick's last advance. His regiment would have marched up this ridge and into battle. The terrain was cleared and free of all trees at the time of the engagement.

---

[19] Distant cousin Edward Wallick is also at the Battle of Opequon. He is deployed just to the north of Elias, fords Red Bud Creek around 3:00 PM and becomes engaged in battle. Edward's regiment is part of the final thrust into the northern Confederate flank that will eventually break the Rebels. The Confederates will retreat through Winchester, giving General Sheridan a great victory.

SEP 23   Elias dies of his wounds   Elias is taken to the army hospital in Winchester, Virginia, suffers for four days then dies of his wounds. [20]

Winchester National Cemetery
Elias B. Wallick is buried in the second row with the American flag.
Location: Section 12, Site 327

The alternate spelling *Wallack* is common with the Wallick soldiers during the war. The death date of this man, together with evidence from the *Official Roster of Soldiers from the State of Ohio in the War of the Rebellion*, confirms this soldier to be Elias B. Wallick, from Strasburg, Ohio.

Comrades-in-Arms

No brothers, uncles or first cousins

Elias is buried as E.B. Wallack.

---

[20] The Battle of Opequon Creek also claims the life of Confederate Colonel George S. Patton, namesake and grandfather of the famous WWII U.S. Third Army general.

Henry M. Wallick - 16th Ohio Volunteer Infantry, Co. G
67th Ohio Volunteer Infantry, Co. C

11

Rank: 16th OVI, Private
67th OVI, Private, promoted to 2nd Lieutenant

Place of enlistment: Holmes County, Millersburg, Ohio

Dates of enlistment: 16th OVI, April 22, 1861
67th OVI, November 19, 1861

Service time: 16th OVI, 3 months
67th OVI, 2 years, 6 months

Born: 1838/39, Holmes County, Ohio

Age at first enlistment: 23 years old

Physical description: height - 5' 10", brown hair, hazel eyes

Civilian occupation: farmer

Family Lineage: Henry, son of "Holmes" Henry, son of "Bedford" Michael, son of Hans Michael Wallick

There is perhaps no Wallick soldier whose Civil War story is more tragic than that of Henry M. Wallick from the little village of Killbuck, Ohio. Henry was a young man whose sense of duty and patriotism was so strong that he enlisted twice in the Union army. His first enlistment was at the beginning of the war for three months with the 16th Ohio Volunteers. He saw some minor action with this unit in the mountains of West Virginia and after fulfilling his term, he took a two-month respite from the service. Henry was a farmer and after going home and harvesting his crops, he reenlisted for three years in a new company that was being organized in Holmes County. Cousin William D. Wallick, also from Killbuck, likewise joined this new outfit. Henry and William became part of the 67th Ohio Volunteer Infantry which was formed in Columbus, Ohio, and then sent east to Virginia. Henry soon learned that the battlefield was not the only place where a soldier could be attacked. Soon after leaving Columbus a case of measles struck and killed cousin William, only two months after he had enlisted. This was a foreshadowing of what Henry would face in the next few years, for Henry would fight a war against disease as well as Confederates.

It is no surprise that Henry was quick to enlist just days after the Confederate attack on Fort Sumter. Military service was part of his heritage. His grandfather, "Bedford" Michael, was a well-known Pennsylvania militiaman during the American Revolution and his father, Henry George Wallick, served in the War of 1812. In the mid-1820s, just after marrying his wife Sarah, and overseeing the settlement of his deceased father's estate, Henry George sojourned west with others from the Wallick clan to Tuscarawas County, Ohio. He had a brief stay there but soon relocated to neighboring Holmes County. Henry George (in the Wallick vernacular "Holmes" Henry) first settled in Millersburg and then purchased a farm ten miles south of Millersburg near the hamlet of Killbuck, Ohio. There he and his wife raised eight children, five girls and three boys. Two of the boys, Henry and David H. Wallick, served in the Union army. A total of five Wallick sons of Holmes County served during the war, the two aforementioned plus William D., his brother Charles and cousin Elijah.

Henry and the 67th OVI were active in the eastern theater of the war. They fought and defeated General Stonewall Jackson in the first battle of his Shenandoah Valley Campaign. In this engagement, the First Battle of Kernstown, the 67th Ohio was active from the opening guns to the Confederate retreat. This engagement was General Jackson's only defeat of his entire Valley campaign. Henry then spent most of 1863 on islands off the South Carolina coast near the city of Charleston. It was there, on Morris Island, that his regiment took part in the futile assault on Fort Wagner, a heavily defended Confederate fortress at the mouth of Charleston Harbor. Some members of the 67th did breech the walls during the famous night attack, but eventually they had to fall back due to the lack of reinforcements.

The failed attack on Fort Wagner.

The 67th Ohio did breach the earthen walls of Fort Wagner during its attack, but their effort was unsupported and eventually all the Federal troops had to withdraw. Out of an attacking force of 5,264 men, there were 1,515 soldiers killed, wounded or missing. A casualty rate of over 25 percent.

In the midst of attacking Rebel positions on Morris Island Henry's strength was being depleted by debilitating attacks of diarrhea. The lack of sanitation, plus bad food and a hot tropical climate, was ideal for breeding diseases and made many soldiers unfit for duty. The unrelenting assaults on Henry's constitution led Dr. Westfall, the assistant regimental surgeon, to request that Henry be given a 30-day medical leave. Instead, a 20-day leave was granted and Henry went home, but still did not improve. He remained so ill in Killbuck that the return to his regiment had to be delayed for over two months. All during that time Henry was considered AWOL by brigade headquarters. In January, 1864, upon Henry's return to his regiment, he began the process of trying to clear himself of the charge. At that time he and his regiment also reenlisted, giving each man a 30-day furlough as a reward. Henry again went home to Holmes County. But this time he was healthy, even healthy enough to marry his Killbuck fiancée, Ellen Wells, the last week of his leave.

In the spring of 1864 the 67th Ohio Infantry moved from the South Carolina coast up to Virginia. Henry continued to work on his AWOL defense while he battled more health problems that eventually hospitalized him. At the end of April he was sent for a week to Seminary Hospital in Georgetown, Washington, D.C. After his discharge from there he rejoined his regiment just before an engagement at Chester Station, VA. This railroad depot was located about half-way between Richmond and Petersburg. It is difficult to say just how effective Henry was on that hot spring day, leading his men into battle after his lengthy illness (the temperature was said to be near 100 degrees). However, his presence would have been valuable since he obviously had the ability to inspire men under his leadership. Henry entered the ranks as a private and was regularly promoted, eventually receiving a 1st lieutenant's commission by the governor of Ohio (although he was never mustered in at that rank).

The Battle of Chester Station, VA, is considered by historians a very minor engagement between the Union and Confederate forces. Most military histories do not include it in their catalogs of battles and skirmishes. But the May 10, 1864, engagement was no small affair to Henry and his regiment. In this one battle the regiment had seventy-six officers and men killed or wounded, Henry being one of the fatalities. His new bride Ellen, all too soon, became a war widow after only two months of marriage and one week of living as husband and wife. With Henry's death, Ellen Wells Wallick is lost to history. Henry's trail also ends after the Battle of Chester Station, for there is no record of where he is buried in Virginia.

And there is no record of Henry being buried in Killbuck, OH, nor any of its surrounding communities. A search in the *Official Roster of Soldiers of the State of Ohio in the War of the Rebellion, Volume V- Roll of Honor*, reveals nothing; he is not included. This Roll of Honor identifies all the men from the 67th Ohio who died during the war and where they are buried. Henry and one other soldier who died at Chester Station, for unknown reasons, are omitted. This reference book, when compared to the official casualty report written by Henry's commanding officer, states that Henry and twenty other soldiers were either killed outright or died of their wounds at the Battle of Chester Station. Nineteen of them were then buried in Hampton National Cemetery. There appear to be two possibilities of what became of Henry and his comrade's bodies after being killed at Chester Station. Either they were buried in Hampton National Cemetery as unknowns, or their bodies were never recovered and remained on the battlefield at Chester Station. There were fires on the battlefield at the close of the engagement, rendering recovery of all the killed and wounded extremely difficult. We may never know the true story behind the final disposition of Henry M. Wallick's body.

Henry Wallick with the 16th Ohio Volunteer Infantry
(3 months service)

<u>1861</u>

APR 22 Henry enlists in Millersburg, OH, in response to President Lincoln's call for 75, 000 volunteers to put down the southern rebellion. Fort Sumter had been fired upon ten days before.

APR 25 The men from Holmes County travel to Camp Jackson, in Columbus, OH, and are organized into Company G, 16th Ohio Volunteer Infantry.

MAY 11 The 16th OVI is mustered into Federal service with General George B. McClellan as its commanding officer.

MAY 25 Henry and his regiment leave for the towns of Farmington and Grafton, WV, where they guard the Baltimore & Ohio Railroad.[21]

JUN 3 Battle at Philippi, WV Federal control of northern West Virginia is very important because it links by rail the eastern and western states of the Union. The Baltimore & Ohio Railroad slices through the extreme northern region of that state and any interruption of service would be detrimental to the North's war effort. Henry and the 16th Ohio see action at Philippi, WV, in what is the first notable land battle of the Civil War. It is a very minor skirmish and mockingly called the "Battle of Philippi Races" because of the hasty Confederate retreat. There are few casualties: 4 Union and 26 Confederate out of a total of 3,800 engaged, but the consequences of this Union victory are huge for General George B. McClellan. He is propelled into the national spotlight as a war hero and within six months General McClellan is made the commander of all the Union forces.

JUN 29 Engagement at Bowman's Place Some companies from Henry's regiment see action in this very small engagement.

JUL The 16th Ohio continues to guard the B&O Railroad and they pursue Confederate forces in West Virginia.

AUG 18 Henry is mustered out of Federal service in Columbus, OH, on expiration of term. During the 16th Ohio's three months of service his regiment had one man killed and two died of disease.

---

[21] In 1861, Farmington and Grafton were still part of northern Virginia. The state of West Virginia was not created until 1863. To avoid confusion, current state boundaries will be applied.

Henry Wallick with the 67th Ohio Volunteer Infantry
(3 years service)

1861

NOV 19 Henry reenlists as a private in a newly organized company from Holmes County. They move to Columbus, OH, and become part of the 67th Ohio Volunteer Infantry.

DEC 31 Henry is promoted to 3rd Sergeant in Company C of the 67th OVI.

1862

JAN - MAR 10 The 67th has guard duty at Paw Paw Tunnel and Great Capapon Creek, WV.

FEB 26 William D. Wallick, who is in the same and company as Henry, dies of measles and is buried in an army hospital cemetery at Cumberland, MD. He is eventually disinterred and reburied at Antietam National Cemetery.

MAR 11 - 21 The regiment advances to Winchester, VA, then makes a reconnaissance to Strasburg, VA.

MAR 22 - 23 First Battle of Kernstown The 67th is opposed by General Stonewall Jackson in this first battle of Jackson's 1862 Shenandoah Valley Campaign. The Confederates want to create a diversion and keep as many Union soldiers as possible deployed in the Shenandoah Valley. This strategy will help relieve some of the pressure put on the Confederate forces that are defending Richmond, VA. On the evening of March 22, Henry's brigade makes first contact with the enemy and draws skirmishing fire. The next day, faulty intelligence given to General Jackson prompts him to engage the Federal army even though he is greatly outnumbered. By 2:00 PM the combatants are in position and the engaged forces begin the battle with salvos of artillery fire. The fighting becomes very intense and by evening, Henry's brigade is thrown into the melee. He and his regiment fight the famous Stonewall Brigade for about two hours and the 67th Ohio makes numerous charges against a stubborn Rebel line. But the Stonewall Brigade eventually runs low on ammunition and must retreat, much to the ire of General Jackson.

Pritchard's Hill, First Battle of Kernstown.
Henry and the 67th Ohio were deployed on this field.

The First Battle of Kernstown is the only engagement in Stonewall Jackson's Shenandoah Valley Campaign where he is defeated. Roughly 8,000 Union soldiers have been opposed by 3,000 Confederates, creating 1,000 combined casualties. Michael Wallick of the 27th Indiana and William F. Wallick of the 13th Indiana also take part in this battle and campaign. William is deployed very near Henry at the First Battle of Kernstown and Michael will be captured on May 23rd at Buckton Station, VA, a casualty from the Battle of Front Royal.

APR - MAY   The 67th OVI marches to Fredericksburg, VA, and then to Front Royal. Stonewall Jackson is still creating havoc for the Federal forces in the Shenandoah Valley.

MAY 23   Henry is promoted from 3rd sergeant, to 1st sergeant in Company C.

JUN 9   The 67th Ohio Infantry helps cover the Union's defeat and retreat at the Battle of Port Republic, VA.

JUN 29   Henry will spend most of the summer at Harrison's Landing, south of Richmond, on the James River.

AUG 16 - DEC 31   The 67th Ohio moves downstream to Fortress Monroe on the Atlantic coast, at the mouth of the James River. They spend a week there and then move inland to Suffolk, VA, for the rest of 1862.

1863

JAN   On New Year's Day Henry makes preparations to travel down the Atlantic seaboard to the islands off the Carolina coast where he will be posted for the next year. His regiment first moves to Beaufort, NC, then they are transported to New Bern, NC. By the end of January he is at Port Republic, SC.

FEB 9   The 67th OVI is deployed for the next two months on the islands of Hilton Head and St. Helena, SC. Now a vacation destination for the wealthy, in 1863 they are swampy lowland islands off South Carolina and breeding grounds for a multitude of nasty insect and diseases.

APR 3 - JUL 9   The 67th Ohio occupies Folly Island, south of Charleston Harbor.

JUN 13   Henry is commissioned a 2nd lieutenant by the governor of Ohio and officially mustered in at said rank on July 1.

JUL 10   Attack on Morris Island   The Union army secures a base at the south end of Morris Island. This island is at the mouth of Charleston Harbor.

JUL 18   Assault on Ft. Wagner   The 67th Ohio takes part in the famous assault on Fort Wagner, Morris Island, SC. A Federal force of ten regiments charges across a narrow strip of beach in an almost suicidal attack on the heavily fortified Confederate stronghold. The Union regiments are led by the 54th Massachusetts Colored Troops whose commanding officer, Colonel Robert Gould Shaw, has passionately lobbied that his men be given the honor to lead the attack. The twilight assault on this fort is dramatically portrayed in the climax to the 1989 film "Glory".

The 67th Ohio is in support of the lead brigade in this night attack and does penetrate the southeast corner of the Confederate fort. They hold the position for about an hour but must eventually withdraw due to the lack of reinforcements. Henry's brigade commander, General H. S. Putnam, is killed in the assault and the Federal casualties are high, about 1,500 versus 200 Confederate. No benefit is gained from the attack. The Union army must now lay siege to the Rebel fortress. It is unknown to what degree Henry is involved in this assault. He may very well have stormed the fortress with his regimental brothers. However, his records from the National Archives show that at this time on Morris Island Henry is sometimes very ill. He may have been sick enough to be unfit for duty that

Storming Fort Wagner, by Kurz & Allison

night, but there is no written record stating this. Even if he were sick, as an officer he would be expected to lead his men into battle, unless the illness was of an extreme nature. Any serious debility of Henry at the time of this attack is unknown. The regiment suffers heavy casualties with many of Henry's comrades being killed.

JUL 19 - SEP 6 Siege of Fort Wagner and movements around Charleston, SC   The Union forces are unable to overthrow the fortified Rebel positions on Morris Island, either by direct assault or offshore naval bombardment. They lay siege to the fortress throughout the summer.

SEP 7 Capture of Fort Wagner   The Union army, with the help of the U.S. Navy, forces the Confederates to abandon Fort Wagner on the night of September 6. The Union army now occupies all of Morris Island.

SEP 8 - OCT 31   The Federals move against Charleston, SC.

SEP 11   Henry has been ill periodically the past three months with chronic diarrhea. The assistant surgeon of the regiment, Dr. James Westfall, makes a written appeal to Lt. Colonel Edward Smith that Henry be granted a 30-day leave of absence to help improve his condition. Accompanying the doctor's recommendation is a note written by Henry making a personal appeal for a 30-day leave. Henry is only granted a 20-day leave of absence.

Henry Wallick wrote this note on September 11, 1863, to his commanding officer requesting a 30-day leave of absence due to "consequences of physical disability". This is the only surviving document that was entirely written in Henry's own handwriting.

Dr. James Westfall, Assistant Regimental Physician, writes an accompanying letter stating "a greater change is necessary in his case to save life or prevent permanent disability." Henry has suffered from chronic diarrhea for the past three months.

Lieutenant Henry M. Wallick of the 67th Regiment of Ohio Vols. having applied for a certificate on which to ground an application for leave of absence. I do hereby certify that I have carefully examined this officer, and find that said officer has Chronic Diarrhoea and has suffered under its effects for a period of Three Months — and that in consequence thereof, he is in my opinion unfit for duty. I further declare my belief that he will not be able to resume his duties in a less period than Thirty Days. In my opinion a greater change is necessary in his case to save life or prevent permanent disability

James Westfall
asst Surg. in chg. 67 Regt OVI

Morris Island S.C.
Sept. 11th 1863

OCT 2   Henry begins his 20-day leave with hopes that his health will improve while at home.

OCT 22 - DEC 28   At the conclusion of Henry's leave he is still too sick to return to duty and must delay his departure from Killbuck. Henry is now considered AWOL by brigade headquarters. It will take another two months for his health to improve so he can leave Holmes County. During his extended absence, Dr. T.G.V. Boling examines him three times (Oct. 25, Nov 12 and Dec 2). This physician writes a certificate after each examination which states that Henry is still too ill to resume his duties. At the close of each certificate Holmes County Justice of the Peace, Robert Justice, writes an endorsement for Dr. Boling, in effect notarizing the document. Robert Justice verifies that Dr. Boling is a legitimate practicing physician in Millersburg, OH.

Henry needs this certificate of examination from a doctor in "good standing" to legally extend his leave. Dr. Boling wrote this note on November 12, 1863. In it the doctor states that "he is suffering from chronic diarrhea and debility resulting there from. I also certify that in my opinion he cannot be able to resume his duties in the field in a less period than twenty days from this date." Certificates written by Dr. Boling and Justice of the Peace, Robert Justice, have the identical wording.

DEC 28 Henry is finally healthy enough to report for duty at Hilton Head, SC. He immediately requests a hearing to present evidence and explain his extended absence.

1864

JAN While at Hilton Head the 67th OVI reenlists as a veteran volunteer regiment. Doing this grants each man a $400 bonus plus a 30-day furlough. It is unclear if Henry ever intended to stay with his veteran regiment after his initial three-year enlistment. There is nothing in his compiled military service record to indicate his intentions. However, he was granted a thirty-day furlough in March of 1864 and that could be an indication that he did intend to stay with the 67th Ohio as a veteran volunteer.

FEB 5 Henry makes another plea to brigade headquarters for a hearing on the charge of being AWOL.

Henry's second appeal to headquarters for a hearing on being AWOL.

Camp Seymour Hilton-Head S.C.
February 5th 1864.

Lieut. Col. Ed. W. Smith
Ass. Adj. Genl.
Sir:

I have the honor to make the following Statement to wit: On the 28th December 1863 I made application for a hearing before a Board on account of overstaying leave of absence by reason of Disability and was referred to the Recorder of the Commission, convened for that purpose at Hilton-Head, S.C. At the earliest practicable opportunity I presented myself with Surgeon's Certificates for examination. No Action was then taken and I have since presented myself at five successive Meetings with the same lack of Success. I do therefore most respectfully ask that some measures may be speedily adopted, by which I can obtain a hearing, as the Regiment has reenlisted and will in all probability leave for the North by next Boat.

Very respectfully
Your obedient Servant
Henry M. Wallick
2nd Lieut. 47th Regt. OVI

Approved:

Capt. 47th Regt. OVI Commdg Co. C.

FEB 18 Henry is commissioned a first lieutenant by the governor of Ohio but must wait to be officially mustered in at that rank (unfortunately, he is killed before that happens).

FEB 24 Henry begins a month-long furlough back home in Killbuck, OH.

MAR 17 While on furlough, Henry marries Ellen Wells, also from Killbuck. They have a one-week honeymoon before Henry must return to the war.

APR - MAY 3 The regiment moves to Yorktown, VA, to be part of General Benjamin Butler's Bermuda Hundred Campaign.

APR 6 Henry is granted permission to appear before a military commission to present evidence that he was too sick to return to duty in October of 1863.

Letter from the Adjutant General's Office in Washington, D.C,
granting Henry a hearing on the charge of being AWOL in the fall of 1863.

War Department,
Adjutant General's Office,
Washington, D. C., April 6 1864.

Major General Silas Casey.
Comdg Provisional Brigades.
Washington. D.C.
General.
I have respectfully to acknowledge the receipt of a letter from 2nd Lieutenant HM Walliek, 67th Ohio Volunteers, charged with absence without leave; and to inform you, that in accordance with your request endorsed thereon, it has been referred this day to the Military Commission in this city, of which Brigadier General Caldwell. U.S. Volunteers, is President.
I am. General. Very Respectfully,
Your Obedient Servant,
Thomas M Vincent,
Assistant adjutant General,

Note written by Dr. James Westfall
requesting Henry's admission to
Georgetown Officers Hospital.

APR 14   Henry is again sent to the regimental hospital due to illness.

APR 25   Dr. James Westfall, Assistant Regimental Surgeon, writes to the medical director at Georgetown Officers Hospital:

Sir,
You will please give Lt. Wallick an order to go to Officers' Hospital, Georgetown, D.C. We are to move this morning & the Lt. is not able to go with us. He has been quite ill but is now improving. Very Respectfully,

James Westfall, Surgeon, 67 O.V.I.

MAY 2   After one week Henry is discharged from the hospital and rejoins his regiment.

MAY 4 - 5   The 67th Ohio is part of General Benjamin Butler's operations on the south side of the James River and Bermuda Hundred. They occupy City Point, VA.

MAY 6 Henry is cleared of the AWOL charge   It is difficult to know exactly when he is notified of this but the bar to his pay, which has been in place since being charged AWOL, is removed on May 6, 1864.

MAY 9   Engagement at Swift Creek   The 67th confronts and drives back Rebel forces at Swift Creek. General Butler does not follow up the attack and is content to only destroy the Confederate railroad.

May 10   Battle of Chester Station   The Confederates send a reconnaissance-in-force to Chester Station to prevent any further destruction of the railroad between Petersburg and Richmond. As the forces assemble (near the present day intersection of US 1 and Highway 10) the 67th Ohio is placed in the front line, near a battery of artillery, where they take heavy casualties as the battle explodes. The near 100-degree heat that day, together with a dry spring season, will set some portions of the battlefield on fire before the engagement ends. Confederate and Union forces try to rescue the wounded, with mixed results. The Federal forces are defeated in this engagement and as night falls, they withdraw with heavy casualties. Whitelaw Reed states this brief account of the engagement in his 1868 chronicle, *Ohio in the War, Vol II*:

> *The Sixty-seventh maintained its position from first to last, presenting an unbroken front to four successive charges. A section of our artillery, for a short time, fell into the hands of the enemy, but was recaptured by a portion of company F. The 10th of May, 1864, will always be remembered as a sad but glorious day by the Sixty-seventh. Seventy-six officers and men were killed and wounded in that battle.*

One day after the battle, Henry's commanding officer of the 67th Ohio, Colonel Alvin Voris, wrote a brief account to his wife about the savage fighting at Chester Station:

> *...I have no time to enter into details, but the 9th and 10th [of May] were really days of intense anxiety and peril to me and my regiment. The 67th lost 71 in killed & wounded, 13th Indiana 163 in killed and wounded & prisoners, the 169th New York 51 killed, wounded and missing... Lts Wallick and Ballard were instantly killed doing their duty like heroes.*

Map 6   **The Battle of Chester Station.**
The 67th Ohio was in the front line at the center of the battle on May 10, 1864.

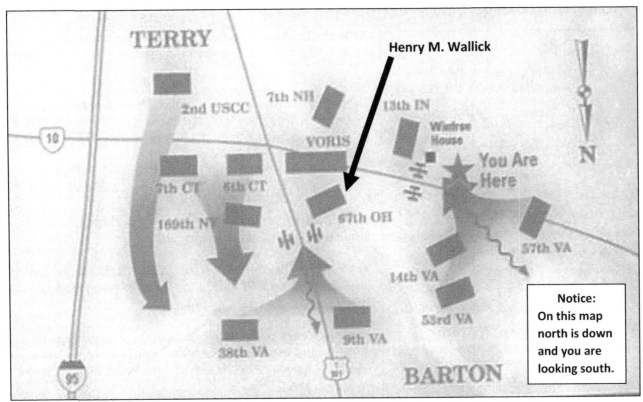

Map is from the historical marker, Civil War Trails - Chester, Virginia.

Epilogue - Henry's grave has yet to be found anywhere in Ohio or Virginia. It is still a mystery what became of his body after he was killed at Chester Station. The author believes there are two possibilities: Henry was either buried in Hampton National Cemetery as an "unknown" (his body being so disfigured from his wounds that he was unrecognizable) or he was left on the field of battle, his body never being recovered. The latter is in all probability the most likely scenario. The Confederates won the battle and had possession of the field at the end of the day and fires engulfed some of the battlefield after the engagement. The muzzleloading type of firearms used during the Civil War generated a great amount of heat and flame when fired. The expelled wadding would sometimes cause the dry leaves and brush on the ground to ignite. Many times during the war soldiers were unable to retrieve the bodies of their fallen comrades because of brush fires.

The case for being buried as an unknown is less likely, but still plausible. There were twenty soldiers killed or mortally wounded at the Battle of Chester Station. By comparing the battle report of Colonel Voris and Ohio's official record of those killed during the battle, every soldier, except two, is accounted for and the dead were buried in Hampton National Cemetery.[22] Second Lieutenant Henry Wallick and First Sergeant Sylvester Matson were included in Colonel Voris' casualty report but left out of Ohio's Roll of Honor. It was an unfortunate mistake made by the State. Two days after the battle an unknown soldier, #4085, was buried at Hampton National Cemetery. He is the only Unknown buried within weeks of the battle. Perhaps there was so little left of that Unknown's body after the battle that it was impossible to identify the soldier. It was not uncommon, particularly after a very heated artillery exchange, for this to be the case. Perhaps this soldier was Henry or Sergeant Matson. The last disposition of Henry's body may forever be a mystery.

---

[22] Source: *Official Roster of Soldiers of the State of Ohio in the War of the Rebellion, Volume V, Roll of Honor,*

Monument to the Battle of Chester Station.
This historic marker is located on the roadside of US
Highway 10, just outside of Chester, Virginia.
It was erected by The Sons of Confederate Veterans.

There are 638 unknowns buried in the Hampton National Cemetery. Only one Unknown Soldier was interred shortly after the Battle of Chester Station - #4085, buried on May 12, 1864. Could he possibly be Henry M. Wallick? It is more likely that Henry's body was never recovered and possibly consumed in the battlefield fires created during the engagement.

Comrades-in-Arms

Brother
David H.   102nd OVI

Cousins
David   139th Ohio National Guard
Daniel   20th OVI
Elijah   102nd OVI
Michael   27th IVI
William D.   67th OVI- died of disease

Hampton National Cemetery

David H. Wallick - 102nd Ohio Volunteer Infantry, Co. G

12

Rank: Private

Place of enlistment: Holmes County, Millersburg, Ohio

Date of enlistment: August 9, 1862

Mustered into Federal service: September 6, 1862

Service time: 2 years 10 months

Born: August 7, 1832 - Holmes County, Ohio

Age at enlistment: 30

Physical description: height: 5' 10", dark hair, dark eyes

Occupation: farmer

Family Lineage: David H., son of "Holmes" Henry, son of "Bedford" Michael, son of Hans Michael Wallick

David H. Wallick had only been married four months when he rode into Millersburg, Ohio, and enlisted in the Union army.[23] At the time he was a thirty-year-old farmer and it would be interesting to know why he left his hearth and home so quickly after marrying his seventeen-year-old bride Sarah Moore. Although he may not have known it when he enlisted, David was a father-to-be. His daughter Margaret was born to the couple sometime in 1863 while David was deployed south fighting the Rebels.[24] The eighteen-month war had already been an intrusion into David's family. His younger brother, Henry M. Wallick, had been swept away by war fever in 1861 immediately after the Confederates attacked Ft. Sumter. At that time President Lincoln called for 75,000 volunteers to serve ninety days to help crush the southern rebellion and more than enough men volunteered, Henry being one of them.   After Henry fulfilled his three-month obligation he returned home to reenlist for three years with the 67th Ohio Volunteer Infantry. Perhaps by the summer of 1862 David believed it was time for him to step up and make a contribution to the Union army's war effort.

We know that Elijah Wallick, David's cousin, enlisted on the same day and that the two served in the same regiment and company. The first two years of their service appears to be somewhat routine. Then, on September 24, 1864, Elijah was chosen to be part of a relief expedition and march to embattled Fort Henderson at Athens, Alabama. About two hundred men from the regiment were dispatched to Athens and twenty of them, including Elijah, were from company G. All the men who were ordered to Ft. Henderson were captured, and then incarcerated at Cahaba Federal Prison in southern Alabama. Fate was more kind to David, as he was ordered to stay in camp with the remainder of his company.

Most of the duties of the 102nd were rear echelon assignments such as guarding trains, repairing bridges and providing post security. Although these duties appear to be mundane and less than exciting, there was always the danger of attacks from Confederate marauders. General Nathan Bedford Forrest became a legend in the war by

---

[23] David H. Wallick married Sarah Moore on April 10, 1862, and enlisted in the Union army on August 9th. However, he wasn't mustered into Federal service until September 6, 1862.

[24] The exact date of Margaret's birth is unknown. Jeff Wallick references her birthday only as 1862/63, and since no furlough is recorded during his enlistment, it can be assumed she was born sometime in the first half of the year 1863. If she was indeed born in 1862, Sarah must have been a pregnant bride when she married David. Either way, the teenage Sarah had to cope with pregnancy and childbirth soon after her new husband went off to war.

attacking Union supply stores and creating havoc in the rear areas of the Federal lines. He is also the Confederate general who captured both Elijah and William Wallick.

The Civil War was hard on the Wallick families from Holmes County. Four of their sons were wounded, captured, killed or physically broken by the end of the war. David's brother, Henry, was killed in action at the Battle of Chester Station, Virginia, and cousin William D. Wallick, who enlisted with brother Henry, died of disease early in the war after being in the army only two months. Cousin Elijah was spared a horrific death in the icy waters of the Mississippi River only because he was so pathetically ill when paroled from Cahaba Prison that he required a long hospitalization and did not return home with his captured comrades. Eighty-one soldiers from David and Elijah's regiment perished when the steamboat *Sultana* exploded. And Charley Wallick was said to have been wounded at the battle of Port Gibson during the Vicksburg campaign. David is the only soldier from Holmes County for whom there is no mention of his coming to any physical harm or illness during the war. That is not to say that he was never sick or injured, only that no incident was severe enough to be recorded in his company's log.

Those Wallicks who survived the war returned to Holmes County, but not for long. By 1869 the three veterans, Charley, Elijah and David, moved all their families out of Ohio to the trans-Mississippi. Charley and Elijah relocated to Iowa and David bought a farm near Olathe City, Kansas. The war deaths, together with the veteran's migration, forever diminished the Wallick presence in Holmes County, Ohio.

David H. Wallick with the 102nd Ohio Volunteer Infantry

1862

AUG 9 David and cousin Elijah enlist in the Union army for three years in Millersburg, OH. Whether David knows it or not, his wife Sarah is pregnant with their first child. The 102nd is organized at Camp Mansfield and, according to their regimental history, they are known for their "gentlemanly qualities" while in camp. Not exactly the "fearsome" reputation most regiments would desire as they march off to war.

SEP 6 - 22 David is mustered into Federal service on September 6th at Covington, KY. As a result of the Confederate invasion of southern Kentucky, David will be posted in and around the defenses of Cincinnati through September 22. He receives $25 of his $100 bounty after his mustering-in.

SEP 22 - OCT 6 The 102nd OVI is moved to Louisville, KY, to bolster the defenses of that city in response to Confederate General Braxton Bragg's move towards the Ohio River.

OCT 5 - 6 The regiment is assigned to guard the brigade wagon trains while pursuing General Bragg.

OCT 8 Battle of Perryville The 102nd is held in reserve and sees no action, but they are close enough to hear the sounds of battle.

OCT 10 - DEC 30 After the Battle of Perryville, David and his regiment move to Bowling Green, KY, where they are given the responsibility of securing the railroad line from Bowling Green to Nashville, TN. On December 19th they are moved to Russellville and then to Clarksville.

1863

JAN - SEP David spends almost ten months in the vicinity of Clarksville, TN, building bridges, forwarding supplies and providing a secure base of operations for the Union army.

SEP 26 - 30 The 102nd is called on to help repel a Confederate cavalry raid by General Wheeler.

OCT - DEC The regiment is moved to Nashville to guard the railroads and supply stores.

1864

JAN - APR The 102nd OVI remains in Nashville where they protect one of the Union's most vital supply bases in the entire South.

APR 26 - JUN 6 The primary responsibility of the 102nd Ohio Infantry is to help guard the Nashville and Chattanooga Railroad from Normandy to Decherd, TN. Thousands of men are needed throughout the war to protect the railroads from attacks by Confederate guerillas. Sometime in the month of May, David is notified that his brother Henry has been killed in action at the Battle of Chester Station (May 10, 1864). On June 6th the regiment crosses over the Cumberland Mountains.

The Nashville Railroad Yard with the State Capitol building in the background.

JUN - AUG The 102nd is part of a defensive line along the Tennessee River from Stevenson, AL, to Seven Mile Island.

SEP 1 - 15 The regiment has duty protecting the Tennessee Railroad from Decatur, AL, to Columbia, TN.

SEP 23 - 24 Union troops at Fort Henderson in Athens, AL, are in battle with Confederate cavalry under the command of General Nathan Bedford Forrest, and the troops are on the brink of surrender. The commanding officer at the fort, Colonel Campbell, requests that a relief expedition be sent to him immediately. This force includes some men of the 102nd Ohio Infantry. David's cousin, Elijah Wallick, is one of twenty men from his company who are sent to Ft. Henderson. For whatever reason, David is not chosen to be part of this expedition. It is indeed fortunate for him. All of the relief force is eventually captured by the "Wizard of the Saddle," General Forrest, and the Federal captives are taken to Cahaba Federal Prison in southern Alabama. Elijah Wallick, and those who were captured with him, will endure great hardships while incarcerated. After their parole, eighty-one of David and Elijah's comrades will lose their lives when the steamboat *Sultana* explodes on the Mississippi River in the early morning hours of April 27, 1865.

OCT - DEC Skirmishes and engagements take place on the Tennessee River against General Hood's Confederate Army. Hood has moved into Tennessee and will soon make a desperate attack at Franklin and Nashville. In these two engagements, the Federal forces totally rout and destroy General Hood's army. It is one of the worst defeats of the entire war for the Confederates.

OCT 26 - 29 The 102nd participates in the siege of Decatur, AL. The city is evacuated on November 25.

NOV 25 - DEC 2 David and his regiment march to Stevenson, AL, and are posted at Fort Harker until May, 1865. One of David's duties at the fort is guarding the stores of ordnance for regiment.

Fort Harker, Stevenson, Alabama.

1865

JAN - MAR 26 The 102nd OVI is at Ft. Harker through the winter of 1865 and in March, David goes on furlough. When he returns to Ft. Harker he continues to guard the stores of ordnance.

APR - MAY The 102nd remains posted in Stevenson, AL, and are detailed to railroad security.

MAY 23 The regiment is moved to Decatur, AL, where they conclude their service in the Union army.

The Silver Cornet Band of the 102nd OVI.
David and Elijah must have spent many
evenings being entertained by these men.

JUN 30 David H. Wallick is mustered out of Federal service in Nashville, TN. He is paid $25.00 of his bounty and is owed $75.00 more. However, he owes the government $33.63 from his clothing account.

JUL 8 When the 102nd Regiment left Camp Mansfield in the summer of 1862, it had over one thousand men in its ranks. Just under three years later the regiment returns to Ohio and musters-out with only 466 men. Over half of David's regiment were captured, killed, died of disease, or replaced for other reasons.

Epilogue - David returned home from the war to his very young family. At Christmastide, 1866, both his father and mother died within five days of each other. With their passing, David sought out new lands in the west and moved from Holmes County. Real estate is very cheap in Kansas and David eventually settled in the little town of Olathe, in 1869. Success followed him to the prairie, where he earned quite a reputation as a rancher and farmer. He died December 1, 1909, and is buried in the Olathe Memorial Cemetery, Kansas.

Comrades-in-Arms

Brother
Henry M.   67th OVI - killed in action

Cousins

Elijah	102nd OVI	David	139th OVI
Daniel	20th OVI	Michael	27th IVI

David H. Wallick
Ron Wallick Collection

Map 7   Journey of Charles Wallick with the 16th Ohio Volunteer Infantry.

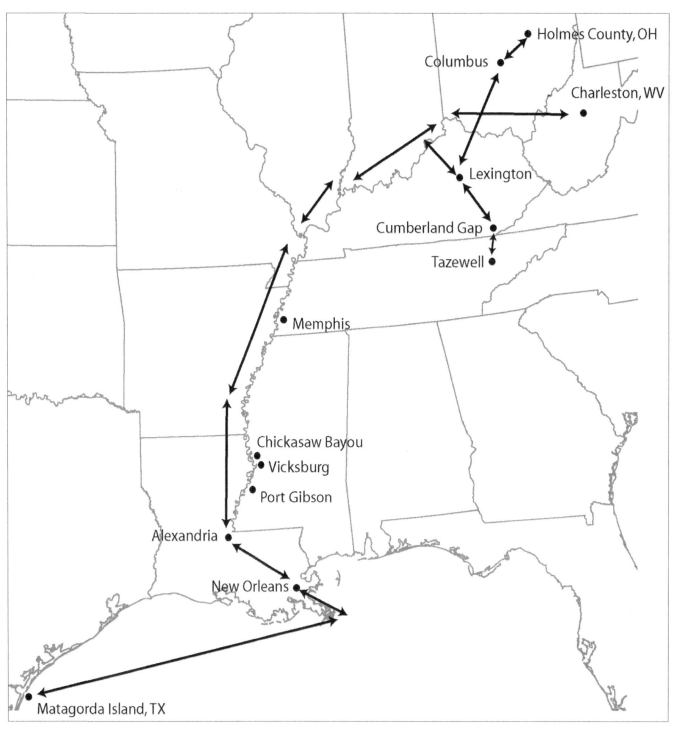

It has been estimated that the 16th Ohio Volunteer Infantry traveled over 6,725 miles by foot, boat and railroad during the three-plus years of its military service.

Charles "Charley" Wallick - 16th Ohio Volunteer Infantry, Co. B

Rank: Private

Place of enlistment: Holmes County, Millersburg, Ohio

Mustered into Federal service: November 4, 1861

Service time: 3 years, 1 month, 3 days

Born: July 8, 1843 - Holmes County, Ohio

Age at enlistment: 19?

Physical description: height - 5' 4", light hair, blue eyes

Civilian occupation: farmer

Family Lineage: Charles, son of "Guthrie" Michael, son of "Bedford" John, son of "Bedford" Michael, son of Hans Michael Wallick

There were two Charles Wallicks who served in the American Civil War. These two soldiers fought in regiments that were engaged in some of the war's most famous campaigns and many times these regiments distinguished themselves on the battlefield. Charles F. Wallick, of Miami County, Indiana, served in the 87th Indiana Volunteer Infantry (IVI), one of the finest volunteer regiments from the Hoosier state. Charles Wallick, of Holmes County, Ohio, served with the 16th Ohio Volunteer Infantry (OVI), whose reputation equals the Indiana men. The two regiments were deployed in different theaters of the war. The 87th IVI fought primarily in the southeast and the 16th Ohio in the west. Charles Wallick, or Charley, as his comrades called him, was a young farmer when he joined the Union army in September of 1861. This biography will use his recorded nickname, "Charley", instead of his given name, Charles, to help separate his identity from distant cousin, Charles F. Wallick.

Charley's father, "Guthrie" Michael (1804-1895), was one of four siblings who were orphaned at a very young age. Michael's father, John Sr., had died suddenly in an accident as a young man and his mother, Margaret Dibert, had died in 1813, possibly in childbirth. Michael grew up in Bedford County, PA, and eventually joined the Wallick family's westward migration to Ohio sometime in the early 1830s, settling in Holmes County. He quickly made a name for himself by demonstrating pyrotechnic heroics when the county courthouse in Millersburg caught fire and nearly destroyed the town.

From the book, *Holmes County, Ohio, Flashes from the Past,* by Donald Egger, an account of the great fire of Millersburg, 1834:

> *The fire destroyed more than half the buildings of the town and decidedly the most valuable ones. The present Court House, then new, was saved by the almost superhuman exertions of Michael Wallick and others, and most of the other buildings were on fire, but saved....At that time Michael Wallick went on top of the Court House and there for six hours, amid fire falling thick as hail, blinding smoke and scorching flame, he succeeded in saving the building. Shortly afterwards the Commissioners voted him $15, as a compensation for the extreme danger he had encountered in saving the house.*

Holmes County Courthouse, c.1840
Photo: Holmes County Public Library

117

Genealogical evidence suggests that Charley was only eighteen years old when he rode into Millersburg and volunteered for a three-year stint with the Union army. This is in contradiction to the war archives which state he was twenty years old. Whichever is true, he was one of thousands from Ohio who volunteered that late summer to help preserve the Union. His younger brother, William D. Wallick, caught "war fever" three months later and enlisted the day after Christmas, 1861. Unfortunately, he also caught a bad case of the measles and was dead within two months, dying in a hospital near Cumberland, Maryland, on February 26, 1862. A soldier in the Civil War was twice as likely to die on an army cot from disease as to die on the battlefield from a wound.

Charley was part of two very famous campaigns in the western theater of the war, one a tremendous success and the other a dismal failure. In the Vicksburg Campaign of 1863, he witnessed General Grant at his very best. The general demonstrated command creativity, improvisation, and determination. In contrast to this was the Red River Campaign led by General Nathaniel Banks. Charley was also part of that debacle, the whole effort being a waste of the soldiers' time, energy, and for some of them, their lives.

There are a few interesting facts about Charley Wallick and his service with the 16th Ohio. During the war he traversed this country's highways and byways more than any other soldier from the Wallick clan. He and his regiment traveled from the Appalachian Mountains of east Tennessee to the Gulf of Mexico. Charley spent a portion of his service time on a beautiful white sand beach off the Texas coast that today is being developed into a tourist playground. However, at the time, the men of the 16th Ohio viewed this sandy, windblown, beachfront property as a cursed abode. They were billeted in army tents where sand found its way into everything and the wind rarely stopped blowing. Charley and the 16th Ohio rode up and down the Mississippi River by steamboat countless numbers of times and by the end of the regiment's enlistment it has been estimated that they traveled 1,620 miles by foot, 1,285 miles by train, 1,200 miles by steamship and another 3,620 miles by steamboat. The war provided a mid-nineteenth century farmer, like Charley, the opportunity of a lifetime. He visited some very distant and exotic places as a young man when most farmers barely traveled outside their own county. Standing 5 feet 4 inches tall, Charley was one of the shortest of all the Wallicks to serve in the American Civil War. Only Abraham Wallick of the 22nd Iowa, standing at a diminutive 5' 3", was shorter. Charley's rifled musket with attached bayonet would have towered above him. However, his slight stature should in no way be taken as the measure of his contribution to the war effort.

Charley Wallick at an unknown age and date.
This image is from an enhanced 16th OVI reunion photograph.

Michael Wood Collection

Charley Wallick with the 16th Ohio Volunteer Infantry

1861

SEP 23 - NOV 3   Charley Wallick travels to Camp Tiffin in Wooster, OH, where the men from Holmes County are organized into Company B of the 16th Ohio Volunteer Regiment.

NOV 4   The 16th OVI is mustered into Federal service at Camp Chase, Columbus, OH.

NOV 28 - DEC 18   The 16th Regiment moves to Camp Dennison, OH, and from there on to Lexington, KY.

DEC 19 - JAN 30.   Charley and his regiment are posted at Somerset, KY.

1862

JAN 31 - FEB 12   The 16th OVI has marched to London, KY, and then moves on to Cumberland Ford to repair and rebuild railroads.

FEB 26   Charley's younger brother, William D. Wallick of the 67th Ohio Volunteer Infantry, dies of measles in an army hospital at Cumberland, MD. William enlisted in the Union army the day after Christmas and was in service only two months. He is the only Wallick to die of disease during the war.

MAR 28 - JUN 18   The 16th OVI participates in the Cumberland Gap Campaign of 1862 and has a skirmish at Elrod's Ridge.

JUN 15 - SEP 15   Charley is part of the occupation force at Cumberland Gap, the "Gibraltar of America," and sees action at Wilson's Gap and Tazewell, TN.

SEP 16 - NOV 10 Charley's regiment is forced to evacuate Cumberland Gap and retreats all the way back to the Ohio River. By the end of the war the Cumberland Gap will have changed hands four times, yet no major engagement ever takes place there. The occupying force always surrenders ground because they were outmaneuvered by the opposing army. The regiment becomes part of an expedition to Charleston, WV, then is ordered to Memphis, TN.

Background to General Grant's Vicksburg Campaign

Vicksburg, Mississippi c. 1860.

 NOV - DEC Charley and the 16th OVI have moved west to become part of General Grant's Vicksburg Campaign. The prolonged siege of Vicksburg, MS, is not the beginning but the capstone to Grant's movements against the Confederacy's bulwark on the Mississippi River. Grant has five months of failed ventures before he conceives of a plan that is not only ingenious, but finally works. Vicksburg is situated on high bluffs that overlook the Mississippi River and with well-placed Rebel artillery, it is nearly impossible to assault by boat (although Grant at first tries and fails, miserably). If he could take the town, the Union would have free navigation into the heart of the nation to move foodstuffs and materiel from the Great Lakes to the Gulf of

Mexico. This would also cut the Confederacy in two and deprive them of agriculture and livestock products from the western Confederacy, especially Texas. It is impossible to go into great detail about the campaign in this brief sketch, however, this background material is necessary to highlight Charley's participation in General Grant's great crusade. Charley fought in a campaign where many historians believe Grant demonstrated his best generalship and this operation rivaled any that were designed by Julius Caesar or Napoleon Bonaparte.

DEC 20 - JAN 3 The 16th OVI is part of General Sherman's Yazoo River Expedition to take Vicksburg by land from the north.

DEC 29 Battle of Chickasaw Bayou Charley and the 16th Ohio are key troops in this battle of the bayou north of Vicksburg. They attack entrenched Rebel positions around noon and take heavy casualties. Charley's regiment storms headlong into Confederate rifle pits that are below the bluffs and they are decimated by murderous Confederate musketry. General Sherman is forced to retreat back up the Yazoo River and this expedition ends in failure. Losses to the regiment are great: 311 officers and men killed, wounded or captured.

Confederate troops were well-entrenched on the distant bluffs. The engagement is called "The Battle of Chickasaw Bluffs" in many historical narratives but the ridge is really called Walnut Hills. The 16th Ohio advanced down this road, moving toward the distant hills, where they met murderous rifle fire, creating numerous casualties and a hasty retreat. The engagement is more accurately called "The Battle of Chickasaw Bayou" and it put an end to General Grant's plan to attack Vicksburg from the north.

1863

JAN - FEB Charley is part of an expedition to capture Ft. Hindman on the Arkansas River. The regiment is so badly shot-up from its engagement at Chickasaw Bayou that they are held in reserve and do not take an active part in this engagement. The regiment is then moved to Young's Point, LA, west of Vicksburg on the Mississippi River.

MAR - APR 15 The 16th OVI moves upstream to Milliken's Bend, General Grant's headquarters. The Union forces are on the west bank (Louisiana side) of the Mississippi River and surrounded by swamps. Vicksburg dominates the heights on the east bank of the river. The general needs his gunboats south of town to transport his troops from the west bank to the east bank of the Mississippi. Grant has devised at least five plans to approach Vicksburg the past few months and every one of them has failed. He now plans to circumnavigate Vicksburg by digging a ten mile man-made canal, parallel to the river and through the Louisiana swamp. By floating his troops down this canal he can be out of range and bypass the big guns of Vicksburg. Charley's regiment spends six weeks in the middle of winter digging through the muck and mud of the bayou and this too, ultimately fails.

APR 16 In the middle of the night, General Grant has eleven gunboats and transports from Admiral Farragut's river fleet run the gauntlet past Vicksburg. There is constant Rebel fire for 2 ½ hours from their big guns but only one river vessel is sunk. Grant now has the means to transport his army on to dry land from the west bank of the Mississippi to the east bank of the river.

Confederate artillery fire on Union gunboats the night of April 16, 1864.

The USS Corondolet was one of the ironclads that ran the gauntlet at Vicksburg.

Illustrated London News

APR 25 - 30 General Grant's Army crosses the Mississippi River at Bruinsburg, MS, and now has a secure base on the east bank of the Mississippi River.

General Grant's Vicksburg Campaign- May, 1864

Map 8

National Park Service Map

Vanguard leaves
Milliken's Bend
March 31

Haynes' Bluff
Snyder's Bluff

Milliken's Bend

Steele's Bayou

Yazoo River

New Orleans, Jackson &
Great Northern Railroad

Vicksburg, Shreveport
& Texas Railroad

Chickasaw
Bayou

Battle of the
Big Black River Bridge
May 17

Wabu

VICKSBURG

Duckport O

Richmond

Roundaway Bayou

Bayou

Grant's
Canal

Southern RR of Mississippi

Clinton

JACKSON

Edwards
Station

Siege of
Vicksburg
May 18-July 4

Battle of
Champion Hill
May 16

Raymond

Battle of
Jackson
May 14

River

Battle of
Raymond
May 12

LOUISIANA

Brierfield

Mississippi River

Big Black River

MISSISSIPPI

Pearl River

Arrives
Hard Times
April 28

Hard
Times

Union fleet bombards
Grand Gulf
April 29

Grand Gulf

Big

Bayou

Pierre

Line of Grant's march

Confederate defense

North

0   10   20 Kilometers

0   10 Miles   20

Crosses
Mississippi
River at
Bruinsburg
April 30

Bruinsburg

Port Gibson

Battle of
Port Gibson
May 1

Little
Bayou Pierre

This picture is a good illustration of the terrain and road conditions where the Battle of Port Gibson was fought. The battlefield has remained unchanged in the years since the engagement. There are some historical markers in the area, but no preserved battlefield.

MAY 1 Battle of Port Gibson (or Battle of Thompson's Hill) This is where Charley is reportedly wounded in the ankle, refuses treatment, binds his wound with a piece of bacon and then secures a mule to ride off and rejoin his regiment. There is no mention of this incident in Charley's extensive compiled military service record. There are a few possible explanations for this: 1. The service records from the National Archives are very incomplete and it could easily have been overlooked. 2. If he refused treatment and was not admitted to an army hospital there would be no official record of his injury and one can then assume that maybe it was a very slight wound. A seriously wounded soldier would have been ordered by his commanding officer to seek treatment and probably would have been absent from duty, which may or may not have been documented. 3. This could be a good soldier's tale, passed down through the years and embellished with each retelling. Perhaps the original account started as no more than a sprained ankle, with no mule or bacon. This story aside, early in the day on May 1st Charley's brigade does drive the enemy back 400 yards to secure a Union victory.

MAY 16 Battle of Champion Hill Both Daniel Wallick of the 20th OVI and Charley Wallick fight in this battle. For months Daniel's regiment has been involved with the Vicksburg Campaign and they have a hard fight on Champion Hill, where they suffer many casualties. Charley's commanding officer is slow to engage the enemy but does eventually join the conflict late in the day. The defeat of the Confederates at Champion Hill guarantees the fall of Vicksburg. With this loss, the Confederate Army is forced back into Vicksburg and the town is condemned to a siege. Without outside help, the Confederates will be forced to surrender.

MAY 17 Battle of Big Black River Bridge The Confederates last natural line of defense before Vicksburg is the Big Black River. There is a morning fight to take the bridge over the river and the 16th Ohio is in the front line of the attack. Charley's brigade commander is wounded during the battle in an exchange of artillery fire.

MAY 19 First Assault at Vicksburg General Grant is impatient with the thought of a siege and fears that the Rebels will be reinforced. The general orders an assault that is very costly and a failure. Charley and his regiment are held in reserve during this first assault.

MAY 22 Second Assault at Vicksburg By mid-morning Charley's regiment is about a 1/2 mile south of the present-day Vicksburg National Military Park Visitor's Center and they charge the Rebel works. Murderous Confederate fire stops the regiment about 200 yards from the entrenched enemy. All of General Grant's forces are pinned down in front of the Vicksburg earthworks and Grant, rightly, calls off the attack. However, Charley's corps commander, General

16th Ohio Infantry Monument at Vicksburg National Military Park.

122

McClernand, has relayed false information to headquarters, leading Grant to believe there is a breakthrough in Charley's sector. Grant orders an afternoon attack with the same results as before. By dark, Charley's regiment has retreated back from the Confederate line. General McClernand is eventually sacked and sent back home to Illinois, his faulty intelligence sent to General Grant being a contributing factor.

MAY 24 The 16th OVI marches about twelve miles east of Vicksburg to be part of Sherman's exterior line of defense against Confederate reinforcements. Charley is temporarily assigned to General Hovey's 12th Division. They are sent to guard the Big Black River railroad bridge, where they fought with the Confederates on May 17th.

JUN - JUL 4 Conditions in Vicksburg have become appalling. The civilian population and soldiers are starving with no food or supplies passing through the siege lines. The Confederate army finally succumbs to General Grant's forces on our nation's birthday, July 4th, believing they can negotiate more favorable terms of surrender from their countrymen on this day. In part they are correct. Grant paroles the men and officers who promise not to take up arms against the United States. However, the Confederate army is disbanded with few ceremonial honors. The town of Vicksburg will not celebrate Independence Day for 82 years - not until after VE Day (Victory in Europe), 1945.

JUL 5 - 17 The regiment participates in the siege of Jackson, MS.

AUG 13 - OCT 3 The 16th OVI is ordered to New Orleans, LA, and then to Brashear City, LA.

NOV 19 - DEC Charley is posted at DeCrow's Point on the tip of Matagorda Island, TX. In his company is a drummer and friend from Millersburg, Thomas B. Linn. In a letter dated December 1863, Thomas gives a good description of where he and Charley are posted. Later in the month he even refers to Charley by name in two entries of his diary. The following is a letter from Thomas B. Linn, 16th Ohio Volunteers, Company B, to his Uncle A. B. Grey, to be reproduced in *The Holmes County Republican*, a local newspaper.[25]

Decrow's Point, Texas, December 2, 1863

> *We are at last on the bleak shores of Texas: landed on a sandy point extending into the sea, dividing Matagorda Bay from its more extensive neighbor, the Gulf of Mexico. This is called Decrow's Point, named after the old planter who owns it. Mr. Decrow is a native of Maine but leaving the old homestead, he wandered through the Eastern States, thence westward through Ohio, Indiana, Illinois, and finally found himself almost at the opposite extreme of his country, and settled. He lived here twenty-five years and is candid enough to admit that he has wandered from the path of his forefathers and now "sympathizes with the Confederates." But I know you would rather learn something of our trip than read about this old secesh Texan. We left Brashear City* [now part of New Orleans] *Sunday morning, November 22, on the cars for Algiers. Arriving at the depot about one o'clock we were met by our paroled men* (former POWs who were captured at Chickasaw Bluffs) *and then such a shout rent the air, such shaking of hands at meeting with old comrades and friends, was only equaled by the meeting of the same men with their friends and relatives when they marched into the Courthouse in Millersburg, on the eventful eve when true valor and bravery were rewarded by the presentation of those beautiful swords to the gallant Lieutenants Corn and Voorhees. This important addition to our numbers raises the spirits of our men, as well as improves the looks and effectiveness of the regiment. Company B can now boast of 47 men, all good and true, instead of 29, as the case less than two weeks ago* [100 men was a company at full strength]. *We pitched our tents near the depot and remain in Algiers two days.*

---

[25] *The Holmes County Republican* had a rival publication, *The Holmes County Farmer,* a Democrat newspaper that would constantly refer to the President as "King Lincoln" in its anti-war editorials. Newspaper publications during the Civil War were unabashed in their biased reporting and felt no need to subscribe to "a fairness doctrine."

The following excerpts are from Private Thomas B. Linn's personal diary:

Wednesday, December 2, 1863

> *Charley Wallick, Frank Wilson and I went down to the beach and took a bath in the bay* [Matagorda Bay, about 60 miles north of Corpus Christi, TX]. *Commenced a letter to Uncle Frey for the Republican, also one to Lizzie. Unloaded ship and go aboard for my drum. Pitch our tent anew. Short of grub.*

Thursday, December 17, 1863

> *Passed an ugly night and this morning are covered with sand.* **Charley Wallick** *and Harry Myers went into the other tent in the night. Wind still blows as hard as ever. Some of Co. A's tents torn to shreds. Wind goes down about noon and we fix up our tent - put cattle skins up at the ends and threw up the sand all around the tent. Fixed up nicely now.*

1864

JAN - MAR   Throughout the winter the 16th Ohio remains posted at Matagorda Island, TX.

MAR 18 - 23   The regiment moves to New Orleans and then to Alexandria, LA.

MAR 26 - MAY 22   The Red River Campaign   The 16th OVI is on Matagorda Island at the beginning of General Nathaniel Banks' Red River Campaign. The purpose of this campaign is to pursue the Rebels up the Red River from Alexandra to Shreveport, LA, and then on into Texas. General Banks makes a poor choice of roads in his advance on Shreveport. Instead of traveling on a road close to the Red River, which can easily supply his army, he chooses one that is no more than a dirt path that runs through the wilderness. This, and other poor choices throughout the campaign, ultimately dooms the expedition to failure. The Federals are driven back and defeated at the battles of Sabine Cross Roads, Pleasant Hill and other minor engagements. The 16th Ohio is ordered to Alexandria, LA to help reinforce the retreating Union army.

APR 26   Charley's regiment arrives and helps construct a dam at Alexandria. LA. It has been very dry during the campaign and a dam is necessary to help raise the water level so Admiral Porter's gunboats can retreat back down the Red River.

MAY 13 - 20   General Banks' Army, including the 16th Ohio Infantry, retreats to Morganza and Mansura, LA.

MAY 30 - June 6   Charley and his regiment are sent on an expedition to the Atchafalaya River.

JUN 22 - JUL   Private Wallick has detached duty as a brigade orderly.[26]

AUG - OCT   The 16th Ohio regiment is posted at Morganza, LA. This is a small town on the Mississippi River between Baton Rouge, LA and Natchez, MS.

OCT   Charley begins his journey home to Ohio.

OCT 31   The 16th Ohio Volunteer Infantry is mustered out at Camp Chase, Columbus, OH. There are so few veterans who wish to reenlist that the regiment is disbanded. Those who do reenlist are transferred to the 114th Ohio Volunteer Infantry.

---

[26] An orderly could have an array of duties and responsibilities. He could be a runner for the staff at headquarters or simply act as a commanding officer's personal valet.

Epilogue - Charley returned to Millersburg, Ohio, after his discharge from Federal service. Ready to rejoin normal civilian life, he married his sweetheart, Mary Gray, on February 9, 1865. Two months later, in April 1865, with the Civil War quickly drawing to a close, the whole family moved west and settled in Iowa. By 1870 none of the Wallick war veterans or their immediate families were living in Holmes County. They all had relocated west, either to Iowa or Kansas. How much Charley's travels and younger brother's death during the war influenced his family's decision to start anew is mere speculation. What is certain is that he and his parents, "Guthrie" Michael and Hannah, along with his older brothers and young sister, all departed for Iowa just one month after Charley's wedding. He had a rough start in his new life. Charley's young bride, Mary, died while giving birth to their daughter, Ada, just months after arriving in Victor, Iowa. He did remarry two years later and had at least twelve more children by Mary Shaull (the exact number is uncertain). Charley died on July 2, 1926; just six days short of his eighty-third birthday.

Comrades-in-Arms

Brother
William D.   67th OVI- died of disease

Cousin
Henry M.   67th OVI- killed in action

Charles Wallick
He is buried between his two wives
in the Victor, Iowa, Memorial Cemetery.

Mary Gray died November 4, 1865
Mary Shaull died August 9, 1919

Scott Alan Wallick Collection

William D. Wallick - 67th Ohio Volunteer Infantry, Co. C

Rank: Private

Place of enlistment: Holmes County, Ohio - December 26, 1861

Mustered into Federal service: January 2, 1862

Service time: 2 months

Born: 1845/46? Holmes County, Ohio

Age at enlistment: 18, probably younger

Physical description: height - 5' 5", light hair, gray eyes

Civilian occupation: farmer

Family Lineage: William, son of "Guthrie" Michael, son of "Bedford" John, son of "Bedford " Michael, son of Hans Michael Wallick

It is truly unfortunate that William D. Wallick will have the shortest biography of all the Wallick soldiers. He only served two months before passing away in an army hospital at Cumberland, Maryland, on February 26, 1862. It also appears that he was the youngest Wallick to have ever served in the Union army. Conflicting records indicate that he could have been as young as sixteen but certainly no more than seventeen years old when he signed his enlistment papers. The National Archives state his age as eighteen years old but considering all the other genealogical evidence, that seems unlikely. William joined the army the day after Christmas, 1861, following his cousin Henry M. Wallick into the 67th Ohio Volunteer Infantry (they were actually first cousins, once removed). Henry was five or six years older than his younger cousin and eager to join the ranks of the new company of soldiers being organized in Holmes County. Perhaps this influenced the family's decision to let William enlist. The two families could draw comfort from the fact that their sons would be serving together in the same company and could look after each other. The irony is that neither William nor Henry would survive the war.

Charley Wallick, William's older brother by three years, had enlisted in the 16th Ohio Volunteer Infantry in September, 1861. It must have pained young William very much to watch his older brother shoulder arms and parade off into military glory while he had to stay home and clean out the barn. Though underage, he was determined to not miss this opportunity of a lifetime. Stretching one's age was done quite often by new recruits and it appears this is exactly what William did.

Many new volunteers, such as William, came from isolated rural farming communities and they had little exposure to what we now consider "childhood diseases" like measles, mumps, chicken pox, etc. This made them very susceptible to sickness in general. The miracle drug aspirin was years away from development, so the slightest fever could be a serious threat. The real life-threatening danger to a Civil War soldier (by a margin of two-to-one) was camp life, not the battlefield. Whereas approximately 200,000 men died in combat during the war more than 400,000 were laid waste by disease. Unfortunately, William was one of them.

The Official Roster of Soldiers from the State of Ohio in The War of the Rebellion, 1861-1865, Roll of Honor, lists William D. Wallick as buried in Antietam National Cemetery, Sharpsburg, Maryland. Obviously, he did not fight in the September 1862 Battle of Antietam, for he died nine months before that engagement ever began. But the soldiers who were killed at that battle are not the only ones buried in the national cemetery. Many soldiers who died during the war were buried in the surrounding countryside and then moved to be reinterred at Antietam Cemetery.

Identification of the dead was a real problem during the American Civil War and Antietam has numerous soldiers buried as "Unknown." A total of 4,776 soldiers are buried at Antietam National Cemetery; one-third of them are unidentified. Dog tags were not used by either side during the war. When fierce battles were anticipated, soldiers sometimes wrote their names on pieces of paper and pinned them to their clothing so they could be identified by their comrades if they were killed.

When there was a major battle with many casualties the army didn't have time to collect all the dead and transport them to proper cemeteries. The fallen were often buried on the battlefield to later be reinterred. The same was true with those who died in hospitals when relatives were unable to claim the bodies. William D. Wallick appears to be just such a case.

Some soldiers who died at the Cumberland hospitals were later transferred to Antietam National Cemetery. All indications are that William was one of those who were moved. But if William was buried at Antietam National Cemetery, why is he not identified in the interment records? The answer may be that his identification tag was lost when he was first buried or when his body reinterred. Grave markers at hospital cemeteries were not intended to be permanent and one can imagine the problems of transporting hundreds of bodies across many miles to be reburied. Burial parties in Civil War armies were sometimes careless and haphazard in their duty, especially after a battle when quick interment was a priority. The labor used for this gruesome work was not always military personnel but sometimes hired civilians or ex-slaves. The opportunity for losing a soldier's identity was great. The mammoth twelve-volume series *Official Roster of Soldiers from the State of Ohio in the War of the Rebellion* is far from perfect in all its documentation, but for lack of any other credible evidence, this author accepts as fact that William D. Wallick is buried as an unknown in Antietam National Cemetery at Sharpsburg, Maryland.

William D. Wallick with the 67th Ohio Volunteer Infantry

1861

DEC 26 William enlists as a very young soldier the day after Christmas, 1861. He joins his cousin, Private Henry M. Wallick, in Company C of the 67th OVI.

1862

JAN 2 The 67th Ohio is mustered into Federal service at Camp Chase, Columbus, OH.

JAN 19 William's regiment departs for West Virginia via the Baltimore & Ohio Railroad..

FEB William is stricken with the measles and taken to one of the many army hospitals in the vicinity of Cumberland, MD.

This country inn at Clarysville, west of Cumberland, MD, was one of the buildings used as an army hospital at the time of William D. Wallick's untimely death. Cumberland and Clarysville eventually had a 1,000-bed complex to help nurse back to health the Union soldiers. Throughout the war, thousands of men were sent to these facilities to recuperate. In the spring of 1864, distant cousin Edward Wallick of the 36th Ohio Infantry was sent to a Clarysville hospital, perhaps this very one.

FEB 26   Private William D. Wallick dies of measles at Cumberland, MD, and is interred in the hospital cemetery. In 1867 he is reinterred as an unknown at Antietam National Cemetery, Sharpsburg, MD.

Antietam National Cemetery, Sharpsburg, Maryland.

Antietam is like many other Civil War cemeteries where unknown soldiers are scattered among those who have known identities. The picture below illustrates the difference between the two styles of stone memorials. One can immediately identify original Civil War unknown markers for they are only small squares with a number etched on top.

Soldier number 1474 may not be William D. Wallick, but his marker in the cemetery would look similar.

William D. Wallick is buried in Antietam National Cemetery with 4,775 other soldiers.

<u>**Comrades-in-Arms**</u>

Brother
Charles   16th OVI

Cousin
Henry M.   67th OVI- killed in action.

Elijah Wallick - 102nd Ohio Volunteer Infantry, Co. G

Rank: Private, promoted to Corporal

Place of enlistment: Holmes County, Millersburg, Ohio

Mustered into Federal service: September 6, 1862

Service time: 2 Years, 9 months, 11 days

Born: April, 1831 - Holmes County, Ohio

Age at enlistment: 31

Physical description: height - 5' 8", light hair, brown eyes

Occupation: farmer

Family Lineage: Elijah, son of Andrew, son of "Bedford" Michael, son of Hans Michael Wallick

Elijah Wallick was a grandson of "Bedford" Michael and the son of Andrew Wallick. Andrew had been born, like all of his siblings, in Bedford County, Pennsylvania, and by 1830 he had migrated west to farm in the picturesque countryside of Holmes County, Ohio. Here, Elijah was born and raised into manhood. He was about thirty years old when the political union of our nation was torn apart by the Confederates' attack on Ft. Sumter. On August 8, 1862, Elijah joined the Federal army; he would serve his country in the western theater of the war for almost three years. His cousin David H. Wallick, also from Holmes County, served with Elijah and was in the same regiment and company, 102nd Ohio Volunteer Regiment, Company G. They were about the same age and shared many of the same wartime experiences. However, on September 23, 1864, their destinies were led in two different directions. Elijah was one of 350 men who were detached from two regiments of his brigade, the 102nd Ohio and 18th Michigan, and sent of help the besieged Federal forces posted at Fort Henderson in Athens, Alabama. Why Elijah was part of this expedition and cousin David remained in camp is unknown. For some reason only 20 men from Company G were selected to be part of this relief force.

Fort Henderson had been under attack for several days by the sly "Wizard of the Saddle," General Nathan Bedford Forrest.[27] As a result, soldiers from the United States Colored Troops, who occupied the fort, were forced to surrender to General Forrest. Elijah and his expedition arrived thirty minutes after the fort had been evacuated and after a brief but fierce firefight, they too were forced to surrender. The men were eventually taken to the Federal prison camp at Cahaba, Alabama, where they were "guests" of the Confederacy the last six months of the war. Elijah became very ill while incarcerated at Cahaba. His service record from the National Archives tells us that, because of his illness, he was one of the first to be paroled and was immediately sent to the Union hospital at Camp Fisk, near Vicksburg, Mississippi. He was diagnosed to have scurvy and had also developed a severe case of rheumatism. Elijah was transferred to several hospitals during the last months of the war. On April 9, 1865, while Elijah was in the hospital at Camp Fisk, General Lee surrendered his forces to General Grant and with the collapse of the Confederacy, all of Elijah's compatriots from Cahaba Prison were released to begin their journey home.

General Nathan Bedford Forrest

---

[27] General Forrest is the same commander who captured William Wallick near Rome, Georgia, on May 3, 1863.

At first glance it seems unfortunate that Elijah's prison experiences had so broken his health that he was unable to celebrate with his comrades their release from prison and the end of the long war. However, the fact that he was so ill and needed to be hospitalized may have rescued Elijah from an agonizing fate. Had he been well enough to stay with his captured brethren he very well could have been on board the ill-fated steamboat, *Sultana*. This vessel's horrific demise on the Mississippi River is still considered the greatest maritime disaster in United States history.

Elijah Escapes the *Sultana* Disaster!

At the end of the war steamboat captains received from the U.S. Government five dollars per enlisted man and ten dollars per officer to transport them back north. However, some of the captains offered army officers a kick-back of $1.15 for every soldier put on their boat, thus resulting in many boats stuffed way beyond their capacity with passengers. The *Sultana* was just such a vessel when it began its voyage April 24, 1865, steamed out of Vicksburg, MS, and headed toward Memphis, TN. Built in Cincinnati, Ohio, in 1863, it was registered to carry only 376 passengers. On its departure from Vicksburg the *Sultana* was carrying over 2,400 soldiers, many of them friends and comrades of Elijah who were captured with him and refugees from Cahaba Federal Prison. Every available compartment was packed with soldiers who hardly had an inch of open space on the decks to maneuver. On April 26, the *Sultana* made a stop at Memphis for fuel and supplies and then continued its journey up the Mississippi. Early the next morning at around 2:00 AM, seven miles north of Memphis, one of her boilers blew up, causing a great fire to break out and the boat to sink.

This photograph of the overcrowded *Sultana* was taken less than 24 hours before she exploded on the Mississippi River. Elijah probably would have been loaded on this boat had he not been so seriously ill. Over 70 comrades from the 102nd Ohio perished when the *Sultana* sank.

Those not killed by the explosion or trapped inside the burning boat jumped into the waters in an attempt to reach the shore. The Mississippi was near flood stage that spring and the passengers and crew found themselves rushed down steam by an incredibly swift current. Those who were not excellent swimmers drowned and many of those who did not drown died of hypothermia from the cold water. Over 1,700 passengers perished that night while another 500 made it to shore and were taken to hospitals, many of them dying after a few days. Unfortunately, the tragic accident received little coverage in the newspapers at the time due to all the events following President Lincoln's assassination. John Wilkes Booth had been cornered and killed the day before the *Sultana*'s sinking and the Presidential funeral procession was winding its way through the American heartland towards Lincoln's home in Springfield, Illinois.

Had Elijah not been so seriously ill upon his release from prison, he could have been another casualty in the *Sultana* tragedy. Had he been on the *Sultana* in his weakened state he most assuredly would not have survived the icy waters of the Mississippi River. In this case, Elijah's broken health just may have saved his life. Many from the 102nd Regiment were not so lucky. Official records state that a least eighty-one soldiers from Elijah's regiment perished in the dark waters of the Mississippi that night. Some fellow POWs escaped; most did not. In the book, *The Sultana* by Jerry O. Potter, Elijah is listed as having been on board the steamboat the night of the explosion and survived. That is an error. Elijah's service records prove that he was never a passenger on the *Sultana*.

Elijah Wallick with the 102nd Ohio Infantry

1862

AUG 9   Elijah and cousin David H. Wallick go into Millersburg, OH, and enlist in the Union army. They agree to donate the next three years of their lives to Uncle Sam and the United States Government. At this time Elijah is living in Killbuck Township, home also to David H. and his brother Henry M. Wallick of the 67th Ohio Infantry. A total of five Wallick men from Holmes County will serve in the Federal army during the Civil War. Elijah and David H. are organized into Company G of the 102nd Ohio Volunteer Infantry at Camp Mansfield, OH. While in camp waiting to be mustered in, the regiment becomes known for their "gentlemanly qualities," not a flattering reputation given to men preparing for war.

SEP 6 - 22   Elijah is mustered into Federal service on September 6th in Covington, KY. Because of the Rebel invasion into southern Kentucky, he will be posted in and around the defenses of Cincinnati, OH.

SEP 22 - Oct 6   In response to Confederate General Braxton Bragg's move toward the Ohio River, the 102nd Regiment is deployed to Louisville, KY, to help bolster the defense of that city.

OCT 5 - 6   The men of the 102nd are assigned to guard the brigade wagon trains while pursuing General Bragg.

OCT 8   Battle of Perryville   The 102nd is held in reserve and sees no action. But they are close enough to hear the sounds of battle.

OCT 10 - DEC 30   After the Battle of Perryville Elijah and his regiment move to Bowling Green, KY, where they are given the responsibility of railroad security from Bowling Green, KY, to Nashville, TN. On December 19th they are moved to Russellville, TN, and from there to Clarksville.

1863

JAN - SEP   The men of the 102nd spend almost ten months in the vicinity of Clarksville, TN, building bridges, forwarding supplies and providing a secure base of operations for the Union army.

JUL - AUG   Elijah is detailed as an honor guard.

SEP 26 - 30   The 102nd is called on to help repel a Confederate cavalry raid by General Wheeler.

OCT - DEC   Elijah and his regiment are moved to Nashville, TN, and continue their rear echelon duty.

1864

JAN - APR   The 102nd remains in Nashville where they protect one of the Union's most vital supply bases.

APR 26 - JUN 6   Elijah's primary responsibility is to help guard the Nashville and Chattanooga Railroad from Normandy to Dechard. Thousands of men were need throughout the war to secure the southern railroads and protect them from attacks by Confederate guerrillas and cavalrymen. On June 6th they cross over the Cumberland Mountains.

JUN - AUG The 102nd is part of the defensive line along the Tennessee River, from Stevenson, AL, to Seven Mile Island.

SEP 1 - 15 The regiment has duty protecting the Tennessee Railroad from Decatur, AL, to Columbia, TN.

SEP 23 - 24 Elijah is captured and becomes a prisoner of war Elijah, with a detachment of soldiers from the 102nd Ohio and 18th Michigan, is sent to help relieve Fort Henderson, in Athens, AL, and is captured by General Nathan Bedford Forrest. Here is an Account of their capture at Fort Henderson from *War of the Rebellion: A Compilation of Official Records of the Union and Confederate Armies:*

> *About the 20th of September the Confederate cavalry, under General Nathan Bedford Forrest, crossed the Tennessee River near Waterloo, Alabama, and appeared in front of Athens, Alabama. Considerable skirmishing took place and the garrison, occupied by the 106th, 110th, and 111th Colored Troops and commanded by Colonel Campbell, withdrew into the fort. By night-fall the town was completely invested and the quartermaster and commissary buildings were destroyed by the Confederates. On the morning of the 24th the Confederates opened fire on the fort with a 12-pounder battery, firing from two different directions, north and west, which was answered by the artillery from the garrison. Later two flags of truce were received demanding a surrender, which was declined by Colonel Campbell. When he was requested to grant Major-General Forrest a personal interview, he complied to meet with the general. At this interview Colonel Campbell allowed himself to become convinced by the Confederate commander that it was useless to contend against the larger superior forces of the enemy.[28] The garrison at the time had overwhelming numbers to General Forrest's Cavalry. Thirty minutes after the evacuation for surrender of the fort, reinforcements consisting of the 102nd Ohio and the 18th Michigan regiments arrived, and after a severe fight were also forced to yield.*

OCT - DEC Elijah is held a prisoner of war in Cahaba, AL, The town of Cahaba, in south-central Alabama, was from 1820-1826 Alabama's first state capital. Frequent flooding of the Cahaba and Alabama Rivers eventually forced the relocation of the capital in 1826 to Tuscaloosa, then to Montgomery twenty years later. The town of "Old Cahaba" is nothing more than a very minor tourist stop now. The antebellum river town died at the end of the nineteenth century but it has recently been reclaimed as an historic park. "Old Cahaba Archeological Park" can be visited today and is located about fourteen miles southwest of Selma, AL.

Artist depiction of Cahaba Federal Prison Camp.
At one point this facility held over 5,000 prisoners.

Site of Cahaba Federal Prison today.

---

[28] This was untrue. General Forrest had his troops simply march in a circle to give the impression that he commanded a much larger force. He used the marching-in-a-circle ruse a number of times during the war to deceive his enemy. William Wallick was captured when his commanding officer was similarly deceived.

1865

JAN Elijah is still being held captive in Cahaba Federal Prison. Conditions are harsh, as are all Civil War prison camps. Cahaba is first used as an overflow for prisoners being sent to Andersonville Prison, in southern Georgia. Elijah could have been a prisoner in that hell-hole. Although the living conditions at Cahaba are not nearly as brutal as at Andersonville, Cahaba is still very overcrowded and the prisoners greatly suffer from poor food and exposure.

FEB Elijah is admitted to the prison hospital with typhoid fever. He will suffer from numerous diseases while a prisoner of war.

MAR 1 Severe flooding of the Alabama and Cahaba Rivers add to the prisoners' misery and force many to stand for hours in knee deep water. Some men take turns sitting on high bunk beds and support beams in the old warehouse prison.

MAR 16 About this time the first group of soldiers from Cahaba begin their journey to Camp Fisk near Vicksburg, MS. Camp Fisk is a parole camp for Union and Confederate prisoners who await exchange. Elijah is one of the first paroled due to his ill health.

MAR 30 Elijah is admitted to Camp Fisk Army Hospital with scurvy and severe rheumatism. He will remain hospitalized for the next few months and, thankfully, be spared the agony his prisoner-of-war comrades will experience on the steamboat *Sultana*.

APR 1 Elijah is sent to the army's General Hospital at Jefferson Barracks, MO, near the city of St. Louis.

APR 24 Those who were captured with Elijah and suffered with him in Cahaba Prison have been paroled and are loaded on board the steamboat *Sultana* to begin their journey home. The *Sultana* is delayed in its departure due to a leak in one of her boilers. The repair is hastily made and the boat departs up river for Memphis. The overcrowded boat carries six times its recommended limit of passengers; over 2,400 persons are packed on board.

APR 27 2:00AM The *Sultana* explodes in a fireball of flames seven miles north of Memphis. Over 1,700 passengers are killed and hundreds of others seriously burned and injured while attempting to reach the shoreline. A great many drown due to the frigid temperatures of the Mississippi River and the weakened condition of the prisoners of war. More lives are lost in the sinking of the *Sultana* than in the sinking of the *Titanic*.

A fate Elijah was fortunate to have missed.
Many friends and comrades perished that night.

Photograph- *Harper's Weekly*

MAY 25 Elijah is transferred from Jefferson Barrack Army Hospital to Benton Barrack Army Hospital in St. Louis, MO. He will stay here one week before going back to Ohio.

JUN 1 Still very ill, Elijah is sent to Camp Chase in Columbus, OH.

JUN 19 Elijah is officially mustered out of service under Government Order #77 while in the army hospital at Camp Chase. This order states that "all volunteers who need no further treatment in army hospitals are to be honorably discharged from service with immediate payment and all prisoners of war treated the same." After two months of hospitalizations and separation from his regiment, Elijah is finally allowed to go home. All of those in the 102nd Ohio Volunteer Regiment who were not part to the Ft. Henderson expedition (which includes Elijah's cousin David H. Wallick) are mustered out of Federal service in Decatur, AL.

Epilogue - Elijah recuperated in a number of army hospitals before he returned home to Holmes County. He eventually married Olive Gibbens and moved to Iowa in the late 1860s. Elijah was part of the Wallick family's post-Civil War mass migration out of Holmes County to the newer western lands. He was a successful farmer for many years and died in Ladora, Iowa, on May 8, 1922, at ninety-one years of age.

Elijah Wallick- Ladora, Iowa

His inscription reads:
E. Wallick
1831-1922
Co. G 102nd Reg Ohio Vol

Scott Alan Wallick Collection

Comrades-in-Arms

Cousins

David H.	102nd OVI
Daniel	20th OVI
David	139th OVI
Henry	67th OVI
Michael	27th IVI

136

Isaiah Wallick - 49th Ohio Volunteer Infantry, Co. G

Rank: Private, promoted to Corporal

Place of enlistment: West Lodi, Ohio - Aug 18, 1861

Mustered into Federal service: September 3, 1861

Service time: 2 years, 3 months, 9 days

Born: c. 1840 - Coshocton County, Ohio

Age at enlistment: 21

Physical description: height - 5' 7", brown hair, gray eyes

Occupation: farmer

Family Linage: Isaiah, son of Samuel, son of "Bunker Hill" Michael, son of "Bedford" Michael, son of Hans Michael Wallick.

The wonders of modern science have helped determine that Isaiah is indeed a descendant of Hans Michael Wallick and that he should be included in the family's roster of soldiers who served in the American Civil War. In 2008, a descendent from Isaiah's family participated in a genetic test which proved Isaiah was of the same heritage as all the other soldiers in this volume[29]. He enlisted for three years and fought in some of the biggest battles of the war. However, his enlistment was cut short and came to a tragic end when he died in a Chattanooga army hospital from the wounds he received while fighting at Missionary Ridge.

In 1840 Isaiah was born to Samuel Wallick of Crawford Twp, Coshocton County, Ohio. Samuel was a farmer, and at some time in the 1850s Samuel moved his wife Margaret and seven children to Hardin County, in northwest Ohio. When the war intensified in the summer of 1861and finally exploded with the Battle of Bull Run, Isaiah went into the small hamlet of West Lodi, in Seneca County, to enlist in the Union army. He was one of 300,000 volunteers who answered President Lincoln's call that summer to quash the southern rebellion. Isaiah was working for the Stumm brothers when he

Isaiah Wallick

joined the army, however, his enlistment papers state that he was a farmer by trade. Whether the Stumm brothers were a mercantile establishment or owners of a farm on which he worked is unknown. Isaiah's younger brother Edward also served in the war and enlisted only three months after the death of Isaiah. Edward was three years junior to his brother, and his enlistment so soon after Isaiah's death is a testimony to both men's honor and patriotism.

The 49th Ohio Volunteer Infantry saw its share of fighting during the war. They had a few skirmishes and minor engagements with the enemy early in the conflict. Then on April 7, 1862, at the Battle of Shiloh, Isaiah's regiment had the first serious test of its mettle when they arrived on the battlefield and helped push the Confederates back to their original pre-battle positions, negating the Confederate successes of the first day's fight. The next great contest for the 49th Ohio was on the last day of December, 1862, at the Battle of Stones River. At the beginning of the battle Isaiah's regiment was overrun by the Confederates and forced to retreat, taking a great many casualties. The regiment had to retire from the field after running low on ammunition and the Confederates captured one of their commanding

---

[29] A great-grandnephew of Isaiah had his DNA compared to others of the Hans Michael Wallick lineage. The test proved positive and because of this confirmation, both Isaiah and his younger brother Edward are included in these biographies.

officers, General Willich. The 49th rejoined the fight on the second day of battle and made a bayonet charge that helped turn the tide against the Rebels and produce a victory for the Union. But of all the battles and engagements that Isaiah and his regiment were part of, it was at the Battle of Chickamauga where they perhaps gave their best performance.

The 49th OVI saw action on both days of battle at Chickamauga. They fought there together with Isaiah's distant cousins Charles F. Wallick, of the 87th Indiana, and Levi Wallick, of the 44th Indiana. All three Wallick regiments were engaged on or near Kelly Field on the second day of battle and all claimed to be one of the last regiments to leave the battlefield as night fell over the Georgia landscape. The Battle of Chickamauga had more casualties than any other two-day battle in the Civil War. Many military historians consider this conflict more like a gigantic brawl between two opposing armies than an organized battle. The undulating terrain and thick undergrowth made it difficult for units to stay together and the result was a great deal of chaos within the ranks. It was more than just a defeat for the Union army. It was a catastrophe. The Federals were smashed, totally routed, demoralized and had to make a humiliating retreat back into Chattanooga, Tennessee. But on the heels of such a loss was to be one of the most remarkable and stunning infantry assaults in military history.

With their defeat at Chickamauga, Isaiah and the Federal army were surrounded at Chattanooga by the Rebels, who held the high ground on both Lookout Mountain and Missionary Ridge. After a six-week Confederate siege of the city, General Grant was brought in from west Tennessee to help break the stranglehold held by the Rebels. On November 24th, Grant ordered his troops to advance and take Lookout Mountain. This dutifully done, he next ordered the assault of Confederate positions on Missionary Ridge.

View atop Missionary Ridge from the Confederate perspective.
Isaiah and the 49th Ohio charged up the hill below, toward the camera.
The City of Chattanooga is three miles in the background.

The Rebels had three rows of entrenched troops across the 600-foot ridge - one line at the bottom, one in the middle and one at the top. By mid-afternoon of November 25th, the Union army was ready to charge the Confederate lines. At about 4:00 PM, General Grant gave orders for his commanders to attack, take the first row of rifle pits at the bottom of the ridge, and then halt. However, the attack was so successful that the Federal troops found themselves in a difficult position. Having quickly taken the rifle pits they were now being fired upon by the Confederate army above them. They had the choice of either continuing to advance up the ridge, or to turn around and retreat; they couldn't just stay where they were in the rifle pits. Without orders and on their own initiative (and to the shock of General

Grant and all his staff who were watching), the soldiers chose to continue their charge up the ridge and force the Rebels out of their entrenchments. The 49th Ohio was one of the first regiments to plant its flag on the summit of Missionary Ridge and all the Union troops were astonished and wild with delight at their success. Unfortunately, by that time Isaiah had been shot and was not among his jubilant comrades.

At some point in the charge Isaiah was wounded by a Rebel ball or shell and he failed to advance with the rest of his regiment. Isaiah died two days after the assault in an army hospital in Chattanooga.

Missionary Ridge is in the far horizon beyond the cannon. This picture was taken from Orchard Knob, where General Grant and his staff watched the Union army's assault. This sector of the ridge is also where Isaiah's regiment charged the Confederate positions on November 25, 1863.

Isaiah Wallick with the 49th Ohio Volunteer Infantry

1861

AUG 18   Isaiah Wallick enlists as a private in the Union army at West Lodi, OH.

AUG - SEP   Isaiah and his comrades from Seneca County are organized into Company G of the 49th Ohio Volunteer Infantry at Tiffin, OH. The regiment then moves to Camp Dennison.

SEP 21   The 49th OVI is ordered to Louisville, KY. They are the first volunteer regiment to enter that state.

OCT - DEC   The regiment is moved to Munfordsville, KY, near present day Mammoth Cave National Park.

1862

JAN - FEB 13   Continued duty at Munfordsville, KY.

FEB 14 - MAR 3   49th OVI moves to Bowling Green, KY, and then to Nashville, TN.

MAR 16 - APR 6   Isaiah and his regiment are marched to Savannah, TN, and then on to Pittsburg Landing, where the first day of the Battle of Shiloh is concluding. They can hear the sounds of combat as they approach the battlefield.

Monument to the 49th Ohio Infantry at Shiloh

APR 7 Battle of Shiloh - Second Day During the night of April 6th, the 49th OVI arrives with General Don Carlos Buell's Army of the Ohio and prepares for the second day's fight at the Battle of Shiloh. General Grant's Army of the Tennessee has been pushed back and nearly destroyed. The arrival of Isaiah and his comrades help save the Federal forces from annihilation and turn an apparent defeat into a great Union victory. The 49th is placed near the center of the Union line in the early afternoon of April 7th. The regiment is in a desperate fight for three hours and is able to regain all that was lost from the previous day's battle. It is a Union victory, but with a terrific loss of life. More American soldiers (combined Union and Confederate casualties) die in this one battle than in all of our previous wars combined. The country is horrified by the lengthy casualty lists and blames General Grant who, although the victor, is nevertheless demoted and has a temporary setback to his career.

APR 29 - MAY 30 The 49th OVI marches to Corinth, MS, and begins to besiege that city.

JUN 10 - AUG 19 The regiment is deployed to Battlecreek, AL.

AUG 20 - SEP 26 Isaiah and the 49th Ohio are moved to Louisville, KY, and begin their pursuit of Confederate General Bragg.

SEP 27 - OCT 15 The 49th is part of the Union forces that pursue General Bragg in Kentucky and they have some minor skirmishing at the Battle of Perryville on October 8.

OCT 16 - DEC 26 Isaiah and his regiment are marched to Nashville, TN, and join the advance brigade that raises the siege of Nashville.

DEC 26 - 30 There is an advance on Murfreesboro, TN, by the 49th Ohio and its division.

DEC 31 The Battle of Stones River: First Day Isaiah and his regiment are heavily engaged in the early fighting at Stones River. They continue to press the enemy for six hours until they must retire to the rear of the Union army, minus one of their commanders. During the morning's battle General Willich, Isaiah's brigade commander, is captured by the Confederates.[30] Distant cousins William and Levi Wallick are also at the Battle of Stones River. By the end of the first day's fighting all three of the Wallick brigades are gathered east of Asbury Road and just north of today's Stones River National Military Park.

JAN 1 New Year's Day, 1863 Both combatants are very unorganized and avoid battle, using the New Year's holiday to consolidate their lines and reorganize their armies.

JAN 2 Second Day of Battle The second day of fighting finds the 49th Ohio held in reserve until late afternoon, then they are ordered to join a bayonet charge to repel a brigade of Confederates and help retrieve lost ground on the Union left. The battle ends in a tactical draw. However, after a few days the Confederate Army retreats, thus providing a strategic victory for the Federal forces.

JAN 3 - JUN 22 Isaiah's regiment is placed on guard duty at Murfreesboro, TN.

---

[30] General August Willich is eventually exchanged and resumes command of his brigade at the Battle of Chickamauga.

JUN 23 - JUL 7   The 49th OVI participates in General Roscrans' Tullahoma Campaign in middle Tennessee.

JUL 8 - AUG 16   The regiment is part of an occupation force that secures middle Tennessee.

AUG 17 - SEP 22   Isaiah and his regiment cross the Cumberland Mountains and Tennessee River in preparation for the Chickamauga Campaign.

SEP 19 - 20   Battle of Chickamauga   The 49th Ohio is active on many parts of the battlefield at Chickamauga and are moved about freely throughout the engagement. It is interesting that three Wallick soldiers, Isaiah of the 49th Ohio, Charles F. Wallick of the 87th Indiana and Levi Wallick of the 44th Indiana, all fight near each other on the second day of battle. At Kelly Field, in the middle of Chickamauga National Military Park, the 49th Ohio and the 87th Indiana have monuments to their respective regiments not more than 100 yards apart (see photo below). However, it is unlikely that Isaiah and Charles ever knew each other due to where they were raised (one in Ohio and the other in Indiana) and the great distance between the branches of their family tree. At the conclusion of the battle Charles and Levi are, again, very near each other as they make a desperate last stand on Snodgrass Hill (for a more detailed narrative, see page 81). Their heroic actions enable the Union army to safely retreat back into Chattanooga.

The regiments of Isaiah and Charles F. Wallick are memorialized by monuments within 100 yards of each other on Kelly Field at Chickamauga National Military Park. The 49th OVI monument is at the bottom left and the crown of the 87th IVI monument is visible under the white arrow. Levi Wallick's regiment, the 44th IVI, was also heavily engaged during this battle. Their regimental monument is located in Brotherton Field, which is just south of Kelly Field.

SEP 24 - NOV 24   Siege of Chattanooga   Isaiah and the Federal army are now bottled up and besieged by the Confederates at Chattanooga. This causes a great shortage of food and supplies that is only broken with the arrival of General Ulysses S. Grant. On October 17, the day of his arrival, Grant immediately takes control of the situation and within two weeks he has routed the Rebels at Brown's Ferry and has created a safe supply line for his army. He then develops a plan that will push the Confederates off the surrounding hills of Chattanooga. By late November everything is in place and Grant starts the Union breakout by taking from the Confederates a small knoll to the west of Missionary Ridge called Orchard Knob. Isaiah and his division are used to accomplish this task. The next day Lookout Mountain is overrun and secured, setting the stage for the assault on Missionary Ridge.

NOV 25 - 27   The Assault on Missionary Ridge & Death of Isaiah   At exactly 3:40 PM on November 25th, Isaiah is one of over 24,000 Federal troops ready to storm the Confederate positions on Missionary Ridge. General Grant has established his command post at Orchard Knob and a cannon is fired as a signal to begin the assault. A thick blue line, two-and-a-half miles long, marches forward to capture the entrenched Rebel positions at the bottom of Missionary Ridge. This quickly being done, the Federal troops are now fired upon from above by the enemy and must either retreat or continue to move forward. En masse they charge out of the captured entrenchments and up the steep slopes of Missionary Ridge to take the remaining Confederate positions. General Grant, watching all of this with great anxiety from Orchard Knob, is overheard saying to his commanders surrounding him, *"Who ordered those men up the hill?"* No one answering he says: *"Someone will suffer for it, if it turns out badly."* It does not turn out badly for the Federals and is one of the most remarkable assaults ever made in military history. The Rebels are totally routed and abandon their almost impregnable position. However, the charge does turn out badly for Isaiah. He is mortally wounded during the assault, which is the day before Thanksgiving, suffers throughout the holiday and dies the day after. As glorious a victory as it is, it comes at a very high price. Isaiah is one of 2,287 Union soldiers killed or wounded in the hour that it takes to capture Missionary Ridge.

Chattanooga National Cemetery
Isaiah is in the second row, third from the left.

Isaiah Wallick

<u>**Comrade-in-Arms**</u>

Brother
Edward   34th & 36th OVI

Epilogue - Unfortunately, Isaiah's given and surnames are both misspelled on his headstone and his date of death is also incorrect. Only the regiment and company inscriptions are without error. Misspellings are common on Civil War memorials. The misspellings of his given name, Isiah, and surname, Wall-a-c-k, do appear in some of his service records. The date Nov 29, 1864, is wrong by a year and two days. Casualty reports and other wartime records confirm that Isaiah was mortally wounded during the assault on Missionary Ridge, November 25, 1863, and that he died two days later.

Isaiah Wallick's gravesite is located in section D, Plot 12110 in the Chattanooga National Cemetery.

<u>**Comrades-in-Arms**</u>

Brother
Edward   34th & 36th OVI

Uncle
Michael   27th IVI

Cousin
Hewit   38th IVI

A Remembrance about Isaiah Wallick

The following is a transcript that was found by Mary Wallick Stierhoff at the Harding County Historical Society. It is part of a volume that identifies who the volunteer soldiers were from Harding County during the American Civil War. Unfortunately, only two pages of the document were copied and the titlepage is missing, leaving us guessing as to its source. This passage was written by Isaiah's family friend, Captain Philip Stumm, of the 74th Ohio Volunteer Infantry. The recorded supper anecdote happened shortly before Isaiah's death, when the Union army was under siege and low on rations in Chattanooga, Tennessee.

This transcript has been copied with few corrections.

49th O.V.I.

Isaiah Wallick, (Brother of Edward) Co. G, Colonel Strong's Co.[31]

Enlisted Aug. 18, 1861, was wounded Nov. 25, 1863 in the charge on Missionary Ridge, and died the 27th, same month.

Isaiah was a good boy. He worked for the Stumm Bros. at the time the war commenced.
    I saw him once during his service. While we were holding Chattanooga, before the battle of Lookout Mountain I went to visit him carrying my haversack with me as we had to do at that time to save what little rations we might be fortunate to have.
    I found him in his pup tent, and he insisted that I remain for supper. Now just think of such an idea. I remained and occupied his tent while he prepared the repast, and in he came into his tent with half of a common canteen for a dish heaped up full of fried whole corn that had been manufactured into hominy by the use of wood ashes. He had some coffee, but one tin cup which we both drank from, one spoon which we used alternately until the corn all disappeared. Before leaving for my quarters, which were about 1-1/2 miles from the 49th, he informed me he would replenish my larder [pantry].
    He made a small excavation in the loose ground in the bottom of his tent and disclosed a gunny sack with about a half a bushel of corn in it, that he said one of the battery guards happened to be going from it and he had wax or something on his fingers and the corn followed him to his tent and was secreted [hidden]. He filled my haversack. Captain Snodgrass and I had several good meals of boiled corn after that trip. Col. Strong informed me one time that Isaiah Wallick was one of the best and bravest men he had in his company and always in a good humor and ready for duty. I like to speak of such noble boys as Wallick was. He was part of our family for many months before he went to the front.

---

[31] Brother Edward's biography begins on page 145. Colonel Luther M. Strong started the war as the captain of Isaiah's Company G. Captain Strong was a good soldier, promoted through the ranks and eventually became the regiment's colonel.

Edward Wallick - 34th Ohio Volunteer Infantry, Co. D
36th Ohio Volunteer Infantry, Co. D

17

Rank: Private

Place of enlistment: Allen County, Lima, Ohio

Mustered into Federal service: February 15, 1864

Service time: 1 year, 4 months

Residence: Ada, Ohio

Age at enlistment: 19

Physical description: height - 5' 9", dark hair, blue eyes

Civilian occupation: farmer

Family Lineage: Edward, son of Samuel, son of "Bunker Hill" Michael, son of "Bedford" Michael, son of Hans Michael Wallick

In the late fall of 1863, the family of Samuel Andrew Wallick had just finished harvesting their crops when they received stunning news from the war front. They had been shorthanded on their Harding County, Ohio, farm for the past two years, ever since Samuel's eldest son, Isaiah, left to join in the fight to crush the southern rebellion. He and his regiment, the 49th Ohio Volunteer Infantry, had been in some of the bloodiest engagements of the war. Before the rebellion names such as Chickamauga Creek, Shiloh Church and Murfreesboro were just remote specks on a southern map. Now they were synonymous with savage, brutal fighting and the 49th Ohio had been in them all. The Union losses in these engagements were staggering. But now, for once, there was good news from the south about this war.

Edward Wallick c.1900

Photo courtesy of Ron Wallick

Shortly after Thanksgiving, Samuel's family learned of the most amazing and glorious victory the Union army had achieved thus far on the battlefield. Perhaps the fortunes of war had now turned in favor of the Federal troops, for they had just made a remarkable charge up Missionary Ridge, just outside of Chattanooga, Tennessee, and thoroughly thrashed the Rebels. Isaiah and his regiment were part of this heroic endeavor. The Union army's line of battle stretched over two miles and was 24,000 men strong. When they stormed out of their positions to dislodge the entrenched Confederates, the Union troops were unstoppable. After taking the works at the base of the 600-foot ridge, the Federals did not halt as ordered but continued to chase the Rebel army all the way up to the summit. The success of this grand assault was an important step toward the death of the Confederacy. For Samuel Wallick the news of this stunning Union victory was soon tempered by news that his son Isaiah had been killed during the battle. The charge up Missionary Ridge took place on the day before Thanksgiving, November 25, and Isaiah became mortally wounded sometime during the attack. He was then taken to a hospital in Chattanooga where he struggled all through the holiday. But his wounds were too severe, and he died the day after Thanksgiving, November 27, 1863.

Edward Wallick was just a few weeks shy of his nineteenth birthday when his brother was killed. He was born in Coshocton County, Ohio (as were all of Samuel's children), but moved to Ada, Ohio, as a youth. When the war broke out in 1861, brother Isaiah was quick to enlist, leaving Edward the only son to help on the farm. Isaiah's death could have brought bitterness to Samuel and his family. However, Edward volunteered for service just two months after the death of his brother. He could have waited to be drafted or tried to avoid military service altogether. He did neither. It seems more likely that Edward volunteered from his sense of patriotism and to honor his brother's sacrifice.

Enlistment paper for Edward Wallick, dated February 3, 1864.
In lieu of his signature, Edward made an "X" as his mark, which was witnessed by W. A. Bearinger.

Edward Wallick with the 34th Ohio Volunteer Infantry

1864

FEB 3 Edward Wallick enlists in Lima, OH, for 3 years as a volunteer recruit. He is paid $60 and due $240 more by the Federal government (although his record states that $84.15 will be deducted "for clothing in kind or money advanced.")

FEB 27 Edward is assigned to Company D, 34th Ohio Volunteer Infantry, and joins the unit as a new recruit at Charleston, WV.

MAY 1   General Crook's Expedition against the Virginia & Tennessee Railroad On April 29th the 34th OVI is divided into two columns. One is mounted infantry, who go with General Averill and his cavalry, and the other is dismounted infantry, who go with General Crook and his infantry division. Edward is with General Crook and is assigned to a brigade commanded by future President Rutherford B. Hayes. On May 1st General Crook sets out from Charleston, WV, to break up the Virginia & Tennessee Railroad and destroy the New River Bridge near Newbern Court House, VA.

MAY 9 Battle of Cloyd's Mountain General Crook learns that the Rebels occupy the summit of Cloyd's Mountain, near Dublin, VA, and prepares to dislodge them. The Federal forces must cross open ground under heavy musket and artillery fire. They make a successful charge and drive the enemy from the field.

MAY 10   General Crook destroys the New River Bridge The main goal of the expedition is achieved when Union forces defeat the Confederates guarding the Virginia & Tennessee Railroad Bridge over the New River. The bridge is totally destroyed. They then move and capture the Confederate stores and supplies at Dublin Depot.

JUN 6   Skirmish at Buffalo Gap Edward and General Hayes' brigade have a skirmish with the Rebels at Buffalo Gap, where they succeed in driving them out of the pass. General Hayes will command Edward's brigade, then his division for all of his enlistment with the 34th Ohio.

JUN 8   General Crook, with Edward and the 34th Ohio, arrive at Staunton, VA, and make their final preparations to join General Hunter in what is to become a disastrous raid on Lynchburg, VA.

JUN 16   The 34th Ohio reaches Liberty, VA.   After crossing the Blue Ridge Mountains, they have a skirmish with the Confederates outside of town.

JUN 17 - 19   Raid on Lynchburg, VA   General Crook sends General Hayes' brigade on a flanking expedition across the James River for the purpose of attacking Lynchburg from the rear while the cavalry on their left makes a diversionary probe. The attack is made late in the day on the 18th and is partially successful. In the opinion of Lt. Colonel Franklin, commanding officer of the 34th Ohio, the attack would have been entirely successful had orders from General Hunter not forbade the Union forces from occupying the city that night. Lynchburg is reinforced overnight by 20,000 Confederate soldiers from General Early's command at Richmond. The next morning the Rebels open the day with a fierce cannonade and the Federals answer back with their own barrage. In the afternoon there is an engagement and the 34th Ohio suffers heavy losses. At dark on the evening of June 19th the Federal forces must retreat. The Rebels pursue the Union forces and there is a second skirmish at Liberty, VA.

JUN 21   Engagement at Catawba Mountain The enemy continues to press the retreating Federals and attack the unsupported artillery of General Hunter's command while it passes through a narrow gap at Catawba Mountain. The Rebels suddenly descend from the hills, dispersing drivers and gunners. They continue their savage attack by shooting horses, cutting their harnesses and blowing up caissons. The mounted portion of the 34th Ohio, being a few miles away, hurries to the scene and counterattacks. The Rebels are driven off after a sharp engagement and the Federal retreat continues.

JUL 1 The Federal forces are continually harassed by the enemy as they march through the eastern mountains of West Virginia. They arrive at Charleston on July 1, 1864, exhausted, ragged and half-starved. General Hunter's "Retreat from Lynchburg" is a disaster and is long remembered by the men of the 34th Ohio.

JUL 12 - 15 34th Ohio is moved to Shenandoah Valley Edward and his regiment move from Charleston WV to Martinsburg, VA, in the Shenandoah Valley.

JUL 20 Engagement at Stephenson's Depot The 34th Ohio Infantry has a forced march from Martinsburg to Stephenson's Depot (two miles north of Winchester, VA) in an effort to check the Confederate advance. The outnumbered Federal forces engage the Rebels, capture their artillery and kill or wound all their brigade commanders. The losses to the 34th Ohio are 10 killed and 20 wounded.

JUL 24 Second Battle of Kernstown Confederate General Jubal Early is attacking in the Shenandoah Valley as a diversion to force General Grant to withdraw some of his Federal troops from besieged Petersburg, VA. The 34th OVI is sent west out Romney Road., just north of Kernstown, to protect the Federal right flank. They are not engaged until the afternoon to help cover the Union army retreat.

AUG 24 The 34th OVI is sent to Harper's Ferry to protect that vital possession from an attack by General Early.

SEP 3 The men of the 34th are moved south to Berryville, VA, about eight miles east of Winchester, VA.

SEP 19 Battle of Opequon Creek On the morning of battle, Edward and his brigade have moved to where the Winchester-Berryville Pike and Opequon Creek intersect, just east of Winchester, VA, and they are held there in reserve all morning. At this time distant cousin Elias Wallick (who is with the 126th OVI) is engaged just north of the Berryville Pike and is mortally wounded. At noon the 34th Ohio moves west toward Winchester and is positioned on the battlefield north of Red Bud Run, where they can support an attack by the Federal right flank. Edward is still in General Hayes' brigade and they deploy for battle about 4:00 PM. The brigade advances parallel and north of Red Bud Run, then pinwheels south and charges into the Confederates flank. There is pressure all along the Federal line of engagement and the Confederates break, run, and stream back as a disorganized mob into Winchester, VA.

SEP 22 Battle of Fisher's Hill Confederate General Early tries to make a stand at Fisher's Hill after his defeat at the Battle of Opequon Creek. The Confederates have chosen a naturally strong position to defend and are well entrenched. General Sheridan orders Edward's division to Little North Mountain where they slam into the Rebel left flank at about 3:30 PM. The Confederate left topples like dominos and the Union army then attacks the center, where the Rebel line breaks from their trenches. By the end of the day General Early has lost sixteen guns and 1,000 men are taken prisoner.

This is the Confederate position at the Battle of Fisher's Hill. The Confederates formed their line of battle in this field, perpendicular to the horizon. The 34th Ohio was positioned on the distant ridge called Little North Mountain. Edward's regiment charged down from the hills, toward the camera, and slammed into the Confederate left flank, forcing them to retreat.

OCT 19   Battle of Cedar Creek   General Sheridan, commander of the Federal army, has continued to press the Confederate forces in the Shenandoah Valley. General Early decides to make one last attempt to push the Federals back down the valley. On October 17-18 he makes his preparations for an early morning attack on the 19th. The Confederates storm into the unsuspecting Union camps that morning, which initiates a Federal panic and general retreat. Edward's VIII Corps are the first camps to be assaulted by the advancing Rebels and they flee for their lives, moving quickly through other Federal campgrounds. The attack happens so fast that by late morning, all seems lost for the Union army.

But out of this disaster comes one of the great legends of the Civil War. General Sheridan had been called to Washington for a few days and has just returned to Winchester when the battle begins. Hearing the faint sounds of battle from his headquarters, at first he is unconcerned, knowing of a scheduled reconnaissance in the area. But as the firing continues, he decides to take a closer look and leaves Winchester around 9:00 AM. Sheridan soon arrives on the battlefield where the Union soldiers are in total disarray. He takes his horse, Rienzi, and makes his legendary ride on the battlefield, rallying his troops to halt the Confederate advance. Sheridan spends the rest of the day organizing his command and deploying his men. By 4:00 PM he is ready to counterattack. Edward's VIII Corps is still disorganized, but a few men are assembled and form a column in reserve (perhaps Edward was a first-hand witness to Sheridan's inspirational ride). The counterattack drives the Confederates back to their original line. As night descends, the Federals pursue General Early's troops back to Cedar Creek and the Federals make camp where they had been positioned before the morning's surprise attack.

Pictured right is artist Louis Prang's portrayal of General Sheridan rallying his troops at Cedar Creek. Shortly after the battle, Thomas Buchanan Read wrote the poem *Sheridan's Ride*, which is as much a tribute to the General's horse, Rienzi, as to the General himself. It became one of the most popular poems of the nineteenth century – at least among Northerners.

To read the poem, *Sheridan's Ride*, see page 151.

OCT 25   Edward becomes sick at Winchester, VA, and is admitted to the regimental hospital one week after the Battle of Cedar Creek.

NOV 5   Edward is transferred to the army hospital in Cumberland, MD. He is diagnosed with typho-malarial fever, or what was known as "camp fever" during the Civil War. The symptoms include a pronounced chill followed by an intermittent fever, abdominal tenderness, nausea, diarrhea, retention of urine and a heavy coating or furring of the tongue.

DEC   Edward is still hospitalized. However, one record states he is on furlough for a time in December. Perhaps he goes home for Christmas.

Hospital Number 11984 Ward E.

Name Edward Wallick
Age 19 Nativity Shackland Co., Ohio.
Married or Single Single.
Residence Harden Co., Ohio.
Post Office address of } Ada,
wife or nearest relative. } Harden Co., Ohio.
Rank Priv. Co. D Regiment 34th Ohio.
When admitted Nov. 5, 1864.
From what source Field Hospl.

Diagnosis: *(In surgical cases, state explicitly seat and character of wound or injury.)*
Typho. Malarial Fever.

Left- This hospital record lists Edward Wallick's birthplace (nativity) as Shackland County, Ohio. There is no such county in Ohio and it is obviously a perverse spelling of "Coshocton."

Right- this country inn at Clarysville, MD, was an army hospital during the Civil War. Edward could have been treated at this facility.

1865

JAN The record is vague, but Edward may have been able to rejoin the 34th Ohio for a time in January and February, 1865.

FEB 22 Edward and the 34th OVI are consolidated with the 36th Ohio Volunteer Infantry. Since being organized in the summer of 1861, the 34th Ohio has lost so many men due to battle and disease that they are well below regimental strength. Edward joined a veteran unit that had already been together two-and-a-half years. This consolidation is a blow to the 34th Ohio because they lose their independent identity as a regimental unit, something prized by the Civil War soldier. Since units are organized regionally (primarily by counties), it is sometimes difficult to blend two veteran regiments together. It appears that Edward is well enough to join the 36th Ohio for a very brief time.

	36	Ohio.

Edward Wallack
Prvt., Co. D, 36 Reg't Ohio Infantry.
Appears on
Company Muster Roll
for Jan & Feb , 1865.
Present or absent Absent
Stoppage $ 100 for
Due Gov't $ 100 for

Remarks: Transferred from 34 O.V.I. Feb 22/65. Sick Clarsville Hosp Since Feb. 26/65.

	36	Ohio.

Edward Wallick
Pvt., Co. D, 36 Reg't Ohio Infantry.
Appears on
Company Muster Roll
for Mar & Apr , 1865.
Present or absent Absent
Stoppage $ 22 05/100 for transpt
Due Gov't $ 100 for

Remarks: Sick at Clarsville Hosp Md since Feb 26 65

These two records show that Edward Wallick was transferred from the 34th Ohio to the 36th Ohio, but spent little time with his new regiment because of chronic illness. Both records state that he recuperated at a Clarysville MD, Hospital. On the March and April records it appears there was a $22.85 stoppage of pay for transportation. Most likely for his journey home on furlough in December of 1864. Notice the two different spellings of "Wallick" on the index cards.

150

FEB 26 - MAY 30 Edward is again admitted to a Clarysville Army Hospital near Cumberland, MD, and will remain hospitalized there for the rest of his enlistment. He is discharged May 30, 1865, under General Orders #77 (same discharge Elijah Wallick received) with a surgeon's certificate of disability. This General Order states that "all volunteer soldiers who need no further treatment in army hospitals are to be honorably discharged from service with immediate payment and all prisoners of war treated the same."

Epilogue - Edward fulfilled his military obligation and returned to Ada, OH, in June of 1865. He married Hanna Jane Stroud on December 18, 1872, and they had five children who survived to adulthood. By 1910 Edward had moved to Portland, OR and there he died on October 20, 1918. Edward Wallick is buried in Multnomah Park Cemetery, Portland, OR.

Edward Wallick's gravestone at Multnomah Park Cemetery, Portland OR.

Ron Wallick Collection

<u>**Comrade-in-Arms**</u>

Brother
Isaiah   49th OVI

Sheridan's Ride
by Thomas Buchanan Read

Up from the South, at break of day,
Bringing to Winchester fresh dismay,
The affrighted air with a shudder bore,
Like a herald in haste to the chieftain's door,
The terrible grumble, and rumble, and roar,
Telling the battle was on once more,
And Sheridan twenty miles away.

And wider still those billows of war
Thundered along the horizon's bar;
And louder yet into Winchester rolled
The roar of that red sea uncontrolled,
Making the blood of the listener cold,
As he thought of the stake in that fiery fray,
With Sheridan twenty miles away.

But there is a road from Winchester town,
A good, broad highway leading down;
And there, through the flush of the morning light,
A steed as black as the steeds of night
Was seen to pass, as with eagle flight,
As if he knew the terrible need;
He stretched away with his utmost speed;
Hills rose and fell, but his heart was gay,
With Sheridan fifteen miles away.

Still sprang from those swift hoofs, thundering south,
The dust like smoke from the cannon's mouth;
Or the trail of a comet, sweeping faster and faster,
Foreboding to traitors the doom of disaster.
The heart of the steed and the heart of the master
Were beating like prisoners assaulting their walls,
Impatient to be where the battlefield calls;
Every nerve of the charger was strained to full play,
With Sheridan only ten miles away.

Under his spurning feet, the road
Like an arrowy Alpine river flowed,
And the landscape sped away behind
Like an ocean flying before the wind,
And the steed, like a barque fed with furnace ire,
Swept on, with his wild eye full of fire.
But, lo! he is nearing his heart's desire;
He is snuffing the smoke of the roaring fray,
With Sheridan only five miles away.

The first that the general saw were the groups
Of stragglers, and then the retreating troops;
What was to be done? what to do?--a glance told him both.
Then striking his spurs with a terrible oath,
He dashed down the line, 'mid a storm of huzzas,
And the wave of retreat checked its course there, because
The sight of the master compelled it to pause.
With foam and with dust the black charger was gray;
By the flash of his eye, and his red nostril's play,
He seemed to the whole great army to say:
"I have brought you Sheridan all the way
From Winchester down to save the day!"

Hurrah! hurrah for Sheridan!
Hurrah! hurrah for horse and man!
And when their statues are placed on high
Under the dome of the Union sky,
The American soldier's Temple of Fame;
There, with the glorious general's name,
Be it said, in letters both bold and bright:
"Here is the steed that saved the day
By carrying Sheridan into the fight,
From Winchester, twenty miles away!"

Daniel Wallick - 20th Ohio Volunteer Infantry, Co. G

18

Rank: Private

Drafted in Van Wert County, Ohio: October 5, 1862

Mustered into Federal service: November 13, 1862

Service time: 9 months, 7 days

Born: October, 1823 - Tuscarawas County, Ohio

Age: 39 years old

Physical description: height - 5' 6", black hair, blue eyes

Civilian occupation: farmer

Family Lineage: Daniel, son of Jacob, son of "Bedford" Michael, son of Hans Michael Wallick

One of the many fundamental changes to American life which was brought about by the Civil War was that the United States and Confederate governments, in order to prosecute that war, began to exert more power and influence into the everyday lives of its citizenry than ever before. Both governments at some point during the conflict suspended the writ of habeas corpus (persons were jailed without being charged with a crime), levied the first ever income tax (3 to 10 percent of all income over $800 in the North and 5 to 10 percent in the South) and both used forced conscription, or the draft, to fill their military ranks. Daniel Wallick was a thirty-nine-year-old farmer living in Van Wert County, Ohio, when his number was chosen in the State of Ohio's draft lottery and he was ordered to serve nine months with the Union army. He was born and raised in Tuscarawas County but in 1852, shortly after he married his wife Sarah, he moved with his father, mother and three brothers to Van Wert County. There, as a middle-aged man, he was drafted on October 5, 1862, and reported for duty three days later at the Van Wert Enlistment Office. He was eventually assigned as a new recruit to the 20th Ohio Volunteer Infantry and joined that regiment on January 11, 1863, in La Fayette, Tennessee.

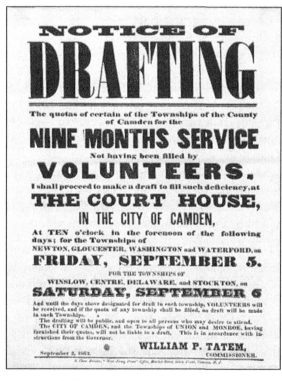

NOTICE OF DRAFTING

The quotas of certain of the Townships of the County of Camden for the

NINE MONTHS SERVICE

Not having been filled by

VOLUNTEERS.

I shall proceed to make a draft to fill such deficiency, at

THE COURT HOUSE,

IN THE CITY OF CAMDEN,

At TEN o'clock in the forenoon of the following days; for the Townships of NEWTON, GLOUCESTER, WASHINGTON and WATERFORD, on

FRIDAY, SEPTEMBER 5.

FOR THE TOWNSHIPS OF WINSLOW, CENTRE, DELAWARE, and STOCKTON, on

SATURDAY, SEPTEMBER 6

And until the days above designated for draft in each township, VOLUNTEERS will be received, and if the quota of any township shall be filled, no draft will be made in such Townships.

The drafting will be public, and open to all persons who may desire to attend. The CITY OF CAMDEN, and the Townships of UNION and MONROE, having furnished their quotas, will not be liable to a draft. This is in accordance with instructions from the Governor.

September 2, 1862.

WILLIAM P. TATEM,
COMMISSIONER.

Ohio was one of the first states during the war to institute a draft in order to fulfill its quota of soldiers for the Union army. The state drafted over 12,200 men in the fall of 1862, which predates by six months the first ever draft held by the Federal government. The draft was used as a threat to entice men to volunteer their services. Those who joined voluntarily received a cash bounty from the federal, state and (in some instances) local governments. In total, it could be quite a sum of money for a young man. But for a middle-aged man like Daniel, it probably was less of an inducement. Those who did not volunteer and waited to be drafted received nothing - no signing bonus at all. Unfortunately for Daniel, he was part of this later group of recruits who were impressed into service for nine months in late 1862. Daniel is the only Wallick to be drafted during the American Civil War.

Michigan recruitment poster. In an effort to avoid drafting men and still fulfill their quotas, some states used creative marketing techniques to induce their citizens to volunteer for the armed forces. The poster below from Michigan highlights the benefits to joining Union army.

The draft, as one can imagine, was not popular and produced some of the worst anti-government riots in American history. The anti-war riots of the Vietnam era pale in comparison to the anti-draft riots in the North, particularly in New York City, during the Civil War. Martial law was eventually declared and the United States Army had to send several regiments of soldiers (some having just fought at Gettysburg) in order to quell the disturbances. Michael Wallick of the 27th Indiana and Elias Wallick of the 126th Ohio were both posted in New York City in response to the rioting during the summer of 1863. It is estimated that 120 civilians were killed and over 2,000 injured as the city spiraled into chaos. It is still considered the largest single civil insurrection in our nation's history (excluding, of course, the Civil War itself).

The streets of New York City erupted into anarchy when its first draft was administered. Federal troops even had to use artillery and bayonets to help suppress the rioters.

When Daniel joined the 20th Ohio Infantry in January 1863, he became part of a regiment who had been together since the early fall of 1861. These were well-seasoned veterans and one can imagine the challenge it must have been for Daniel to "fit in" with his new comrades. The 20th Ohio was in some of the biggest battles and victories in the western theatre of the war. They were at the capture of Forts Henry and Donelson, the Battle of Shiloh, the siege of Corinth, and some other minor engagements.

Daniel was attached to the 20th Ohio Infantry just as it became part of General Grant's campaign against Vicksburg. This movement against the Confederate army's bastion on the Mississippi River produced a spectacular victory for the Union forces in the summer of 1863.[32] The 20th Ohio Regiment was very active in Grant's movements towards Vicksburg and took heavy casualties at the Battles of Raymond and Champion Hill. Daniel was present at the final capitulation of Vicksburg, and then two weeks later he was discharged from service, having fulfilled his military obligation.

---

[32] Refer to Charles Wallick's biography for more information concerning General Grant's movements against Vicksburg. Map #8 on page 121 shows how Grant approached the city.

Daniel Wallick with the 20th Ohio Volunteer Infantry

1862

OCT 5   The State of Ohio holds its first state-wide draft lottery.

OCT 8   Daniel Wallick reports to the enlistment office in Van Wert, OH.

NOV 13   Private Wallick is mustered into Federal service at Camp Mansfield, OH, and is then assigned to the 20th Ohio Infantry. The regiment is located in southwestern Tennessee and part of General Grant's Central Mississippi Campaign.

1863

JAN 11   Daniel joins the 20th Ohio Volunteer Infantry at Lafayette, TN.

JAN 26   The 20th Ohio moves to Memphis, TN, and becomes part of the Vicksburg Campaign.

FEB 22   Daniel and his regiment move down the Mississippi River by steamboat to Lake Providence, LA and spend the next two months aiding Admiral Porter's river fleet, which is pursuing the Confederates in the swamps and bayous of Louisiana. When Daniel joins the 20th Ohio in January, he becomes part of an outfit that is attached to General Grant's Army of the Tennessee, the same outfit as distant cousin Charley Wallick.

APR 19   Activity in the wetlands of Louisiana do not agree with Daniel's constitution, for he becomes very sick and confined to a hospital bed at Millikin's Bend, LA (on the west side of the Mississippi River). Meanwhile, the rest of his regiment is marching down to Hard Times, LA to be ferried across the river to Bruinsburg, MS. This movement is part of Grant's masterful Vicksburg strategy to circle back around that city and attack it from the rear. Exactly when Daniel becomes ill and when he returns to duty is unclear. According to his compiled military service record he has reported present for duty as of April 10th, but is "left in hospital at Millikin's Bend April, 19, 1863." Daniel is then listed "present" for duty for the months of May and June.

MAY 1   Battle of Port Gibson   The 20th Ohio is held in reserve during this battle. Daniel has recovered from his illness and is counted present for duty. It is at this battle (also called The Battle of Thompson's Hill) that Charley Wallick is said to be wounded in the ankle.

MAY 12   Battle of Raymond - Fourteen Mile Creek   The men of the 20th Ohio bore the brunt of the fighting at Fourteen Mile Creek, two miles southwest of Raymond, MS. The regiment straddles what is today's State Route 18 and they jump into the creek bed for cover. The Confederates know that Raymond is the last line of defense for their state capital and railroad hub, Jackson, MS. If Jackson is taken, there is no hope of resupplying Vicksburg by rail. The 20th Ohio is engaged in heavy fighting for an hour and is decimated by Rebel musketry.

Ahead is the intersection of Mississippi State Route 18 and Fourteen Mile Creek. The 20th Ohio straddled this road then fought in the creek bed on May 12, 1863, during the Battle of Raymond.

Below is a description of the battle from *Ohio in the War*, by Whitelaw Reid:

On the 12th of May the Twentieth deployed in advance of the Seventeenth Corps as it approached Raymond, Mississippi, and while resting with arms stacked, was fired upon from a dense thicket beyond a small stream [Fourteen Mile Creek]. The regiment immediately formed and advanced across the creek, using the bank on the opposite side as a breastwork. For an hour the struggle was severe, and especially so to the Twentieth, as regiments on the right withdrew their lines a little distance to the rear, and the flank of the Twentieth was exposed to a raking cross-fire. Every man stood firm until the line again advanced, and the Rebels gave way. The regiment lost in this engagement twelve killed and fifty-two wounded.

Private Osborn Oldroyd, Company E, gives this account of what he witnessed when he reported the battle losses of his company to Colonel Force, commanding officer of the 20th Ohio:

I took the roll-book from the pocket of our dead sergeant, and found that while we had gone in with thirty-two men, we came out with but sixteen - one-half of the brave little band, but a few hours before so full of hope and patriotism, either killed or wounded. Nearly all the survivors could show bullet marks in clothing or flesh, but no man left the field on account of wounds. When I told Colonel Force of our loss, I saw tears course down his cheeks, and so intent were his thoughts upon his fallen men that he failed to note the bursting of a shell above him, scattering the powder over his person, as he sat at the foot of a tree.

Above is Fourteen Mile Creek, southwest of Raymond, MS, and site of fierce fighting by the 20th Ohio Infantry in its drive toward Vicksburg. The Union forces advanced from left to right, using the creek bank as a breastwork. The 20th Ohio sustained heavy casualties during the engagement.

MAY 14 The Battle of Jackson, MS Daniel's regiment remains in the rear guarding the wagon trains.

MAY 16 The Battle of Champion Hill This battle is one of the most critical engagements of the Vicksburg Campaign. Daniel's brigade sees some of the heaviest fighting on the Union right. Again, we turn to Whitelaw Reid for a brief description of the 20th Ohio's contribution:

The regiment moved on through Clinton [Mississippi], Bottom Depot, to Champion Hill, when the regiment was early pushed forward to a strong position in a ravine, under such a fire that it was dangerous for a staff officer to approach with orders. Though the adjoining regiments on each flank were pushed back as the enemy moved up in mass, the Twentieth held its ground without wavering till its ammunition was exhausted; it then fixed bayonets and prepared to maintain its position, but the Sixty-Eighth Ohio came to its assistance from the reserve and the enemy was driven back.

With this Union victory the Confederate army is eventually driven back into Vicksburg and the city must now withstand a siege.

MAY 19 First Assault at Vicksburg The 20th Ohio's brigade is held in reserve during a disastrous frontal assault ordered by General Grant.

MAY 22 Second Assault at Vicksburg Daniel's division is part of the Union army's charge down Jackson Road, where they take tremendous casualties in a frontal attack of the Confederate earthworks. Private Osborn Oldroyd writes in his book, *A Soldier's Story of the Siege of Vicksburg*, a description of the assault.

About 11 o'clock came a signal for the entire line to charge upon the works of the enemy. Our boys were all ready, and in an instant leaped forward to find victory or defeat. The Seventh Missouri took the lead with ladders which they placed against the fort, and then gave way for the others to scale them. Those who climbed to the top of the fort met cold steel, and when at length it was found impossible to enter the fort that way, the command was given to fall back, which was done under a perfect hail of lead from the enemy.

Monument to the 20th Ohio at Vicksburg Military Park.
It is located just east of Shirley House.

Stone marker on Jackson Road
showing the furthest advance
made by the 20th Ohio during its
May 22nd assault.

MAY 26 - June 4 Blair's Mechanicsburg Expedition Daniel and his brigade are temporarily attached to General Blair's command and ordered by Grant to "lay waste" the country between the Yazoo and Big Black Rivers. The Confederate army, which is bottled up in Vicksburg, will receive no support or supplies from outside the city.

JUN 22 Sherman's Exterior Line at Vicksburg The 20th Ohio is now attached to General John McArthur's Provisional Division and is ordered to guard Messinger's Ferry on Bear Creek, a tributary of the Big Black River. General Grant posts Daniel's regiment here to help prevent a rear attack by the Confederate army. This is the last posting Daniel will serve with the 20th Ohio Volunteer Infantry.

JUL 4 Surrender of Vicksburg With the collapse of the Confederate citadel on the Mississippi, the Union will soon be able to navigate freely from Minnesota to the Gulf of Mexico. Daniel and Charley Wallick have both served in this campaign, however, it appears their regiments never crossed paths since they were in two different army corps.

JUL 14 Daniel is mustered out of Federal service ten days after Vicksburg surrenders to General Grant.

Epilogue - Daniel returned home to Van Wert, Ohio, in the summer of 1863. The 1870 United States census records Daniel as a single, divorced laborer living with his 84-year-old father Jacob, in the home of Samuel Dibert. It's unknown when he and his wife Sarah ended their union. Jacob died in 1874, and by 1880 Daniel moved in with his niece Elizabeth and her husband, Peter Prophet, who was from Germany. In the late 1880s Daniel moved west to Oregon and became a sheepherder in beautiful Wallowa County, which is located in the northeast corner of Oregon, bordering Washington and Idaho.

In the late winter of 1906, Daniel had a heart attack while preparing a bath and fell against a hot stove that caused horrible burns to his arms and face. He was living with his nephew, Urias Wallick, at the time of his accident. Urias moved out to Oregon to live with his uncle sometime after 1900. Daniel died of his injuries on March 13, 1906, and was buried in Prairie Creek Cemetery, southeast of Joseph, Oregon.

Inscription:

**Daniel Wallick
1823 - 1906
Private Co. G 20th
Ohio Vols.
1861 - 1865**

The dates of service give the impression that Daniel was in the 20th Ohio for four years. However, he was only in the army for nine months.

Comrades-in-Arms

Brother
David   139th - Ohio National Guard

Cousins
David H.   102nd OVI
Henry M.   67th OVI
Elijah   102nd OVI
Michael   27th IVI

David Wallick - 139th Ohio National Guard, Co. H

19

Rank: Private

Member of Van Wert County Battalion, Ohio National Guard

Mustered into Federal service: May 15, 1864

Service time: 100 days

Born: November 21, 1827 - Tuscarawas County, Ohio

Age when mustered in: 37 years old

Civilian occupation: farmer

Family Lineage: David, son of Jacob, son of "Bedford" Michael, son of Hans Michael Wallick

In 1813 David Wallick's father, Jacob, moved from the hill country of Bedford County, Pennsylvania, to the beautiful Tuscarawas Valley in eastern Ohio. This valley in Ohio was the conduit through which most of the descendants of Hans Michael moved in their migration to western lands. By 1853 Jacob was sixty-eight years old and had raised all seven of his children. Both he and his wife, Elizabeth, then accepted the late-in-life challenge of leaving forever Tuscarawas County after calling it home for nearly forty years. He trekked across the state with four of his sons, John, Daniel, Emanuel and David, and settled on the rich northwest farmlands of Van Wert County, Ohio. Jacob and his sons were all farmers and well trained in agriculture. All of his sons were married when they left Tuscarawas County but only David had any children, an infant son named John Wesley. David's family grew very quickly as he cultivated the Ohio prairie and by 1864, we find him a middle-aged man with a farm to tend and five children to raise. However, the war was to very suddenly intrude upon David and his family's pastoral life. He never volunteered nor was he drafted, like his brother Daniel, but he did serve in the Ohio militia, later called the Ohio National Guard.

The Ohio National Guard can directly trace its roots to the American Civil War. From colonial days there had always been a local militia system in our country, but during the Civil War the term "national guard" was adopted for local militia organizations. At the beginning of the 1861 war, most of the existing state militias were incorporated into Federalized volunteer regiments, so the mission of local defense and order fell to new units of men who were exempted from Federal service: youths, middle-aged men and a few veterans who had completed their active duty.

In the spring of 1864 David Wallick was a member of the Ohio National Guard and his company, like many others across the North, was called into active duty for 100 days. President Lincoln had asked the northern state governors that thousands of these "One Hundred Days Men" be mustered into Federal service and sent to less dangerous rear areas for duties such as guarding railroads, supply depots and enemy prisoners.[33] Ohio alone supplied over 35,000 troops who were organized into regiments, federalized, then transported to the eastern theater of the war. This call-up of the state militias allowed more experienced volunteer regiments to be free for combat duty. The massive buildup of soldiers was needed in Virginia for the Union army's spring offensive of 1864, which is commonly referred to as General Grant's Overland Campaign. A few national guard units did see combat during this bloody thrust into the Confederacy, but David's regiment was not one of them. David and the 139th Ohio National Guard were first deployed in Washington, D.C. for garrison duty; they then moved to a little peninsula called Point Lookout, Maryland, that jutted into Chesapeake Bay, to guard Confederate prisoners of war.

---

[33] There were four Wallicks who served as One Hundred Days Men in the spring of 1864: Wesley, David, Benjamin and Benjamin Franklin.

Point Lookout State Park is located at the mouth of the Potomac River on Chesapeake Bay. Today, the 1,042-acre facility offers numerous vacation activities plus a Civil War Museum. Before the war the peninsula had primarily been a destination for tourists. But by 1862, the strategically located cape was only used for military purposes. Many Rebel soldiers suffered greatly at Point Lookout, which was one of the worst of the northern prison camps.

With a wife and five children, David may have thought it better to join one of the home guard units than take a chance on being conscripted into Federal service. David's age and familial status would not have made him exempt from the draft. Exactly when he became a guardsman is unknown. He could have been a militiaman well before the war. Or he could have joined the national guard shortly after seeing his older brother, Daniel, drafted into military service in the fall of 1862 (see page 153). Whatever the truth may be, we find David in the spring of 1864 a farmer with a large young family, living in Van Wert County, and receiving news that his national guard company has just been called up for active duty by President Lincoln for the next 100 days.

David Wallick with the 139th Ohio Volunteer Infantry – Ohio National Guard

1864

MAY 11 - 20 The 139th Ohio National Guard Regiment is organized from nine companies of the 9th Regiment, Ohio National Guard from Cincinnati; one company from the 82nd Battalion, Ohio National Guard, Van Wert, County (David's Company); and one company from the 73rd Battalion, Ohio National Guard, Ottawa County.

MAY 21 The 139th travels to Washington, D.C. via the Central Ohio and Baltimore & Ohio Railroads, where the regiment performs garrison duty.

JUN 1 David and his regiment are moved to Point Lookout, MD, at the mouth of the Potomac River, to guard Confederate prisoners of war. Point Lookout Confederate Prison Camp (officially called Camp Hoffman, but rarely referred to by that name) is one of the worst of the northern prison camps. At the beginning of the war the Union army established a hospital at Point Lookout, with twenty buildings configured as if spokes in a wheel. However, because there are a large number of prisoners taken at the Battle of Gettysburg, the peninsula is soon transformed into a Confederate prison. By the summer of 1863 the camp is constructed to house 10,000 prisoners, but within a year it is home to as many as 20,000 Confederates. The prison camp is operational for almost two years and over 50,000 soldiers are incarcerated during this time. According to historical records, there are no permanent barracks erected for the prisoners. The barracks in the prison picture on the following page are for the Union soldiers. The Rebels are confined to 40 acres of sandy beach within a fifteen-foot stockade fence that surrounds the camp. It is located one-half mile northeast of the Union army hospital. The climate is brutal, especially in mid-winter and summer, and the prisoners have only tents for shelter throughout the year. The northern prison guards are harsh (we can assume the men of the 139th are no different) and there is little food, fresh water or firewood for comfort or cooking. Officially, in twenty-two months 3,584 prisoners die at Point Lookout. However, depending upon whose narratives one reads, some death tabulations climb as high as 14,000. Accounts vary widely between northern and southern writers, with both sides providing unreliable information. What is not in dispute is that this prison has horrible living conditions with inadequate shelter and little food (most of that being bad) and it is garrisoned by some very tough soldiers.

160

David Wallick and the 139th Ohio National Guard spent the summer of 1864 here, at Point Lookout, Maryland, guarding Confederate prisoners. The conditions were harsh and extremely brutal for the Rebels. Below is a deceivingly pleasant picture of the landscape. At the tip of the peninsula is the army hospital and the prison camp is in the upper right-hand corner on Chesapeake Bay.

Map 9

Point Lookout Confederate Prison

Potomac River

Chesapeake Bay

JUL 10 The Confederates plan a cavalry raid that will liberate all 17,000 prisoners at Point Lookout. It is hoped that a quick cavalry strike, timed with a heavy bombardment by off-shore gunboats, can create enough confusion in camp to enable a mass escape of the prisoners. It is a fanciful idea, devised because of the manpower shortage in the Confederate army due to the North's stoppage of the prisoners of war parole in the exchange system. After the July 9th Union defeat at Monocacy Junction, the Rebel high command sends General Bradley Johnson and his men on a raid that is to cover 300 miles in four days. As General Early advances his own army on Washington, General Johnson's cavalry is to wreck railroads and telegraph communications as they go down the Maryland peninsula toward Point Lookout. The scheme begins to unravel when a captured Confederate deserter betrays the plan. The Federals double their own off-shore gunboat patrols and the prison guards are put on high alert. When General Early's attack on Washington stalls before the ring of forts that surround the capital, he commands General Johnson and his cavalry to rejoin his retreating army. With the alarm passed, the men of the 139th continue their mission and monotonous duty as prison guards.

AUG 22 The 139th Ohio begins their return to Camp Chase, in Columbus, OH.

AUG 26 David is mustered out of Federal service on expiration of term. President Lincoln is limited by law as to how long he can use the national guard for Federal purposes.

Epilogue - David returned home to Van Wert County just in time for the fall harvest of 1864. His wife, Mary Ann, had to rely on help from family and friends throughout the summer to keep the Wallick farm and household together. When David marched off to war earlier that spring, he left behind five children ages twelve, ten, eight, three and an infant. The only other Wallicks to have left behind so large a brood while serving his country was "Daviess" Michael from Indiana, who also had a wife and five children, and Abraham Wallick, from Iowa, who enlisted with six children and, unbeknownst to him, twins on the way. Michael and Abraham, however, left their large families for three years, not just three months. David continued to farm in Van Wert County for the rest of his life. And there he died on May 24, 1911, at 83 years old.

David and Mary Ann Wallick are buried in Tomlinson Cemetery, Van Wert, Ohio.

Scott Alan Wallick Collection

**David Wallick
Ohio National Guard, Co. H**

Comrades-in-Arms

Brother
Daniel   20th OVI

Cousins
David H.   102nd OVI   Elijah   102nd OVI
Henry M.   67th OVI   Michael   27th IVI

Benjamin Wallick - 162nd Ohio National Guard, Co. K

20

Rank: Corporal

Place of enlistment: Stark County, Canton, Ohio

Mustered into Federal service: May 2, 1864

Service time: 100 Days

Born: January, 1828 - Dover, Ohio

Age at enlistment: 35 years old

Physical description: height - 5' 10", dark hair, gray eyes

Civilian occupation: wagon maker

Family Lineage: Benjamin, son of George, son of "Peru" Benjamin Senior, son of Johannes, son of Hans Michael Wallick

When "Peru" Benjamin Sr. moved his family to Miami County, Indiana, in 1841, George, one of his five sons, did not go with him but stayed in Tuscarawas County. He was a carpenter who built canal boats in Dover, Ohio, a small town on the Ohio-Erie canal system. Canals were the super-highways of the early nineteenth century and this particular canal wound its way from the Ohio River through the eastern heartland of the Buckeye State and on to the shores of Lake Erie.

In 1828, George had a son, Benjamin, who became a carpenter like his father and specialized as a wagon maker. By the spring of 1864 Benjamin and his wife, Ann, had moved northeast of Dover to Magnolia, Ohio, a small village on the Stark-Carroll County border. While living there, and as the Civil War raged on, the thirty-five-year-old was called to active duty as a member of the Ohio National Guard.

In the spring of 1864 General Grant began what is now called his Overland Campaign. He wanted to press the Confederate armies simultaneously on all fronts, which would stretch the Rebel re-

Canal boat and towpath on the Ohio-Erie Canal System.

sources to their limits and prohibit them from reinforcing one another. In order to implement this strategy Grant needed a great infusion of new troops. President Lincoln asked the state governments for 300,000 more men to serve as One Hundred Days Men to help bolster the manpower needs of the army. These soldiers were assigned mostly rear echelon duty to help secure railroad lines, guard prisoners and perform tasks that were very necessary but far less hazardous. This also released more experienced veterans for frontline combat. Ohio called up 35,000 militiamen for 100 days to serve as Federal troops in May, 1864, and Benjamin was one of these soldiers. Little is known about Benjamin's service other than he spent all his time in Columbus, Ohio, at Tod Barracks. This was one of five army posts in the Columbus area that served as a recruiting station, administration headquarters and a center where soldiers were mustered out after their Federal service. Tod Barracks had a parade ground that was flanked by six barracks, a hospital, mess hall, guardhouse, and officers' quarters. It could accommodate up to 5,000 troops. Benjamin could have performed any number of duties while posted there. Tod Barracks was on nine acres, near today's intersection of High and Goodale Streets, where the Columbus Convention Center is located. Only four companies from his regiment drew this assignment; the rest were sent to Carrollton and Covington, Kentucky, for their service.

Benjamin Wallick with the 162nd Ohio National Guard

<u>1864</u>

MAY 2 Benjamin's Ohio National Guard unit is mustered into Federal service at Camp Chase in Columbus, OH, for 100 days and posted just a few miles away at Tod Barracks. All but one company of the 162nd Ohio Volunteer Infantry (national guard) are from Stark County and most are men of wealth or from wealthy families. Companies A, C, F, and K remain at Tod Barracks while all the other companies move to Covington and Carrollton, KY. Soldiers in those units search for Moses Webster's men, arrest prominent Confederates and help in recruiting of the 117th United States Colored Troops. Benjamin has probably the least interesting service of all the Wallick Civil War soldiers (a distinction the thirty-five-year-old may well have relished). The only noteworthy comment in his compiled military service record is that he owes the U.S. Government $.49 for a haversack.

Tod Barracks before its 1911 demolition.

SEP 4 After 100 days in Columbus, OH, Benjamin is mustered out of Federal service and the regiment returns home to Stark County. The regiment has lost 20 men to disease.

Epilogue - Benjamin Wallick spent the rest of his life as a carpenter in Magnolia, Ohio, and died on June 20, 1920, at age 92. He lived to be the oldest Civil War veteran from the Wallick family.

Benjamin Wallick is buried in Magnolia, Ohio Cemetery

Scott Alan Wallick Collection

Comrades-in-Arms

Uncles

Benjamin Jr.	109th IVI
Christopher	109th IVI
Wesley	109th & 138th IVI

Cousins

William	51st IVI
Charles F.	87th IVI
John Wesley	138th & 151st IVI
Christopher	109th IVI
Jeremiah	109th IVI
William F.	109th, 13th & 151st IVI

From Kansas

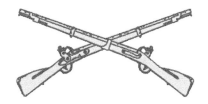

166

Benjamin Franklin "Frank" Wallack - 17th Kansas Infantry, Co. D

Rank: Private

Place of enlistment: Atchison County, Kansas

Mustered into Federal service: July 28, 1864

Service time: 100 Days

Born: September 10, 1844 - Tuscarawas County, Ohio

Age at enlistment: 20 years old

Physical description: height - 5' 9", dark hair, blue eyes

Civilian occupation: farmer

Family Lineage: Benjamin Franklin, son of "Kansas" Benjamin, son of John Junior, son of "Bedford" John, son of "Bedford" Michael, son of Hans Michael Wallick.

During the American Civil War it was not uncommon for soldiers to have different spellings of their surnames written in their service records. The surname Wallick can be found on military documents with alternate endings of "a-c-k" and "e-c-k" (it is clear that most of the time the changes were due to clerical errors). Two of the three Wallick soldiers buried in our national cemeteries have variant spellings of Wallick on their headstones. Both Isaiah Wallick, buried at Chattanooga, Tennessee, and Elias Wallick, buried at Winchester, Virginia, have their names spelled Wall-a-c-k. People were not as careful with spelling in the nineteenth century and many times if a spelling mistake was made, rather than correct it, people just let it go. Ulysses S. Grant is a prime example.

Hiram Ulysses Grant (his real name) was nominated to West Point by a congressman who, in a rush to secure the appointment, didn't just misspell Grant's name but completely changed it to Ulysses Simpson Grant (Simpson coming from his mother's maiden name). When the young cadet went to register at West Point, rather than argue with the enrolling officer about the mistake, he just let it go. He also was painfully aware that the initials to his legal name spelled H.U.G, and that could make life a little more difficult for a plebe at West Point. The mistake, however, proved to be a boon for U.S. Grant, both during the war and later in civilian life. After his glorious victory at Ft. Donelson, he became a hero and famous throughout the North, known in the newspapers as **U**nconditional **S**urrender Grant, thanks to his congressman's careless error.

Frank Wallack, 1870.
Photo- Lola Purdy Thompson Collection

There is one Wallick soldier who spelled his name Wall-a-c-k and it was not a clerk's mistake or careless penmanship but a deliberate change made by that soldier. All of Benjamin Franklin Wallack's service records are consistent in spelling his last name Wall-a-c-k, from his signature on his enlistment papers through his compiled military service record. Benjamin Franklin Wallack was also called "Frank" by his family and friends, and so he will be called in this biography to avoid confusing Frank with his father "Kansas" Benjamin and all the other Benjamins from the Wallick clan.

One family account states that Benjamin Franklin Wall-i-c-k deliberately changed his name to Wall-a-c-k early in his young adult life. The story is told that Frank's wife, Ellen Green, had pressed the matter of changing the spelling of his surname and that Frank finally agreed. This well-educated eastern woman felt that the spelling of Wallick had somehow become corrupted through the years. Her rationale was that back east, every Wallick she knew ended their name in A-C-K. Two brothers, John and Charles, had business ties with Frank and they also agreed to change their names. It is said that this irritated and angered their father "Kansas" Benjamin so much that he threatened to disinherit them all.[34] In order for this story to be true, Frank and Ellen Green had to have met and agreed to the name-change before he enlisted, for all of Frank's service records are spelled Wall-a-c-k. However, their marriage did not actually take place until seven years after his enlistment, making the truthfulness of this story suspect. In any case, the name change did happen and there is a line of the Hans Michael Wallick family that spells its name Wall-a-c-k and that can be traced back to Benjamin Franklin Wallack (1844-1887).

Frank Wallack's early childhood days were spent in Tuscarawas County, Ohio. Then in early 1850, Benjamin's father learned of the fertile farmlands in DeKalb County, Indiana, and decided to move his family there, settling in the little town of Butler. After ten years Benjamin again decided to move his family still farther west to the Kansas Territory, an exploding war zone since the mid-1850s.

The Kansas/Missouri border war was an ugly affair; a bloody insurrection that preceded our national civil war by nearly a decade. Small groups of anti-slavery zealots called "Jayhawkers," and pro-slavery partisans called "Bush-whackers," waged a fanatical war against each other. These were really marauding bands of partisans rather than an organized militia. Stephen Douglas, the senator from Illinois, crafted the Kansas-Nebraska Act of 1854 that gave new territories the right of self-determination in choosing to become a slave or free state. Election fraud and voter intimidation was rampant along the Kansas-Missouri border and citizens resorted to force-of-arms to settle their political disputes. For a time, Kansas would have two state governments with two different constitutions: one that included slavery and one that did not. For many years guerrilla warfare reigned in the region. Benjamin knew he was moving into a viper's den when he decided to relocate his family to Atchison County, Kansas, in March of 1860.

Why would Benjamin willingly move his family into a region where violent civil insurrection was common place? He had no encouragement from his wife Mary to move. When she first saw the miles upon miles of bleak, treeless prairie land she became desperate to return to her home back in Indiana. Benjamin on the other hand saw the treeless

Benjamin Wallick, 1870.
Lola Purdy Thompson Collection

landscape as a positive. Kansas had very fertile grasslands and the lack of trees meant that a farmer didn't have to spend years clearing the land and removing old stumps from his fields. This new land also opened up more opportunities for his sons and it appears that first-born Frank took advantage of them. Benjamin also had a pioneer's spirit, just like his forefathers, and held some very strong personal beliefs. He was an ardent Unionist and Republican (though not an abolitionist), puritanical in his religious beliefs and a strong disciplinarian. Benjamin was not one to let a little adversity, such as unrestrained guerrilla warfare, interfere with the pursuit of his lifelong goals. He couldn't serve in uniform himself due to a hernia, but he did actively support the Union's cause by becoming the Enlistment Officer and Sheriff of Atchison County. As sheriff he saw to the needs of Unionist families while their husbands and fathers were off fighting the war. The story has been told by Frank Wallack's descendants that he was a substitute soldier for his father, but apparently that is not so. There is nothing in Frank's compiled military service record to support such a claim. Frank signed regular enlistment papers for the 17th Kansas Volunteer Infantry and he was mustered into Federal service for 100 days in the summer of 1864. If he had been a substitute, it would be stated somewhere in his military service records.

---

[34] The source for this story is *My Wallick Family,* by Vesta Beatrice (Wallick) Kaufman and Adelaide (Covell) Wallack, transcribed by Scott Alan Wallick in his book, *Hans Michael Wallick's Descendants in America, 1732 - 2012.*

Frank Wallack's enlistment paper. If Frank had been a substitute soldier for his father, a different document would have been signed. (See Hewit Wallick's substitute soldier document on page 68).

VOLUNTEER ENLISTMENT.

STATE OF *Kansas*

TOWN OF *Atchison*

I, *Benjamin F Wallack* born in *Tuscarawas* in the State of *Ohio* aged *twenty* years, and by occupation a *Farmer* Do HEREBY ACKNOWLEDGE to have volunteered this *eighteenth* day of *July* 1864, to serve as a **Soldier** in the Army of the United States of America, for the period of *THREE YEARS*, unless sooner discharged by proper authority. Do also agree to accept such bounty, pay, rations, and clothing, as are, or may be, established by law for volunteers. And I, *Benj F Wallack* do solemnly swear, that I will bear true faith and allegiance to the **United States of America,** and that I will serve them honestly and faithfully against all their enemies or opposers whomsoever; and that I will observe and obey the orders of the President of the United States, and the orders of the officers appointed over me, according to the Rules and Articles of War.

Sworn and subscribed to, at *Leavenworth* this *26th* day of *July* 1864.   *Benj F Wallack*
BEFORE *D C Simmonds*

I CERTIFY, ON HONOR, That I have carefully examined the above named Volunteer, agreeably to the General Regulations of the Army, and that in my opinion he is free from all bodily defects and mental infirmity, which would, in any way, disqualify him from performing the duties of a soldier.

EXAMINING SURGEON

I CERTIFY, ON HONOR, That I have minutely inspected the Volunteer, *Benj. F. Wallack,* previously to his enlistment, and that he was entirely sober when enlisted; that, to the best of my judgment and belief, he is of lawful age; and that, in accepting him as duly qualified to perform the duties of an able-bodied soldier, I have strictly observed the Regulations which govern the recruiting service. This soldier has *blue* eyes, *dark* hair, *dark* complexion, is *five feet nine inches* high.

D C Simmonds
1st Lieut 17th Regiment of Kansas Volunteers,
GOV. PRINT. OFF. July, 1862
RECRUITING OFFICER.

169

1864

JUL 28 Frank Wallack is mustered into Federal service with the 17th Kansas Infantry Regiment at Ft. Leavenworth, KS, for 100 days. He is twenty years old.

AUG - SEP Frank and his company are sent to Lawrence, KS, site of the famous 1863 massacre by Confederate partisan and Tuscarawas County native, William Clarke Quantrill.

William Clarke Quantrill – from Dover, Ohio.

Historical Note - If Frank Wallack did go to Lawrence, Kansas, in the summer of 1864, he undoubtedly saw some of the lingering devastation created the year before by William Clarke Quantrill and his Confederate raiders. Both Frank Wallack and William Quantrill were born and raised in the small town of Dover, Ohio, within the Wallick enclave of Tuscarawas County. However, Quantrill was six years senior to Frank. William had a gifted intellect and became a school teacher immediately upon his graduation from Dover High School. A few years later he went west to seek his fortune. He was a Unionist when he left Dover, Ohio, but turned pro-southern in his sympathies after experiencing some personal challenges and failures in Colorado and Kansas. He never joined a regular Confederate militia group but was recognized as the leader of an independent band of guerrillas by the Rebel government under the Partisan Ranger Act. He was one of the most notorious outlaws of the entire Civil War. On August 21, 1863, Quantrill and his gang of 450 men attacked, sacked and burned to the ground the town of Lawrence, KS, killing approximately 180 men and boys in the town, many of them execution style. Jesse James and his brother Frank began their careers as outlaws riding with William Clarke Quantrill and his bushwhackers.

The raid on Lawrence, Kansas, in the summer of 1863 was perhaps the most savage attack perpetrated on a civilian population during the entire Civil War. Company D of the 17th Kansas Infantry was posted in Lawrence a year after the massacre. Frank Wallack would have seen first-hand the devastation that was leveled on that community.

OCT - NOV The regiment helps repel Confederate General Sterling Price's invasion into Kansas. They march to the relief of Mound City in Linn County, near the site of the Mine Creek Battlefield. On October 25, 1864, Confederate cavalry under General Price engages a vastly outnumbered Union force near Mine Creek, however, it is the Confederates that are soundly defeated. Much of the credit for the lopsided victory is due to the Union's superior weaponry (estimated Union casualties were 100 and the Confederate 1,200). The Union Soldiers have revolvers and breech-loading carbines while the Confederate forces only use muzzle-loading muskets. It is one of the largest cavalry engagements of the Civil War and the largest battle in Kansas.

NOV 16 The 17th Kansas Infantry is mustered out of Federal service at Ft. Leavenworth and Frank returns to Atchison County.

Epilogue - Frank Wallack returned to Effingham, Kansas, after his 100 days of service. He continued to farm and eventually opened a hardware business. He was a strong supporter of public education and worked hard to establish the high school for Atchison County in Effingham. He finally succeeded in his mission and because of his hard work, he became known as the "Father of Atchison County High School." Frank was active in local politics and in 1896 he was elected to the Kansas State Senate. Unfortunately, his term was cut very short. Six months after his election he had an accident where he was thrown from his surrey and severely injured. He died of a heart attack on May 11, 1897, and it was believed that the accident was a contributing factor to his heart failure. Frank Wallack was buried in the Effingham Kansas Cemetery. Tributes to Senator Benjamin Franklin Wallack were read into the official record of the Kansas State Senate on December 23, 1898. The eulogies can be read today online by visiting the Kansas State Senate Archives.

Inscription on the stone:

B.F. Wallack
Sept. 1844-May 1897
One of the Founders of the Atchison
County High School
Bravely He Met Both Life And Death

Comrades-in-Arms

No brothers, uncles, or first cousins

Scott Alan Wallick Collection

171

From Iowa

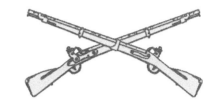

Abraham Wallick – 22nd Iowa Volunteer Infantry, Co. D
Veteran Reserve Corps, 3rd Regiment

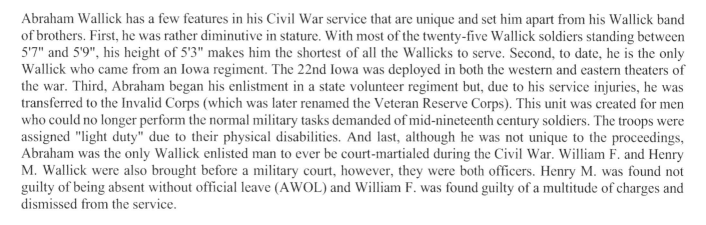

22

Rank: Private

Place of enlistment: Albia, Iowa – July 26, 1862

Mustered into Federal service: September 9, 1862

Service time: 3 years

Born: January 7, 1819, Ohio County, Indiana

Age at enlistment: 43 years old

Physical description: height - 5' 3", black hair, brown eyes, dark complexion

Civilian occupation: carpenter

Family Lineage: Abraham, son of John Abraham, son of "Switzerland" Philip, son of Hans Michael Wallick

Abraham Wallick has a few features in his Civil War service that are unique and set him apart from his Wallick band of brothers. First, he was rather diminutive in stature. With most of the twenty-five Wallick soldiers standing between 5'7" and 5'9", his height of 5'3" makes him the shortest of all the Wallicks to serve. Second, to date, he is the only Wallick who came from an Iowa regiment. The 22nd Iowa was deployed in both the western and eastern theaters of the war. Third, Abraham began his enlistment in a state volunteer regiment but, due to his service injuries, he was transferred to the Invalid Corps (which was later renamed the Veteran Reserve Corps). This unit was created for men who could no longer perform the normal military tasks demanded of mid-nineteenth century soldiers. The troops were assigned "light duty" due to their physical disabilities. And last, although he was not unique to the proceedings, Abraham was the only Wallick enlisted man to ever be court-martialed during the Civil War. William F. and Henry M. Wallick were also brought before a military court, however, they were both officers. Henry M. was found not guilty of being absent without official leave (AWOL) and William F. was found guilty of a multitude of charges and dismissed from the service.

Abraham Wallick with the 22nd Iowa Volunteer Infantry

1862

JUL – DEC On July 1, 1862, President Lincoln issued an executive order requesting an additional 300,000 Federal volunteers to serve in the army for three years or to the conclusion of the war, whichever came first. Recruitment drives were quickly organized and men who the previous year had balked at volunteering were now sought-out by recruiting officers. It would be interesting to know why Abraham Wallick, a 42-years-old carpenter with no prior military experience, decided at his age to enlist in an adventure that was usually reserved for younger men. Not only was Abraham middle-aged, but he was a husband and father of three boys and three girls (one of the daughters being only six months old). And unbeknownst to Abraham or his wife, Mary (Johnson), she was pregnant with twin boys when he enlisted.[35] Nevertheless, on July 28, 1862, Abraham rode into Albia, Iowa, and joined the Union army. He and his Monroe County boys became Company D of the 22nd Iowa Volunteer Infantry (IVI). All were mustered into Federal service at Iowa City, Iowa, on September 9, 1862.

---

[35] Mary Hazel Johnson was born in Fulton, Illinois, and could trace her lineage back to the famous Boone pioneers of Kentucky.

The regiment left Iowa City under the command of Colonel William M. Stone[36] on the evening of September 14 with orders for Davenport, Iowa. They first traveled by rail, then loaded onto a steamer and chugged down the Mississippi River to St. Louis. Three days later they arrived at Benton Barracks. It was there that the 22nd Iowa received their basic military training. After a quick two-week session in the manual-of-arms, the men were again loaded onto rail cars and transported to Rolla, Missouri. They arrived at that small town on September 23 and stayed there approximately four months. The 22nd Iowa's principal responsibilities at Rolla were guarding the supply stores and serving as train escorts for the Army of Southeast Missouri.

Colonel William M. Stone

1863

JAN - MAR On January 27, 1863, the 22nd IVI was ordered to West Plains, Missouri, a march of five days from Rolla. West Plains is in southcentral Missouri, about 25 miles north of the Missouri/Arkansas border. When the 22nd IVI arrived at their new posting they combined with two other Iowa regiments to create the 2nd Brigade of the 2nd Division of the Army of Southeast Missouri. This unit consisted of the 2nd, 22nd, and 23rd Iowa Volunteers. At West Plains the regiments practiced the military maneuvers that were required of a brigade on the battlefield. After a few weeks of intense drilling, the brigade received orders to proceed to Iron Mountain, Missouri.

The march up to Iron Mountain was a grueling winter affair for Abraham and his comrades. When the brigade left West Plains on February 9, they quickly ran into inclement weather. There was a great amount of suffering in the brigade as they tramped through the Ozarks. Not only was the journey physically difficult and exhausting, but there were many nights the troops slept out in the cold with little or no cover. There was also a severe shortage of food rations. In the book, *Historical Sketch from The Report of Adjutant General, 1863,* Volume 1, page 560, it states, "...they endured the hardships and privations to which they were subjected without complaint..." It is almost certain that there was at least a little grumbling from the men along the way.

The 22nd Iowa arrived at Iron Mountain on February 26 and were soon folded into the 23rd Army Corps. This unit was under the command of General Ulysses S. Grant. The regiment had passed a fortnight at Iron Mountain before Colonel Stone was ordered to muster his men and begin a 45-mile trek to Ste. Genevieve, Missouri. They arrived at that Mississippi river town on March 12. It was during this march that Abraham Wallick recorded his first instance of lameness in the right leg and foot. There were no ambulances available, so Abraham rode to his new posting on a cannon carriage.[37] This lameness to his right extremities would hound him throughout the rest of his enlistment. But for now, the injuries were not too severe and with rest, he eventually recovered enough to stay with his comrades.

MAR 9 – APR 27 Abraham's brigade had to wait ten days in Ste. Genevieve before they boarded the steamboat, *Blackhawk,* which transported them down to Millikin's Bend, Louisiana. This assemblage point was about fifteen miles northwest of Vicksburg. Here, the 22nd IVI was again reorganized and they became part of the 2nd Brigade, 14th Division of the 13th Army Corps. The 22nd Iowa was no longer part of the Army of Southwest Missouri but was now part of the Army of the Tennessee. The men still had General Grant as their overall commander, but the corps leadership was under the command of Major General John C. McClernand, one of Grant's bitterest military rivals.

---

[36] Colonel William M. Stone was born in New York State but moved to Coshocton, Ohio, when he was five years old. He was raised in that small town and as a young man, he studied law. William was admitted to the Ohio Bar in 1851. In 1854 he moved from the Buckeye State and set up a law practice in Knoxville, Iowa. William M. Stone became extremely successful in Iowa Republican politics. He was also present at Ford's Theater the night President Lincoln was assassinated.

[37] Pension files of Abraham Wallick, National Archives: Declaration for Original Invalid Pension, November 14, 1878.

Abraham's stay at Milliken's Bend ended on April 12, 1863, when the regiment was ordered to Richmond, Louisiana. This town was twenty miles due west from Vicksburg. At Richmond, there was a small Confederate cavalry detachment that skirmished with the 22nd Iowa. The mid-westerners quickly drove the Rebels from the field. After that engagement, the men proceeded to Carthage and then to Perkin's Landing, where the regiment waited for the rest of the 13th Corps to join them.

On April 27, just after dark, Abraham and all of 13th Corps were transported by a multitude of river vessels down to Hard Times Plantation, where they bivouacked for the night. Two weeks earlier, General Grant had ordered a small flotilla of gunboats to float in the night's darkness past the mighty artillery batteries that were perched on the high riverfront bluffs of Vicksburg. But the river armada was

Abraham Wallick was transported on this river steamer to Millikin's Bend, LA.

soon discovered and fired upon by the Rebels. Nonetheless, the nocturnal venture was successful. Out of 12 boats attempting to sneak past Vicksburg, only one was sunk. However, there were some craft that required varying degrees of repair after running the river gauntlet.

Vicksburg was nicknamed "The Gibraltar of America" and was believed to be impregnable by both the Federals and Confederates. Grant had tried for months to conquer the city by attacking it from the north. All these earlier efforts were disastrous affairs. Now he was going to land his forces south of Vicksburg, move diagonally north up to Jackson, Mississippi, then turn back toward Vicksburg and approach the city from the east (or its landward side). It was a risky operation, for Grant had to sever his army's supply lines and live off the land for this operation to succeed. He also did not know what Confederate forces he might encounter once he crossed the Mississippi River.

MAY 1 – 15 Battle of Port Gibson Abraham and all of the 13th Army Corps were loaded onto the same gunboats that just weeks before had evaded the Vicksburg river artillery. They steamed downriver to Bruinsburg, Mississippi. On May 1, the Federals disembarked and marched inland toward Port Gibson. A few miles outside of the town the Rebel army was waiting for the Federal troops. With the 22nd Iowa at its vanguard, a sharp engagement ensued.

Map 10

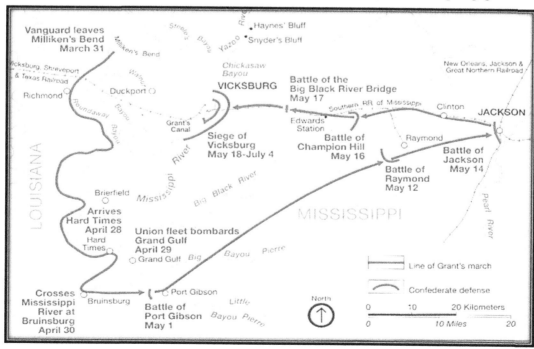

National Park Service Map

At that time, Colonel Stone was in command of the entire 2nd Brigade, which left Major B.J. Atherton in command of the 22nd Regiment. The major later filed a report to Colonel Stone, giving this account of how the men under his command performed at the Battle of Port Gibson.

I received an order from you to hurry my regiment forward and form it in line on the left of our artillery, then hotly engaged with the Rebel batteries. This order was promptly obeyed, and the men came up quickly and in good order, forming at the point designated.

We were then under the enemy's fire, yet my men manifested great coolness and self-possession. We remained in line for two hours in support of the batteries, until the battle ceased for the night, and we lay down on our arms, but not to sleep, as we were in momentary expectation of a renewal of the combat. Soon after sunrise we were again in line and under the enemy's fire, in support of our batteries, until near 10 o'clock, when we were led forward to charge on the Rebel lines. This movement was executed with great deliberation and accuracy, and when their lines were broken and they were driven in rout from the field, we were among the first to occupy their field. In the long and hotly contested fight of the afternoon, my regiment was all the time in the face of the enemy and under the severest fire. Three times we were ordered against the Rebel infantry and under the range of his batteries. Each time we drove them from the field...Throughout this series of engagements, the officers and men of my regiment behaved with great coolness and gallantry. I found them always ready and eager to obey the order to move on the enemy. So well did the entire command acquit themselves, I cannot, with seeming invidious, enter into particulars. It is sufficient to say that they acted nobly, and well sustained the honors already earned by Iowa soldiers...[38]

The morning immediately after the Battle of Port Gibson the 22nd Regiment chased the enemy to Bayou Pierre. However, their pursuit was interrupted when later that night, they came to a halt and repaired a bridge that had been destroyed by the retreating Rebels. This action took a few days. The evening of May 4, the brigade continued their northeasterly march with Colonel Stone back in command of the 22nd Iowa. Abraham and his regiment were eventually ordered to Raymond, Mississippi, and arrived there on May 13, the day after the Confederates had retreated from the town. They were assigned security detail for the railroad that ran through Raymond.

MAY 16 – Champion Hill Campaign On May 16, the men were hastily marched toward Edwards Station to help cut off the Rebels retreat from the Battle of Champion Hill. This Confederate engagement was the most savage and hotly contested battle of Grant's entire Vicksburg campaign. Out of 54,000 troops engaged, total casualties numbered 6,297. The Second Brigade arrived at Edwards Station late in the evening and captured the Rebel's food stores and ammunition, plus 200 prisoners. With the Confederates' defeat at Champion Hill and loss of their supplies, the Rebels had no choice but to withdraw into Vicksburg. However, before they recessed into that fortified city, the secessionists made one last stand.

The 22nd Iowa continued to chase the Rebel army throughout the day of May 16. By nightfall, the enemy had reached the Big Black River Bridge and the Confederates on the east side of the river quickly established a line for defense by using bales of cotton as breastworks. The Rebels were determined to at least delay the Federal advance long enough for them to strengthen the defensive ring of earthworks that were built around Vicksburg. The next morning, the 22nd Iowa was placed on the extreme right of the Federal line that charged the enemy's works. They did not come under direct enemy fire but were part of a mop-up operation that pursued the fleeing Rebels. The retreating Confederates used the railroad bridge and three river steamers as their primary means of escape. Some soldiers tried to swim across the Big Black River but they were either shot, captured or drowned. Once all the enemy were across the river, the Rebels destroyed the bridge. On the whole, regimental losses for the 22nd were light. But the Federal army captured 18 Confederate field artillery pieces, a large quantity of ammunition, thousands of small arms and 3,000 prisoners. These were losses the enemy could ill afford. The night after the battle all of 13th Corps camped on the battlefield. Army engineers worked throughout May 18 to construct a pontoon bridge that would span the Big Black River. By

[38] Roster and Records of Iowa Soldiers, War of the Rebellion Historical Sketches of Volunteer Organizations, Vol. III, 561.

early evening the makeshift bridge was completed and Grant's army started their advance toward Vicksburg. They marched all night and arrived at the heavily-fortified city about noon on May 19. Given Abraham Wallick's past history with lameness, he could have had a very difficult time staying up with his company during these maneuvers. In a November 14, 1878 pension file, Abraham states,

> *Although I suffered much from my right leg and foot, I continued with my company marching through Mississippi and around about Vicksburg.*

It is possible that he could have had trouble keeping up with his comrades and maybe arrived late into camp with the other stragglers. Stragglers were not necessarily individuals who refused to put forth the required effort or shirked their responsibilities. Yes, there were some soldiers who did fit that description, but sometimes soldiers failed to keep up with their units because their bodies would simply breakdown under the constant physical strain. Even today, the official Department of Defense definition of straggler is, "...any personnel, vehicles, ships, or aircraft which, without purpose or assigned mission, become separated from their unit, column, or formation." One needs to remember that the soldiers were usually carrying a full pack on their back, a ten-pound rifled-musket and heavy weapon accoutrements while they marched. The activity was hard enough for a man in his prime. But Abraham was middle-aged, not very large and probably never had to walk so much in his life. As is the case with many injuries, once the physical damage has been done, it is very easy to reinjure the muscles and nerves. He may have been constantly aggravating his past injuries and in constant pain.

MAY 22 – JUL 4 Vicksburg Assaults and Siege As the 22nd Iowa approached Vicksburg, they came under heavy artillery fire. The men advanced parallel to a railroad cut made for the Southern Railroad of Mississippi. Had they been able to continue on this path, the regiment would have been led straight into the center of town. For two hours the men withstood a fierce artillery barrage. Then about 2:00 PM, the 22nd skirmished with some Rebel infantry, gradually moving forward to within 500 yards of the Vicksburg works. After a few hours the attack stalled with the men anchored to their posts. The terrain in front of the Confederate bulwark was hilly, and this provided enough cover for the men to safely rest. The night of May 20 found the regiment building their own earthworks for protection and preparing for the much-dreaded frontal assault of a heavily-fortified position. Throughout the next day, Rebel sharpshooters targeted the Federals. However, their accuracy failed them and only two men from the regiment were wounded. Earlier in the day, the 16th Ohio Battery was able to install two twenty-pound Napoleon guns at the crest of a hill near the regiment. The counter-barrage from this battery helped keep the Rebels cowering behind their fortifications. That evening, Colonel Stone received orders from General Grant to have his men move under the cover of darkness to a midway point between the lines. Quietly, the 22nd led others from their brigade over a hillcrest and down a steep ravine. It was slow work, for the Rebels had cut down trees and then carved the branches into sharp points so the Federal forces would get ensnared in the obstacle. This abatis (French origin) was the predecessor of barbed wire. Wading through the wooden obstruction took several hours, but they finally reach their designated positions. Quietly, they laid throughout the night with their weapons tucked beneath them. At 10:00 AM the next morning, Grant unleashed this Federal juggernaut across a three-mile front. But the Confederates had prepared well and were ready for the attack. The May 22 assault on Vicksburg was the singularly most devastating engagement ever fought by the 22nd Iowa during the American Civil War. They were but a small part of a mammoth effort by the Union army to puncture a hole in the Confederate's defenses that surrounded the town. It was hoped that a victory on this date would avoid a prolonged siege at Vicksburg. At 9:30 AM, the 2nd Brigade, which consisted of the 21st Iowa, 22nd Iowa and the 11th Wisconsin, formed in column just south of the railroad cut. The 22nd Iowa was the lead regiment, followed by the 21st Iowa and then the 11th Wisconsin. At 10:00 AM, a signal cannon was fired and Colonel Stone, with the shout of "Charge," commanded the brigade to advance toward the Rebel works known as the Railroad Redoubt, or Fort Beauregard[39]. The enemy was not taken by surprise and calmly watched hundreds of gleaming bayonets advance toward them. Iowa's postwar publication, *War of the Rebellion Official Records*, Series 1, Vol. 24, page 130, gives an account of the attack at the Railroad Redoubt.

---

[39] Railroad Redoubt is Stop #13 on the Vicksburg Auto-tour. It was built by the Confederates to protect the Southern Railroad of Mississippi that traveled through Vicksburg. Opposite the redoubt is where the 22nd Iowa formed to attack. Today, a handsome monument stands where Second Brigade was deployed.

Map 11

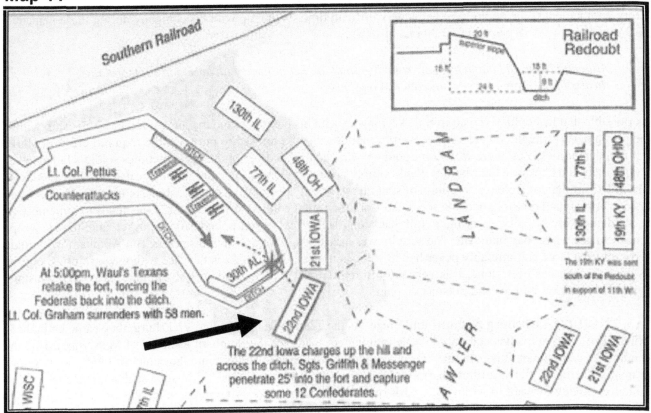

Attack of the 22nd Iowa at the Railroad Redoubt, May 22, 1863.
Illustration: *From Vicksburg to Cedar Creek,*
The 22nd Iowa Volunteer Infantry in the Civil War, by Thomas P. McKenna.

The strong work against which the main attack was directed covered about a half an acre of ground, the walls being about fifteen feet high, surrounded by a ditch ten feet wide. A line of rifle pits connected it with others of the same kind, each of which was so arranged as to enfilade the approach to the other. The regiment succeeded in reaching, under a concentrated fire of grapeshot and musketry, an almost impenetrable abatis, forty yards from the work, where it became necessary to reform the line, the men having become separated in crossing the obstructions. They [the 22nd Iowa] promptly rallied to the flag and were again leading the charge. Colonel Stone was there wounded, while gallantly directing the charge and was compelled to leave the field. Lieutenant Colonel Graham then assumed command and, with a few officers and about fifty men, succeeded in reaching the ditch surrounding the fort, but, having no scaling ladders, they were unable to enter the works. Sergeant Joseph I. Griffith, with some fifteen or twenty men, succeeded by raising one another up the wall, gaining an entrance and capturing a number of prisoners. But the fire from the enemy's rifle pits in the rear of the fort, and the lack of reinforcements coming to their aid, rendered the lace untenable.

The attack was not well-supported and proved to be a failure with only a few survivors of the regiment able to retreat back to the Federal lines. Nevertheless, the three regiments of 2nd Brigade remained on the field, both receiving and returning enemy fire. They were anticipating a supply of reinforcements, but none arrived. The brigade stayed engaged until they exhausted their ammunition and were forced to withdraw.

Everywhere the Federals attacked that day failed. In fact, the men in the 2nd Brigade were the only units to successfully penetrate and enter a fort along the entire Confederate front. The Iowans planted their flag on the Rebel parapet but could not hold the redoubt because they lacked support. The losses for the 22nd Iowa were 27 killed in action, 118 wounded (many of them would later die of their wounds) and 19 captured. They suffered the highest casualty rate of any attacking force at Vicksburg. In a postwar report from the Adjutant General of Iowa, he estimated "...the average loss in killed and wounded of the regiment was 85 percent of the numbers engaged."

The 22nd Iowa's assault at Vicksburg
Painting by the artist, Thure de Thulstrup.

Abraham Wallick's military files do not mention his participation in that day's events. It is clear he was with the regiment, but at that time, the number of soldiers fit for duty was very low due to illness and the effects of three weeks hard campaigning. And it could be that his age, height and past injuries may have prevented any consideration of him being part of the assault force. Height must be considered because at 5'3", his weapon with the attached bayonet would have towered above him, making Abraham far less agile and effective in combat. But there was still plenty of danger and hard work ahead for Abraham, now that the Federal's were reduced to waging siege warfare at Vicksburg.

From May 22 to July 4 the Confederate army and citizens of Vicksburg were strangled by a land blockade where all basic provisions were withheld. As the siege continued, even rats and horses were consumed to alleviate starvation. Soldiers and citizens alike carved dugouts into the hills to escape the round-the-clock bombardment of heavy siege gun and mortar shells that rained down on the city. Sleeping for all combatants, both friend and foe, was nearly impossible.

The Union army was also digging. General Grant tried to use tunnels as a means to break through the Rebel earthworks. For millennia this was done in warfare so soldiers could enter a walled city from underground. Tunneling could also weaken the foundation of the walls so the ramparts would collapse, allowing entry into a city from above ground. The walls of Vicksburg were of earth, not stone or brick. Grant hoped to fill these tunnels with gunpowder and blow holes in the Confederate line.

A civilian neighborhood populated with dugouts during the siege of Vicksburg.

Abraham Wallick was ideally suited to be a tunneler. A 6"8' man can have a huge tactical advantage on a battlefield but put the same man in a tunnel, and he won't fare so well. As short sailors have an advantage in the submarine corps, so short soldiers have an advantage when tunneling. And a tunneler works primarily with his hands and arms, not legs and feet, where Abraham was impaired. Private Wallick speaks of his activity as a tunneler in his November 1878 affidavit.

On the last day of June, 1863, I was set to work in a mine [at] Vicksburg. I had mined several days and nights when one night, about midnight, the Rebels exploded a counter-mine to the right of us, which pressed in the side of our mine and threw dirt on us and around us. The concussion was so great that it stymied me so that I did not have full control of my senses and from which time I have been subject to dizziness, pains in the head and nervous affliction, generally. The concussion and weight of dirt upon my leg and foot did not materially affect them at the time but on the 7th of July, 1863, I was compelled to give up marching on account of pains. I stayed with the miners and sappers corps[40] for a day or two, then I went forward with my company to Jackson, Mississippi.

In this account, Abraham comments that his head was injured when the Confederates created an explosion in their counter-mine. Counter-mining was a common check against an enemy's burrowing activity. Usually, the army that had mines dug under their fortifications would start their own tunnels in order to disrupt the enemy's works. The challenge was how to locate the opposing mine. Abraham Wallick was caught inside or at least near a Federal tunnel when the Rebels detonated their counter-mine. In other pension files he mentions that not only was his head injured, but also his back. He was granted a week's rest to recuperate from the blast.

JUL 4 Surrender of Vicksburg The official end to the siege of Vicksburg occurred on July 4, 1863. Even before that time it was obvious to all combatants that the Confederate stronghold could no longer resist. General John C. Pemberton, a 25-year career army officer, believed he could receive more generous terms from General Grant by surrendering the city on Independence Day. There was some truth to his logic. At first, General Grant only offered unconditional terms of surrender. But what was eventually negotiated was that all soldiers would be paroled and not taken as prisoners of war, staff and field officers would be allowed to take one horse, and all officers could keep their sidearms. Just under 30,000 Confederate soldiers, 172 cannon and 50,000 rifled-muskets were no longer in the service of the Confederate government. With the loss of Vicksburg, the Father of Waters flowed freely from Minnesota to the Gulf of Mexico. Vicksburg was one of the most devastating defeats for the Confederacy. The city did not celebrate the 4th of July for another 81 years.

Abraham Wallick rejoined his Company D comrades at Jackson, Mississippi, on July 10. Due to the devastating number of casualties inflicted on the regiment, there were only 150 officers and men who were healthy enough to make the trek to Jackson. The regiment had become attached to the command of General William Tecumseh Sherman, who was overseeing the siege of Mississippi's capital. The 22nd Iowa (or more accurately, a remnant of the 22nd Iowa) was posted safely to the rear at Jackson and well behind the siege lines. However, this did not mean the men had hazard-free duty.

JUL 14 Injury at Jackson, Mississippi With his right leg and foot again recovering from lameness, and his head and back aching from the mine blast a fortnight before, Abraham became part of a detail ordered to tear up railroad track a few miles south of Jackson. His 1878 affidavit continues:

After the siege of Jackson, I was ordered with others, about the 14th of July, 1863, to tear up the RR track about 4 miles south of Jackson, Miss. While engaged in the work and after one side of the track had been lifted, by some mistake the RR track fell back upon us and pinned me down on the ground. The weight and strain were most severe on my right-side leg and foot, which caused my right leg and foot to swell so that I could not wear my shoe [and] pained me so bad that I had to ride a mule back to Vicksburg.

---

[40] The difference between a miner and a sapper is that a miner works underground, while a sapper works above ground. Sappers were men who dug trenches that zigzagged across a battlefield toward an enemy's fortified position, thus minimizing the attacker's exposure to enemy fire. Usually, the work was done at night to conceal the operation. But sometimes, as at Vicksburg, there would be separate day and night shifts. Since the miners were never exposed, they could work 24/7.

Union soldiers tearing up Confederate railroad track in Mississippi.

JUL – AUG The accident outside of Jackson eventually put an end to Abraham Wallick's enlistment in the 22nd Iowa Volunteers. He remained with the regiment for six more months, but it appears he was unfit for duty during most of that time. Jackson, Mississippi, was taken by the Federals on July 16. The regiment left the city and destroyed Rebel track from the Mississippi Central Railroad all the way back to Vicksburg. On July 24, they arrived at the city and soon after their return, Colonel Stone submitted his resignation. He had been nominated by the Iowa Republican Party to run for governor and that November, he was successfully elected.

AUG – NOV Abraham remained at Vicksburg for three more weeks. On August 13, the 22nd was steamed down to Carrollton, Louisiana (which is just a few miles upriver from New Orleans). They camped there until September 4, then the regiment boarded trains and moved to Bayou Boeuf, Louisiana. Immediately upon their arrival they were ordered on their feet and marched to Berwick. From Berwick they made an expedition to Lafayette, Louisiana, a road which follows today's US Route 90. During that journey the 22nd Iowa had several small skirmishes with the Rebels. After a respite in Lafayette, the regiment countermarched back to Berwick, arriving there November 10.

NOV – JAN, 1864 For the rest of November the regiment bounced along the coastal islands of Texas. First, they steamed down to the mouth of the Rio Grande and camped at Brazos Island. Soon the men were ordered to march north and take the enemy's Fort Esperanza, at the entrance to Matagorda Bay. They arrived at that installation on December 1, ready to begin their assault. But the night before, the Rebels had already abandoned the post, allowing the Federal expedition to walk into Fort Esperanza unopposed. In mid-December, the 22nd Iowa marched to Decros Point, a settlement on the Matagorda Peninsula. They stayed there until January 3, 1864, when the men went into their winter quarters at the nearby town of Indianola. It is difficult to tell how well Abraham traveled with his regiment after leaving Vicksburg. The annals are void of any details. What is clear in his record is that he was with his regiment at Indianola, for it is was there that Abraham had his court-martial.

1864

JAN- 20 The Court-martial of Abraham Wallick The military trial of Abraham Wallick is lean on specifics. We do know the date of the trial, January 20, 1864, and its outcome – guilty. Although he was convicted of being AWOL, he was excused from any consequences and after the proceedings, free to rejoin his regiment. A brief summary of the court's findings concluded that:

> After a careful examination of the evidence adduced, the court finds the accused
> Private Abraham Wallick, Co. D, 22nd Iowa Vols, as follows:
> Of the Specification – 'Guilty.'
> Of the Charge – 'Guilty,' but we attach no criminality, as it appears he was quite unwell
> and direct he be returned to duty. Findings and sentence approved.

What caused this blot on Private Wallick's record was when Abraham marched from Aransas Pass, Texas,[41] to Fort Esperanza, he left his unit without telling either of his company or regimental commanders. The exact circumstances are not mentioned in his record, but it could be that Abraham's injuries had overtaken him to the point where, being unable to keep pace with his comrades, the common straggler became an absent soldier. He was AWOL between November 3, 1863, and January 12, 1864, the day he rejoined his regiment. History is silent as to where he was during his absence. One can speculate that perhaps Abraham was somewhere in a south Texas field hospital and was slow or unable to notify his commanding officers. The leniency of the court would indicate that medical treatment was the cause for his absence. After his court-martial, the army transferred Abraham Wallick to the Invalid Corp. He officially joining that branch of the military on February 22, 1864.

The Invalid Corps had been in existence in some form during the days of the American Revolution. It was then disbanded and reactivated for three years during the American Civil War. Over 60,000 men served in the twenty-four regiments of the corps. The National Archives describes the units as:

- Officers and enlisted men unfit for active field service because of wounds or disease contracted in the line of duty, but still capable of performing garrison duty.
- Officers and enlisted men in the service and on the Army rolls otherwise absent from duty and in hospitals, in convalescent camps, or otherwise under the control of medical officials, but capable of serving as cooks, clerks, orderlies and guards at hospitals and other public buildings.
- Officers and enlisted men honorably discharged because of wounds or disease and who wanted to reenter the service.
- The Invalid Corps was renamed the Veteran Reserve Corps (VRC) on March 18, 1864. Confusion with the damaged goods stamp "I.C." (inspected-condemned) affected volunteer morale.[42]

One can understand how crates sent to the Invalid Corps could be inadvertently tossed if the army also used "I.C." as an abbreviation for inspected-condemned. The "I.C." designation quickly proved an impediment to the corpsmen. To alleviate the problem, the War Department renamed the unit Veteran Reserve Corps only weeks after Abraham joined Company I of the 3rd Regiment.

There were two classifications of soldiers in the corps. First, those who were partially disabled and their periods of service had not yet expired (like Abraham). And second, soldiers who were discharged because of disease, wounds or other disabilities but wanted to reenlist. The corps had their own distinctive uniforms and even brass bands for military ceremonies. Even so, to some there was a stigma attached to being members of the Veteran Reserve Corps.

Members of the 10th Reserve Veteran Corps, Washington, DC.

---

[41] Aransas, Texas, is about twenty miles north of Corpus Christi.

[42] National Archives and Records Administration, RR# 920, Rev. December, 2010.

The reality was that the VRC soldiers had many important responsibilities and their presence relieved more able-bodied troops for combat. Some VRC units were assigned provost duty (military police) in towns and cities. Provost soldiers from the corps became combatants in July of 1864 when Fort Stevens, just outside of Washington, DC, was attacked. This was a highly unusual and emergency response for the VRC, for they were never to be employed as combat troops. That being said, without the corps' help, Confederate soldiers would have entered our nation's capital, causing a political and international crisis of immeasurable proportions. Later, units from the VRC were used to search for John Wilks Booth and were responsible for carrying out the executions of the Lincoln assassination conspirators.

FEB 1864 – July 1865 Unfortunately, there is little to report on Abraham's service in the Veteran Reserve Corps. He certainly was not involved in any of the events that surrounded the attack on Washington, DC. To date, there is little information concerning his whereabouts and the activities of his unit. However, judging by rules of human gestation, Abraham must have had a furlough from his regiment sometime in the fall of 1864 for his son, Wallace, was born on July 26, 1865. It is unlikely that Mary was involved in any extra-marital affair, for that would be very inconsistent with the recorded testimonials of her strong Christian character. Other than that speculative event, very little is known about Abraham's service apart from his entry into the Veteran Reserve Corps on February 22, 1864, and his discharge at Burlington, Vermont, on July 14, 1865.[43]

In the 1880s the War Department gathered company muster rolls, hospital records, descriptive rolls, pay records and enlistment papers to create a soldier's compiled military service record. This was done in part to help verify pension applications. All the infantry, artillery and cavalry units were later microfilmed for preservation and public distribution. However, the compiled military service records of the Veteran Reserve Corps have yet to be filmed, making for a void in the knowledge about those soldiers' service in the corps.

Epilogue- After his discharge, Abraham Wallick traveled from Burlington, Vermont, to Fulton County, Illinois, to rejoin his family. Fulton County had a history with Abraham and his wife. Mary Hazel (Johnson) was born there in 1835 and in 1850, the 15-year-old bride and 31-year-old Abraham established their first home in Fulton County. In 1853, the couple and their infant daughter, Elizabeth, moved to the sparsely populated prairie town of Albia, Iowa. They lived in a cabin (presumably built by Abraham) in a wooded section of the prairie that was frequented by packs of timber wolves. By the time the Iowa carpenter had left for war, he had fathered eight children, six children were already born and twin boys were on the way. Indeed, Mary must have been a very brave and determined woman to accept the responsibility of governing, as a single mother, such a lively brood during Abraham's three-year absence. With the father off fighting Confederates, it is not surprising that after the twins were born Mary and the children went back to Fulton County to live with her brother, the Reverend Elijah Johnson. Abraham reconnected with his family in Illinois after the war and between 1865 and 1868, two more sons and a daughter were born in Fulton, County.

In 1868, with a serious war disability and eleven children under age sixteen, Abraham sold most of his family's possessions and with a covered wagon, two horses and a cow, he began a migration across the plains of Iowa. After traveling three weeks and 250 miles, the weary settlers stopped at Seward County, Nebraska. They were truly a family of pioneers who were content to live in a 10x14 rough slab board house that was dug into a ravine. There were few comforts and many privations. The following year Abraham added a room to the structure and a year after that, Abraham and Mary had twin girls, Addie and Jane. The following record is a list of the thirteen children born to Abraham and Mary Wallick between 1853 and 1870. Those not born in Fulton, County, or Iowa City, were born in a cabin on the prairie.

> Elizabeth Victoria- b: 25 Feb 1853, Fulton County, Illinois
> Christian J – b: Aug 1854, Iowa City, Iowa
> John Franklin- b: 04 Mar 1855, Monroe County, Iowa
> Sarah Ellen- b: 01 Apr 1859, Iowa

---

[43] Some documents in Abraham Wallick's files state that he was discharged June, 14, 1865. One family record even says the date of his discharge was July 27, 1865. In fact, there are many conflicting dates associated with his pension and military records. This is not unusual for a Civil War soldier's record.

Abraham Moses- b: 1860, Illinois
Martha Viola- b: 28 Jan 1862, Iowa
Elijah Scott- b: 14 Mar 1863, Albia, Iowa (twin)
William Melville- b: 14 Mar 1863, Albia, Iowa (twin)
Wallace Grant- b: 26 Jul 1865, Fulton, Illinois
Mary Louisa- b: Nov 1866, Fulton, Illinois
Henry C- b: 1867, Fulton, Illinois
Addie Ada- b: 10 May 1870, Fulton Illinois (twin)
(Amanda) Jane K- b: 10 May 1870, Fulton, Illinois (twin)

Having a wife and thirteen children must have been quite a burden for the old soldier to bear (although, in 1870, the seventeen-year-old Elizabeth was married). But Abraham's life became even more burdensome when Mary, only 36 years-old, contracted pneumonia and died on February 21, 1871. The infant twin girls were only nine months old at her passing. Mary is memorialized in the 1888 book, *History of Seward County, Nebraska*,[44] where it states, "Mrs. Wallick is remembered by all the older settlers as a very worthy Christian lady, who went through great tribulation to her brighter home in the skies to receive her crown."

Abraham Wallick and his family lived on the Nebraska prairie in a dugout similar to this one.

Mary's death destroyed the family. Abraham's twelve-year-old daughter, Sarah Ellen, had nursed her ill mother while caring for her infant sisters. Sarah stayed on the homestead to help her father while all the remaining children were dispersed to other households. It was impossible for Abraham to care for such a large family by himself. As for the children, they not only lost their mother but their entire family was wrecked and ruined because of the separation of all the siblings. They were all placed in different homes, except the twin boys, Elijah Scott and William Melville, who were raised by an aunt. Even the twin girls were separated, with Jane becoming the foster child of Joseph and Lucy Kimball, who gave her the new name of Amanda Jane.

From the time he was discharged in 1865 to the time of his death, Abraham Wallick received a military pension as compensation for the disabilities he acquired while in the service of his country. However, starting in 1878, he had to submit affidavits and doctors' examination certificates in order to continue his pension. Through these pension documents we are able to learn the details of how and where Abraham was injured during the war. These affidavits also help cast a light on his medical condition as he grew older. One such document was written to the Board of Pensions by his minister, Revered E.W. Johnson (most likely his son-in-law), of the United Brethren Church. It states the following:

Seward, Neb.   *Aug 19, 1880*

Dear Sir,
In answer to your questions [I] would say that Mr. Abraham Wallick at the time of his discharge and since up to [this] date has been lame in one of his legs, which he says was injured while in the service of the U S. Last summer there was quite a while that he could not walk at all. He is also troubled with a dizziness in his head which he claims is caused from an explosion in a mine at Vicksburg. He is a carpenter and from the two ailments he is rendered almost worthless as such,

---

[44] *History of Seward County, Nebraska*. Lincoln, Nebraska: State Journal Printing Company, 1888.

[and] I would further add that his complaints are growing worse every year. While I offered him a job of painting (which he also understands) he painted ½ day and had to give it up, [for] he could not stand on the ladder. My judgement is that since his discharge, he has been disabled at least one half, say $20 or $25 per month.

> *Respectfully yours,*
> *Rev. E.W. Johnson*
> *U.B. Minister, Seward, Nebraska*

There are other affidavits that speak to the difficulties Abraham encountered when preforming tasks of physical labor or work requiring long periods of concentration. After the war, he never totally healed in body or mind. The day after his July 14, 1865 discharge, Abraham received his first pension payment of four dollars. As the years progressed there were increases to these monthly allotments. Unfortunately, those increases never kept pace with the wages he lost due to his injuries. On March 16, 1882, his payment was raised to six dollars per month and in 1890, eight dollars per month.

Abraham remained on his 85-acre homestead until 1881, then he moved to the town of Seward, Nebraska. It could be that the property required too much work for the old carpenter to stay on his land. Abraham first boarded with Henry and Mary Miller, then with his twin sons. This move also made it more convenient for Abraham to attend his Grand Army of the Republic meetings, where he had been a founding member.[45]

Abraham Wallick died on January 17, 1892. The *Blue Valley Blade,*[46] a local Seward newspaper, published his obituary soon after his death. He was part of a brotherhood that helped keep our republic united and a generation that understood the meaning of duty, honor and sacrifice. Abraham lived a hard life, but it was a life full of incredible experiences. He left us a rich, yet tragic, story about his life as a Union soldier and Nebraska pioneer.

This is the last surviving photograph of Abraham Wallick and his wife, Mary. This picture was taken shortly before Mary's death. Abraham and Mary are seated. Standing behind Abraham are Mary's sister, America (Johnson), and her husband, Thomas Skillman. Standing behind Mary are her sister-in-law, Sarah Jane (Street) and her brother, the Reverend Elijah Johnson, whom she would visit in Fulton, County, Illinois. All were amongst the earliest settlers in Nebraska.

---

[45] Nebraska Local #3 of the Grand Army of the Republic was organized in 1880.
[46] *Blue Valley Blade* was a weekly newspaper named after the Big Blue River, which runs through Seward, Nebraska.

ABRAHAM WALLICK.

Before the BLADE went to press last week we had been unable to get any of the life history of Abraham Wallick, but are now enabled to do so through the kindness of a member of his family.

Abraham Wallick was born in Ohio county, Indiana, January 1, 1819, and died at his home in Seward, Nebraska, January 17, 1892, and was consequently 73 years and 17 days of age at the time of his death. *1892*

Mr. Wallick removed from Indiana to Fulton county, Illinois, in 1840, where he was married to Mary H. Johnson in 1850. In 1854 Mr. Wallick moved to Monroe county, Iowa, where he resided when the rebellion broke out. He enlisted in the 22nd Iowa Infantry at Albia, Iowa, July 26, 1862, and was mustered out of the service of the Union July 14, 1865, having served his country faithfully for three years. After Mr. Wallick entered the service of his country his little family returned to Fulton county, Illinois, where he joined them after the close of the war, where they remained until in August, 1868, when they came to Seward county and settled down on a homestead three miles west _____ where Mrs. Wallick died in _____ 1871. Mr. Wallick remained _____ homestead until 1881, when he removed to Seward, where he has since resided.

Mr. Wallick and his family were among the early settlers of Seward county, and shared in all the privations and drawbacks incident to a new country. Mr. and Mrs. Wallick had a family of thirteen children, seven sons and six daughters, and it required a good deal of energy and pluck to take care of such a large family in Nebraska at that early day. The oldest daughter married and moved to Pennsylvania, where she died several ago, but the other five daughters and seven sons are still living.

Mr. Wallick was a member of the Christian church, and was perfectly resigned to the call of his Master, saying that all was well with him.

Card of Thanks.

We wish to thank all those who assisted us during the sickness and death of our beloved father.

C. J. WALLICK.
H. C. WALLICK.
MRS. S. P. HAGEMAN.
MRS. G. ODELL.
MRS. G. W. NIGH.
MRS. E. S. SMITH.

Abraham Wallick is buried in Seward Cemetery, Seward, NE.

Comrades-in-Arms- No brothers, uncles or first cousins

188

From Pennsylvania

Washington Wallick – 1st California Infantry, Co. N
71th Pennsylvania Volunteer Infantry

23

Rank: Private

Place of enlistment: Philadelphia, Pennsylvania

Date of enlistment: July 8, 1861

Mustered into Federal service: August 29,1861

Discharged: August 18,1862

Service time: 354 days (due to injury, active service only 53 days)

Born: 1836, Tuscarawas County, Ohio

Age at enlistment: 25 years old

Physical description: height - 5' 9", light hair, gray eyes

Civilian occupation: Carpenter

Family Lineage: Washington, son of Zachariah, son of "Peru" Benjamin Senior, son of Johannes, son of Hans Michael Wallick

Washington Wallick was part of the Benjamin Wallick Sr. clan who in the mid-nineteenth century migrated from Tuscarawas County, Ohio, to Miami County, Indiana. The family settled in the small town of Peru, Indiana. In April of 1861, President Lincoln made a call to arms for all the northern states to put down the southern rebellion. Three months later, Washington became yet another member of the Miami County Wallick family who volunteered to quash the Rebel insurrection. However, although he was raised in Peru with nine close relatives who also served, by 1861, Washington had moved to Philadelphia, Pennsylvania, and it was there where he enlisted in the Union army. There is little mystery as to why Washington left his Indiana hometown to became a Philadelphian. We know that he and his wife, Ellen, married in Peru at a young age in 1854 (both were 18 or 19 years old) and by the summer of 1861 they had moved and established their home in Philadelphia. The 1860 United States census states that Ellen was from Pennsylvania, so it seems Washington decided to leave his mother, father and six siblings in order to live near Ellen's relatives. No one else from Washington's branch of the family ever moved so far away from Peru. Other than his wife, all of Washington's immediate family members are buried in and around Miami County, Indiana.

Washington was recruited to be part of a new four-regiment brigade of eastern men. The creation of this brigade has a few interesting features in its origins when compared to how most Civil War units were formed. At the beginning of the war most regiments and brigades were organized by highly-esteemed, ambitious men from one specific state. And the companies within the regiments were generally men from the same town or county of that state. But Washington Wallick joined an outfit organized by an Illinois lawyer, who at the time was an Oregon Senator that had recently moved from San Francisco, and who was commissioned by President Lincoln to raise a brigade of soldiers from Philadelphia and New York City, all to fight in the name of the State of California. Immediately after the firing on Fort Sumter, the President had assigned his close friend and ally, Senator Edward D. Baker, the job of raising a brigade of four regiments of soldiers who would fight as surrogates for the citizens of California. California had come into the Union as a free state in 1850 and, considering the great distance troops and matériel had to travel in order to engage in battle, some thought it was best to let eastern men fight under the Golden State banner. This arrangement also gave the commander-in-chief the opportunity to add California's quota of soldiers to the Federal ranks, since Pennsylvania and New York already had a surplus of volunteers. Lincoln awarded Senator Baker, who also had extensive military experience, a colonelcy of volunteers to lead this new brigade.

Washington enlisted on July 8, 1861, just a few weeks before the First Battle of Bull Run. Seven weeks later, he was mustered into Federal service and became part of the 1st California Infantry Regiment. This outfit had fifteen companies instead of the usual ten (that is why Washington was in Company N) and they were mostly comprised of Philadelphians. There were three other regiments organized that summer by Senator Baker: the 2nd, 3rd, and 5th California Infantry. All four regiments became known as "The California Brigade."

The brigade had its first real taste of combat on October 21, 1861, at the disastrous affair called the Battle of Ball's Bluff. It was by no means a major engagement, but it did have huge political ramifications. Officers' incompetence combined with inexperienced troops and that created the expected result… a defeat and major embarrassment for the Federal army. Also, one of the more capable commanders was mortally wounded in the battle, Senator Edward Baker. He is still the only sitting senator ever to be killed in action on an American battlefield. After his death, a congressional committee called Joint Committee on the Conduct of the War was created to investigate Ball's Bluff and oversee the Federal army's future military affairs. Throughout the war, this collection of congressmen became a constant thorn in the side of the President and his generals. After the Ball's Bluff fiasco the California Brigade was reorganized into four Pennsylvania Volunteer Infantry (PVI) regiments: the 69th, 70th, 71st, and 109th. These four regiments then became known as the "Philadelphia Brigade." Washington was "officially" assigned to the 71st PVI. This regiment has a wonderful history in the Civil War and it fought in some of war's most famous battles:

Ball's Bluff (as the 1st California Regiment)
Battle of Fair Oaks
Battle of Seven Pines
Malvern Hill
Battle of Antietam
Battle of Fredericksburg
Chancellorsville
Gettysburg- The Angle
Wilderness
Spotsylvania Court House
North Anna
Cold Harbor

The 71st PVI Monument at The Angle.
One of the most Hallowed Ground
sites in all of the American Civil War.

When this author saw the stellar resumé the 71st PVI had acquired during the war, it was with tremendous excitement and anticipation that he began his research into Washington Wallick. However, the author soon discovered a disappointing reality to the Philadelphian's war story. Unfortunately for the author, but fortunately for his subject, Washington was in none of these battles. On September 20, 1861, at Falls Church, Virginia, even before the regiment's engagement at Ball's Bluff, Washington was kicked and tramped upon by a horse, which severely injured his left knee. This injury ended his useful service to the Union army and the disability plagued him for the rest of his life. Below is what little we know about Washington's service in the American Civil War, as can be gleaned from his compiled military service records (CMSR) and pension records.

Washington Wallick with the 1st California and 71st Pennsylvania Regiments

1861

JUL 1861 – OCT 1862 Washington Wallick is enlisted by Captain Keffer in Philadelphia on July 8, 1861, and is to serve for three years. He then goes up to Fort Schuyler, located at the tip of the Bronx, New York, and waits for the rest of the California Brigade to be organized. All of the soldiers are mustered into Federal service on August 29, 1861. On September 1, the brigade is moved to Fortress Monroe, Virginia, and then on to Washington D.C. to help defend the capital. The regiment is involved in a minor skirmish on September 20 near Falls Church, Virginia, which is about ten miles west of the capital. It is there that Washington Wallick is kicked in the left knee by a horse. One pension medical affidavit, dated January 12, 1880 and filed by Jacob M. Price, is more specific and states:

"At the Battle of Falls Church, VA, September 20, 1861, Washington Wallick received a compound fracture of the left knee by a horse knocking him down and tramping on him while in action and engaged with the enemy. I have knowledge of [the] occurrence by being an eyewitness, being in the same company and regiment, and helped him to bandage the limb and helped him to treat the same, before he could get medical treatment."

Washington Wallick's Certificate of Disability for Discharge dated, August 18, 1862.

Washington's surname is spelled both "Wallack" and "Wallick" in his military and pension files.

In an 1896 affidavit seeking an increase in Washington's pension, a medical examination board claimed, *"He had it dressed but was not confined to a hospital. Was furloughed on account of the accident and did not receive proper attention until he reached home."*

Washington began his home furlough on October 26, 1861. This means it was well over a month before he had proper treatment for his injured knee. His company records also state that he was recuperating in Philadelphia during the months of November and December, with nothing written for January and February, 1862. March and April found Washington back with his unit. But how effective he was as a soldier is questionable, for in May, June and July his CMSR only states, "absent, sick and missing." And although he was "officially" transferred to Company A of the 71st PVI, he never appeared on the company's muster roll. His knee affliction was permanent. He was granted a disability discharge on August 18, 1862, while recuperating on David's Island, which is located just off the coast of New Rochelle, New York. He stayed on the island until October 18, then returned to Philadelphia as a civilian.

Washington Wallick's service as a Federal soldier had ended before it ever began. There is little to say about his time in the Union army other than after seven weeks as a private, he was kicked in the knee by a horse and disabled for life. Had that incident not occurred, and given the history of his regiment, he could have had one of the most interesting narratives of all the Wallick soldiers who served in the American Civil War. After months of waiting for his knee to heal, Washington returned home to Philadelphia and was immediately granted a pension of six dollars a month. In 1890 his pension was increased to eight dollars a month; little consolation for his lifelong disability.

Epilogue - After he was discharged from the army, Washington wasn't able to return to his old ways of carpentry because of his mobility issues. His 1871, 1880, 1890 and 1896 pension affidavits state that the war injury made him limp and constantly drag his left leg. However, to make a living, he did apply his knowledge of carpentry in another way; Washington went into business for himself as a picture frame manufacturer. It is possible that he could have overseen a thriving business for many years. But as the adjacent undated newspaper notice states, The Wallick Manufacturing Company eventually had some very serious economic troubles. It appears that the money problems continued up to his death and well beyond, for he left his wife, Ellen, in a severe financial mess.

When Washington died on May 7, 1899 of uremia (blood poisoning due to kidney disease), Ellen was left with two mortgages on their house, unpaid utility bills and overdue property taxes, all totaling over $16,000 (over ½ million dollars in 2023 dollars). It is stated that their home was mortgaged at twice the market value and was in Ellen's name alone. Perhaps this was done to shield their home from Washington's business woes. And according to her widow's pension affidavits, Ellen was totally unaware of how badly Washington was in debt.

RECEIVERSHIP AND ASSIGNMENTS.

Probable Consequence of the Wallick Manufacturing Company's Troubles.

Washington Wallick, picture frame manufacturer, has made an assignment to S. Horace Alleman. Mr. Wallick is an officer of the Wallick Manufacturing Company, which went into a receiver's hands last August. On the 19th execution was issued against him at the suit of Eva C. Haines for $5732.10 on a one-day judgment note. Mr. Alleman said yesterday that his appointment was too recent to permit him to give any account of Mr. Wallick's assets.

The debts of the manufacturing company were $19,921.51 and its capital stock $50,000.

The Common Sense Bicycle Manufacturing Company has made an assignment to Frank W. Parvin.

By June of 1900, Ellen was 64 years old and destitute. Her pension application had yet to be approved by the government and, other than being paid for some "day labor", she had received no income for 13 months. At that time there were very few government-sponsored safety nets for a widowed spouse. Elderly care was mainly left up to the family members. Unfortunately, Washington and Ellen had no children. However, she did receive some assistance from her relatives in Philadelphia. Ellen died of bronchial pneumonia March 30, 1916. In a very comprehensive affidavit from Ellen's file, the only assets she owned at the time of her death were "$30 cash and a few household effects of no value." The information was part of a deposition made by Washington's second cousin and executor of Ellen's estate, Maude Wagner. In this document, Maude is asking the Bureau of Pensions to reimburse her for Ellen's funeral expenses. The extense ledger is very detailed, down to the cost of Ellen's $8.03 dress, in which she was buried, and the $180 undertaker's fee.

Washington and Ellen are buried in the Philadelphia section, plot 166, of the West Laurel Hill Cemetery. They have no stone but are buried just to the right and out of the picture of the largest headstone.

Elizabeth Dyer
Plot 167

George Faulkner
Plot 164

Alexander Dambly
Plot 165

According to the West Laurel Hill Cemetery database, Washington & Ellen Wallick are buried in the Philadelphia section, plot 166. There is no stone.

This is a photo of the Philadelphia section, plot 166

Photograph courtesy of findagrave. com

Comrades- in- Arms

Brother
Jeremiah   109th IVI

Uncles
Benjamin Jr.   109th IVI
Christopher   109th IVI
Wesley   109th and 138th IVI

Cousins
William   51st IVI
Charles F.   87th IVI
John Wesley   138th & 151st IVI
Benjamin   162nd OVI
William F.   13th, 109th & 151st IVI

Appendix I

The Wartime Diary
of
Charles F. Wallick

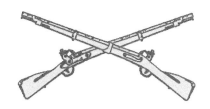

Charles F. Wallick's diary was transcribed by Walter Reyburn in two sections. The first portion was written between April 25 and July 3, 1864, when Charles was fighting in northern Georgia and advancing toward Atlanta. The second was written at the close of the war, between January 1 and April 23, 1865, when the Union army moved up through the Carolinas toward Virginia. It is unfortunate that the middle six months of Charles' diary were never transcribed, for it was during this time that his regiment participated in General Sherman's "March to the Sea."

The Wartime Diary of Charles F. Wallick, 87th Indiana Volunteer Infantry

Monday, April 25, 1864

The night was very cool. Two or three woolen blankets are very comfortable to sleep under at this time. The day was very warm. I received a note from Isaiah Shafer. He is at Indianapolis at the Soldiers' Home. He was very unwell. He sends me this book [the diary] and a hat that father sent with him for me. The day wore away without any movements on the part of the Rebs. The boys were all looking for Dangerfield and his recruits but they come not. The boys that went down to the train were bored for the fortieth time I believe.[47]

Tuesday, April 26, 1864

I was detailed to go on picket. The day was a fine one. We had a nice time picketing. The officers tried to capture some Rebel's pickets post but did not succeed in taking them. I received a letter from reserve toward noon. The day was very warm and sultry. It appeared like the middle of summer to me. I was so lazy I could hardly see nothing of very much importance transpired at Ringgold [GA] to say that the troops drill twice today. Company drill, Battalion and Brigade.

Wednesday, April 27, 1864

I come into camp. The morning was very cool, the day was very hot and sultry. I took a wash in the creek for the first time this spring. We had drill as usual in the afternoon. Dangerfield's long expected recruits came up today. They have meeting every night in the church in town. There have been a large number of soldiers joined the church in the last few days. The glorious mark of Religious Principles are carried on finely at the present and I hope it may continue on in peace and success.

Thursday, April 28, 1864

The weather is still warm and dry. The night is somewhat cool; the morning was a very pleasant one indeed. The golden sun arose over the Ridge and lightens up our camp with his bright beams of golden light. The beauties of nature are fast unfolding their green callers to our view and the beautiful songster is warbling his musical notes among the saucy bowers of some nice tree as the sun rolls on the noonday approaches. Dinner is then served in our camp. Plenty of hardtack and sowbelly. Supper comes also and at last the night descends.

Friday, April 29, 1864

The morning is a very pleasant one. The program for the day was spent early in the morning with a right sharp skirmish with the Rebels. General Kilpatrick is driving them back a few miles. The result was that about 10 of our men were wounded. The fight did not last very long. The day passed away without further molestation from the post of the Rebels. The time was passed away in playing games of almost all kinds. The health of the Company is very good at the present time. The scene closes by going to bed to sleep.

---

[47] Isaiah Shafer, John Dangerfield and Charles F. Wallick were all comrades in Company C.

Saturday, April 30, 1864

The night was cold with some rain. The morning was very pleasant. The rain commenced falling about two o'clock P.M. and continued to fall in showers all day. I tried for a pass to go to Chattanooga to see Bill Wallick [brother William of the 51st IVI] but failed to get the commanding general to sign it for me.[48] I was very much out of humour all day. My health is very good excepting a very severe cold I caught carelessly. There was a detail sent out of the Division to Nashville after mules for the Company and Regimental teams.

Sunday, May 1, 1864

The night was somewhat rainy, the morning was cool. The day was very pleasant. I tried again for a pass but failed getting it. I wrote a letter to Bill. I was detailed on Company guard. We had a preaching a nine o'clock, our chaplain preached a very good service. The [train] cars run into this town, Ringgold about twelve o'clock P.M. I have got a bad cold. We have plenty of rations now. They consist of hardtack, sowbelly, sugar and coffee, because that is the principal part of our grub now.

Monday, May 2, 1864

The morning was very cold. The day very windy. The regiment went out on a scout. There were two brigades that went as far as the tunnel [Tunnel Hill, GA]. The Rebels falling back after some fighting. Our troops come back to camp. The Rebels follow our men up to their old positions where they are picketing again. They seem very saucy and drive very stubborn as though they were determined to hold this position at all hazards. There were some half dozen wounded and killed. The day closes very blustery. The sun is gone down.

Tuesday, May 3, 1864

I was on guard last night. It was very cold for the time of year. The morning is a very pleasant one. I attended surgeon's call this morning for some medicine for the kidney complaint of which I am bothered a good deal with at the present time. This day one year ago, Captain Wallick was captured near Rome, Ga. He is now at Chattanooga with his regiment. The first red bird I saw this year was this morning. The cars are running all the time now. They are rushing the rations through here very fast. We had [illegible] this evening.

Wednesday, May 4, 1864

The night was very pleasant and had a good nights sleep. This morning is a very nice one. They have company drill as usual. I attended surgeon's call to get some more medicine. They excused me from heavy duty. The rail train has just come in but it brings no mail for me. The day is a very business one in camp. We had orders to send extra baggage to the rear. General Palmer has his headquarters close to our camp. He come here today. The prospects of a forward movement is very good at this time. The scene closes by eating supper.

Thursday, May 5, 1864

The night was cold, this morning is a very pleasant one. I attended surgeon's call for medicine. We shipped our extra baggage to the rear today. The day became very warm toward noon. We had company drill. I received a letter from William. He was well. I wrote him one in answer to his. We had no orders to march yet today. We drew rations among them we drew some pickles. The evening was very pleasant. The boys all gathered together in headquarters for a chat.

---

[48] The commanding general probably denied Charles' pass because the Union army was within days of marching out of Tennessee and into northern Georgia. General Sherman was about to begin his Atlanta Campaign.

Friday, May 6, 1864

The night was warm and the morning a very pleasant one. The day was very warm and sultry. Troops are moving all around our camp and vicinity. We receive orders to march at daylight. The next morning there was a bustle in camp making preparations to leave our old camp at Ringgold. I wrote a letter to Bill today. Alfred Koons was at our camp today. He was on his way to his regiment. He was well and thus the busy day passed.

Saturday, May 7, 1864

The first thing on docket was to get up about 3 o'clock in the morning and get breakfast, strike tents, pack knapsacks and we move at seven o'clock P.M.[49] The day was intolerably hot but they marched very steady and rested several times. We camped about one mile southwest from Tunnel Hill. Our troops skirmished here today with the Rebels. Our men fire a shot from the bridge with our cannon. We went into camp about three o'clock A.M.[?] and pitched our tents and took our rest of which we needed.

Sunday, May 8, 1864

The night was very warm. We were up before daylight. We served breakfast and marched about seven o'clock. We moved farther to the right about 3 miles and camped there all day and night. I received a letter from Bill. He was well, he sent me some venison and a calico shirt. The day was very warm. Our men skirmished all day with the Rebels. The right and left wings of our army have not taken their positions yet as I can learn. The evening was a very pleasant one.

Monday, May 9, 1864

The night was very pleasant. I had a good night's rest. The morning was fine and still skirmishing is going along our lines. We had orders to draw two day's rations and be ready to move at 10 P.M. We moved forward in line of battle to a hill about a half mile and in the meanwhile our men were skirmishing steadily all day. We moved forward in line and took another position and camped for the night. Our men were skirmishing till after dark. So the day ended.

Tuesday, May 10, 1864

The night was pleasant, the morning was cool. Firing was heard all along our lines. The day was nice until toward the afternoon. Then it set in and rained all day. The skirmishing was heavier than it has been yet. We had orders to draw two days rations. I feel somewhat under the weather this morning. The kidney complaint is my common enemy. So the day past away. There has not been any regular engagement yet with the Rebels. God only knows when there will.

Wednesday, May 11, 1864

The weather is getting colder with some rain. Our men are still shelling the Rebels at this point. We receive good news from the Army of the Potomac. We draw another day's rations and had orders to be ready to march. I received a letter from Peru today. All the folks are well. This afternoon our men succeeded in getting some very good positions for our artillery. They could throw shells so they would burst on the ridge every time.

---

[49] The use of A.M. and P.M. seems to be reversed at times in Charles' diary. Here, for example, it makes more sense that the regiment was up at 3 o'clock in the morning, started marching at 7 o'clock AM and made their camp at 3 o'clock PM. It needs to be remembered that the author did not transcribe his own diary, that was done by Walter Reyburn. Perhaps Walter wrote it with no input from Charles. It also needs to be remembered that the army can create some very unusual and demanding schedules while campaigning.

200

Thursday, May 12, 1864

The night was very cold. The morning is a fine one for marching. We left camp about seven o'clock in the morning. The day was very pleasant. We marched all day halting occasionally for a rest. The 14th Army Corp moved to the right of our lines of battle about 18 miles, passing through Snake Gap. The roads and fields were all full of wagons and troops of all kinds. We went into camp about ten o'clock at night. I was very tired and wearied out. The night past quietly.

Friday, May 13, 1864

The morning was very cold. We had orders to leave our knapsacks and did leave them and our woolen blankets. We drew three days rations and received orders to move at any time called for. There was a guard left on our baggage. Our men had extensive breastworks thrown up here and had a splendid position. We marched about noon and took our position on the center of our line. Skirmishing was very heavy along in the evening. The day passed without a regular engagement.

Saturday, May 14, 1864   [The Battle of Resaca]

The night was very cold. I did not get much sleep. I had nothing but a rubber blanket and tent bed. The morning was very calm and still. The skirmishing began about seven o'clock and our division was in the second line. We moved forward till the balls commenced whistling around us. Our rations were out and we drew here in line of battle and about 11 o'clock we moved forward and our men made a charge. It was the most awful musketry I ever heard and in the evening the cannonading was the hardest. The fight has begun sure.

Sunday, May 15, 1864

The night was very pleasant and the morning finds us a little to the left of where we were yesterday. Our boys built works and fortified all night. It was a very commanding position for artillery. The ball opened [colloquialism for "the fighting began"] soon in the morning. A couple of batteries were place in position here and opened out on them in fine style. A portion of our brigade were on the skirmish line. Our corps were returning, relieved and we moved to the right. Our regiment has not been engaged yet. The fighting was hard today.

Monday, May 16, 1864

The night was a very disagreeable one to sleep. There were several charges made by the Rebels to retake their fort and entrenchments that our men captured yesterday but they did not succeed in doing it. They were pushed back last night. The Rebels evacuated their stronghold here at Coosa River. We moved camp about twelve o'clock P.M. We moved further to the right. We are about 26 miles from Dalton [GA]. We camped today at a little town called Resaca on the bank of the river. The day was very cold and windy.

Tuesday, May 17, 1864

The night was very cold. Our knapsacks come up last night. We were ordered to be ready to march at three o'clock in the morning. We moved out about day light and marched some four or five miles and halted. It commenced raining and rained till near noon then it cleared away but has clouded up again and more rain fell along in the afternoon. We marched on about five miles. Farther on we passed through a town by the name of Calhoun. It was a nice town.

Wednesday, May 18, 1864

The night was very damp and cold. We were ordered up at two o'clock. Our regiment was led back to guard the train. We marched about two miles and passed through a small town by the name of Adairsville. It was a nice town. The country is very beautiful here and the land is very rich. I was very much fatigued after this day's march. We marched until about ten o'clock at night. I had a good night's sleep. Once more we have been kept up, day and night for some time, about a week.

Thursday, May 19, 1864

The night was cold. We moved out of camp about nine o'clock P.M. and marched on the road to Kingston. I was a very nice town. The railroad connects here with the one that runs to Rome. We moved on through the town and come on the enemy about 4 miles on the other side of town. A brisk skirmish ensued. We were drawn up in line of battle facing to the east. Skirmishing was kept up till dark. The country was very beautiful and rich here and thus the day closes.

Friday, May 20, 1864

I had a good night's rest. My feet were very sore from yesterday's march. My health is good at the present time. This morning a few shots were fired occasionally. The morning is a very beautiful one. The Rebs have fallen back. We went into camp for the day. It was a very warm day. I wrote a letter home. Today, our mail did not come. Our sutler[50] come up. He had a tolerable good assortment of goods. No news from the Potomac today. The cars come in today also.

Saturday, May 21, 1864

The night was cold and a very heavy dew fell. The morning was a pleasant one, the day was very warm. We are still here in camp. The boys passed the time washing and cleaning up. Today the 9th Ohio [a regiment from Cincinnati, OH, who were in Charles' brigade] starts home to be mustered out of service. They were all very happy for the chance of returning home once more. Nothing of any importance transpired today and the long day passed away in peace.

Sunday, May 22, 1864

The morning is very beautiful and the golden sun shines down upon us in all his glory and richness. The mail come this morning but did not bring any news for me. The day passed away and we did not move along in the evening. The mail come. The captain received a letter that stated that William was wounded but it was only a report. I do not know whether it is so or not. Our chaplain preached to us today and received good news from the Potomac.

Monday, May 23, 1864

The night was cold and the morning clear and warm. We marched out of camp about the hours of ten and twelve. We march very steadily all day. About two o'clock come to the River Ettowa [Etowah] and had to wade it. It was a very fine stream about as large as the Wabash at home. We march very fast after we were across the river. We went into camp about 8 o'clock at night. I was very tired and very much vexed and the long day passed away.

---

[50] A sutler was an army peddler who followed the soldiers in the field and supplied them with an array of personal items such as tobacco, stationery, snack foods, etc.

Tuesday, May 24, 1864

The morning was very pleasant and the forenoon was very warm. It set in and rained all the forepart of the night. The afternoon was cloudy. Nothing of any importance transpired today. The boys helped themselves to all kinds of vegetable they could find in the vicinity of the camp. The mail did not come today. The boys were engaged in all kinds of amusements. I had touch of the chronic diarrhea today. I feel very weak and mean and thus the day passed away in all its beauteousness.

Wednesday, May 25, 1864

The night was warm and it rained occasionally through the night. This morning was very unpleasant and I felt very unwell. I attended surgeon's call for medicine for the diarrhea. The day was cool and cloudy. The mail did not come in today. We drew one day's rations. Along in the evening we heard very heavy cannonading in the front. The result is unknown to us now. Nothing of any note has transpired in camp worth mentioning. No late news from the Army of the Potomac.

Thursday, May 26, 1864

The morning was a pleasant one, it rained some through the night. We received orders to march at sunrise. We moved out of camp and the roads were very slippery and in some places it was very muddy. We had a hard march. Our road lay over a broken piece of country, as poor a country as I ever saw. I was covered with heavy pine timber. We went into camp about 8 o'clock in the evening. I was very tired and much fatigued. We are about 35 miles from Atlanta Ga. Our division was left back as train guards.

Friday, May 27, 1864

The night was warm and I had a good night's rest. The morning is clear and cool. The sun is out very bright. We march out of camp about ten o'clock and marched about 6 miles. We were guarding a train to the front. We march back almost to where we started in this morning and went into camp for the night. I was somewhat tired and a good night's rest revived me very much. We drew beef today. No mail came in today.

Saturday, May 28, 1864

The morning was clear and the day was very warm. Heavy cannonading was heard along the front this morning. We are now about 30 miles from Atlanta. Our front is about six miles ahead of us. We moved out of camp about 12 o'clock P.M. and marched about two miles farther to the front and went into camp for the night. There was heavy skirmishing all day, today. The mail come in but I did not receive anything from the north and the day wore away in all its glory.

Sunday, May 29, 1864

The morning was very pleasant, the day was very warm. The roads are very dirty and it is hard marching for the dust we have. We have good water on our road now all the time. We march out of camp at 11 o'clock today and march toward Kingston. We went into camp at a place called Burnt Hickory. No mail come in today. We received good news from the Potomac army. The day closes with us very pleasant and merry.

Monday, May 30, 1864

The night was warm. I had a good night's rest. The sun rose in the morning very bright. The day was very warm and we laid in camp all day. The boys brought in several hogs and some beef. We drew three day's rations. We have all the rations we want excepting beef. It is tolerably scarce at the present time.

There has been skirmishing along the lines today. The mail did not come in today and so the day passed away in peace.

Tuesday, May 31, 1864

The morning was very pleasant, the day was warm. We could hear occasional shots fired along the line. We are about six miles from the front. The mail did not come in today, I sent one home to father. While we are in this camp, the woodticks were very thick and bothered the boys considerable. I had the luck to get poisoned, my health otherways is very fine at the present time. We are in the gold region of Georgia. The surface of the ground is covered with isinglass.

Wednesday, June 1, 1864

The morning was very pleasant, the day very warm. We received orders to march at one. We move out at the above time mentioned. We moved to the extreme left of our line of battle. There was heavy fighting today and last night. We marched about ten miles today. My health is good, my poison was some better then it was yesterday. The poison, sumac is very plenty here. I rode today in the ambulance. The roads are very dusty and the weather continues to be very dry and warm.

Thursday, June 2, 1864

The night was warm, the morning was pleasant and toward noon it clouded up and rained very heavy all afternoon. I was completely soaked through to the skin. We move to the front and relieved Johnson's division. We have good breastworks here. The skirmishers have kept up a continued firing all the time till night. Once awhile through the night you could hear musketry along the lines. I had a good night's rest and my health is good.

Friday, June 3, 1864

The morning was cloudy and cool. Skirmishing is kept up all the time. Along about noon it rained a shower, then the sun came out very warm. You could hear the roar of cannon to the right and left of our position. We worked on our entrenchments today. The mail did not come in today. We are tolerably slim in rations now. We have been carrying three or four days rations for some time. Along in the morning it clouded up and rained some. The skirmishing was kept up all night strong.

Saturday, June 4, 1864

The night was very damp and disagreeable. The morning was very wet and the rain was falling. We are laying here in line behind our entrenchments. Yet there has been heavy skirmishing all the time. The mail did not come in, but we can send mail out. The Rebels have heavy works here and fight very stubbornly to hold the ground. The country is very poor here. Forage [livestock and other food stuffs generally acquired from the civilian population, with or without payment] *is tolerably scarce around here. It rained several showers through the day but the sun went down clear.*

Sunday, June 5, 1864

The morning was very cloudy and wet and muddy. The skirmishing is still going in good style. About ten o'clock P.M. the Rebels left their works in front of us. There was some firing could be heard through the day. The mail did not come in today. The clouds disappear and the sun comes out very warm. The mud dries up very fast. My health is very good at the present time. I have not heard from home for some time and so the day passes away in all its glory and peacefulness.

204

Monday, June 6, 1864

The morning was very pleasant. We marched out of camp about 8 o'clock. We marched a northeast course all day. We went into camp about 6 o'clock in the evening. I was very much fatigued and my clothes were all wet with sweat. I was out of hardtack and sowbelly. The roads are in good condition for marching. The country we are in now is tolerably good. I saw some Rebs, prisoners today. They said they were tired of fighting against the government.

Tuesday, June 7, 1864

The night was warm, the morning pleasant. I had a poor night's rest. My health is very good at the present time. We went into camp here and built good summer bunks as if we would stay here some time. The water is very handy here and plenty of it. The mail did not come in today. We drew rations this evening. They came in very good play here. I was very hungry. The weather is very warm and sultry, so much so that I go all the time with my coat off. I hauled off my pants for the first time last night.

Wednesday, June 8, 1864

The morning was warm, the day was pleasant. Showers fell frequently through the day. The mail come in today but I received nothing, as usually. We had orders read to us today to the effect of reducing two non-commissioned officers of our regiment in rank for stealing while the regiment was in front of the enemy, by orders of Colonel P. Gleason, Commander. The day was passed away by writing letters home and lolling around in the shade for rest, washing clothing without soap and so forth.

Thursday, June 9, 1864

The night was warm, the morning was pleasant. The weather is very warm now. The mail come in today. My health is very good at the present time. We had strict orders read to us today about straggling. We drew rations today. They are somewhat scarce at the present time. The health of the company is good. Tobacco is a very scarce article now. The country here is very poor. The timber is principally pine and oak. There are numbers of creeks and rivers through the country here.

Friday, June 10, 1864

The morning was cool and cloudy. We had marching orders. We moved out of camp at seven in fine glee and marched until about two o'clock in the afternoon and went into camp in view of the Rebels. Our batteries fired an occasional shot all day long. In the afternoon it commenced raining and all afternoon until evening and the clouds went away and the moon and the stars shown very bright. My hardtack is very scarce at the present. I went to bed with a light heart.

Saturday, June 11, 1864

The night was clear and warm, the morning cloudy. It set in and rained showers all through the day. We moved camp about 7 o'clock P.M. and marched about one half mile to the left and went into camp but did not get to stay the night over there. About 3 o'clock A.M. we moved out of camp. We moved farther to the front, pitched tents for the second time in scarce one hour; we struck tents and moved farther to the left and went into camp about 11 o'clock A.M.

Sunday, June 12, 1864

The morning was cloudy and it was raining and continued to rain all day. The mud from six inches to two feet deep everywhere you might go; you would be in the mud. All we could do was to build fires and dry our clothes the best we could. Skirmishing was kept up all the time. There was heavy cannonading along the line. We lay some two miles west of the railroad here in line for fight if the Rebs come.

Monday, June 13, 1864

The night was very disagreeable. It rained all night and I was tired, wet and wore out when I arose in the morning. The sky was dark and the atmosphere was heavy. The roads are intolerably muddy and are getting worse all the time. The boys will stand around and sing and the rain pouring down. For all that our grub is very scarce with us. The Rebels are determined to contend for every inch of ground we gain. The mail did not come in today, and still it rains all the time.

Tuesday, June 14, 1864

The morning was clear and the sun rises in all his glory. We had orders to march at six o'clock A.M. but did not move until 10 o'clock A.M. We moved to the front and skirmished with the Rebels until night. There were several wounded in our regiment and one killed in company F. His name was Henry Irwin. While the skirmish was going on, our main lines were building breastworks. The day was cool and pleasant. Grub continues to be scarce.

Wednesday, June 15, 1864

The night was warm. I did not feel very well this morning. The day was warm. Skirmishing was kept up all day. I could see our shells burst up along the mountain, our men were shelling a wagon train. They succeeded in exploding several caissons, at least we thought so by the cloud of smoke that come up through the timber. We move our line to the right, some two miles and throwed up more entrenchments at night.

Thursday, June 16, 1864

The morning was clear. The skirmishing was again on all the time. Our men just more than shelled the Rebels today. I never heard such a furore. We could see the Rebels taking their train to our right. Our batteries were playing on them all the time. My health is tolerably good at the present time. The mail come in today. The mud dried up some but the signs for more rain are very good. The boys here are in good spirits.

Friday, June 17, 1864

The night was warm. I did not sleep much last night. This morning is very pleasant. Skirmishing was resumed early this morning. Artillery firing was very heavy today. We moved forward one-half mile at one o'clock to a position in our front, throwed up heavy entrenchments. I was very tired. The weather was fair. Firing could be heard along the whole line. Our right wing is pushing the Rebs very fast. Our lines are in the shape of a half circle.

Saturday, June 18, 1864

The morning was very wet and disagreeable. It rained very hard in the night and early in the morning. We moved forward about 7 o'clock. We marched about a half mile and threw up more works. We were in a desperate mud hole, our company in the worst place. The skirmish was very hot. There were a good many men killed and wounded, one in Company C.; John Busey in the right arm. The roar of artillery was loud and awful.

Sunday, June 19, 1864

The morning was very wet. The mud was of various depths, from one inch to three feet deep. We had orders to move at once about the hours of 9 or ten o'clock and moved to the front where the Rebels were strongly entrenched. In the rear of their works, every tree and grub was full of our bullets. We flanked the

206

position at the point. *We were drawn up in line in full view of the Rebs. They are on the mountain [Kennesaw Mountain]. We moved from this position farther to the left and entrenched for the night.*

Monday, June 20, 1864

The morning was very wet and the rain continues to fall. The roads are almost impassable for our teams. There has been more heavy cannonading today than ever I heard before at one time. Our shells would burst on the very top of the mountain. The Rebels shell more today than they have since we left Resaca. They have a very strong position here for artillery. The mail did not come in today. I had my shirt hit today by a ball from a Reb and the day was noisy.

Tuesday, June 21, 1864

The morning is warm and the sun is out, but it is very muddy. There has been very heavy cannonading today. The Rebels replied very sharp to our batteries. We strengthened our works today. I was not very well. I took medicine for the diarrhea and kidney complaint. The mail did not come in. It rained showers through the day, enough to be disagreeable for us. I could see the Rebs very plain through a glass from our camp. We are faced here nearly east. We have been here one day in camp. It affords me much rest to camp once more.

Wednesday, June 22, 1864

The morning was warm and it continued through the day until dark. The joke turned, the Rebs shelled us good today but did not do us much damage; only it kept us close to our works. The cannonading on both sides was very heavy and the skirmishers are busy all the time. The mail come in but as usual none for me. We have had no official news from the Potomac Army. The mud is disappearing fast. We have plenty of good water and enough to eat.

Thursday, June 23, 1864

The morning finds us somewhat further to the left and building breastworks. I spent a sleepless night. I was very badly used up with the diarrhea. The boys are in good spirits. The Rebels opened on us last night and shelled us very hard today, but there was no one hurt in our regiment. The mail come in today. I am not well. I took some medicine, it helped me very little. Our company was detailed on picket this evening. Firing was heavy today.

Friday, June 24, 1864

The morning was very pleasant, the day hot. The sun come down as though he would burn us up. The Rebels on the mountains, Allotoona is the name of this mountain.[51] I believe they shelled us more on the left than in our front. Their sharpshooters are very busy all the time. The mail come in but I was among the unlucky ones of the band. The day was passed away, laying around under the shade of the forest. Our company has just returned.

Saturday, June 25, 1864

The morning was cool, the weather continues very warm and sultry. I attended surgeon's call this morning. The diarrhea troubles me a good deal at this time. The Rebels opened from the mountain with some dozen guns, but our batteries poked the shells in their forts; every shot so that they dried up in a hurry. The mail come in today. Skirmishing is kept up all the time. Nothing is heard from the Army of the Potomac.

---

[51] The Rebels were on Kennesaw Mountain, which is south of the Allatoona Mountain Range. This range is the southern most spur of the Appalachian Mountains.

Sunday, June 26, 1864

The morning was very pleasant, but the day was very hot. The Rebels were the quietest that they have been for some time. The mail come in today. The diarrhea has taken a strong hold on me again. I am taking some medicine. Along in the evening we had orders to move at 12 o'clock P.M. at night, but we marched about ten o'clock at night. We moved to the right and went into camp about two o'clock at night. I was wet with sweat and very tired from marching.

Monday, June 27, 1864   [The Battle of Kennesaw Mountain]

The morning finds us some four miles from where we were yesterday. We moved in to position in the rear of the 2nd division of our corps. We were hardly in our place when the 2nd division made a charge on the Rebels works at this point, with what success I am not able to tell yet; but there were several hundred killed and wounded. The day was as warm as ever I saw. The majority of our wounded were slightly wounded. Our division was not in the engagement today. We were held in reserve.[52]

Tuesday, June 28, 1864

The morning was cool, the day was intensely hot. Skirmishing is again on all the time. Heavy cannonading could be heard frequently through the daytime. The mail come in today but it brought no news for me. I saw in the Peru Republican that father [Benjamin Jr.] had met with a serious fall, but was doing well. I am still bothered with the diarrhea, which is not very agreeable on this campaign, and thus the warm day passed.

Wednesday, June 29, 1864

The morning was pleasant but the day was very hot. There was a cessation of hostilities today until our men could bury our dead. Our men and the Rebels were all together during the time of the flag of truce. When the time was up, a good many of them deserted and ran and jumped into our entrenchments. Our line of battle is in a stone's throw of the Rebel's works. Our works are at the foot of a hill and the Rebels are of the top of it. We are all massed up here together yet.

Thursday, June 30, 1864

The morning was clear and the day was very warm. Nothing of anything occurred today. The mail come in but with the same result as usual, nothing for me. Along in the evening, a mild shower fell. It cooled the air and it was pleasant. We received orders to move at dark and struck tents and at the appointed time we marched to the right about a mile to the right of where we were today and went into camp.

Friday, July 1, 1864

The morning was pleasant the day was very warm. Nothing unusual occurred today. The mail come in. Skirmishing was again on all day, but not so very strong as heretofore. I was unwell and attended surgeon's call for medicine for the diarrhea, which is very troublesome with me. We have a nice camp here. Water is somewhat unhandy but good when we get it. We have no late news from the Army of the Potomac. The boys are all glad to be in camp for a few days.

---

[52] The Battle of Kennesaw Mountain was the only engagement during the Atlanta Campaign where General Sherman tried to dislodge heavily entrenched Confederate troops by a frontal attack. This action created extremely high casualties for the Union army. Sherman never made that same mistake again.

Saturday, July 2, 1864

The morning was pleasant, the day was hot. The mail come in today. The skirmishing is still going on. We are taking it somewhat easy now. The Rebels say they intend to celebrate the Fourth of July by whipping us out of our works. Let them come on. That is what we want them to try. We think we will be rid of here and that the Rebels will make a permanent stand here. The weather is dry and the roads are full of dust. Every place that you would go is so.

Sunday, July 3, 1864

The morning is a pleasant one and the Rebs are still here. The skirmishing is very li ....

Thus ends, in mid-sentence, the 1864 portion of Charles F. Wallick's diary. The entries for July 4, through December 31, 1864, are missing.

Charles F. Wallick and the 87th Indiana Volunteer Infantry participated in the siege of Atlanta, GA, during July and August of 1864. In early September the Confederates abandoned "The Gateway of the South", and the Union army was left to occupy the Rebel's most important railway hub. By November General Sherman was ready to prove that the Union army could march anywhere it pleased within the Confederacy and that he could supply his army by living off the land. Sherman also set out to destroy everything he considered to be of military value in his "March to the Sea." Unfortunately, none of these months are included in the Walter Reyburn transcription of Charles F. Wallick's diary.

By January 1, 1865, the Federal army had accomplished its goal of devastating the Georgian heartland and it occupied the Atlantic coast port of Savannah. General Sherman then prepared to move into South Carolina and lay waste to what he considered, "The Cradle of the Rebellion." Charles' diary continues on January 1, 1865, while being posted north of Savannah, GA.

Sunday, January 1, 1865

This is New Year's Day. We had a very dry time in camp. The weather was very cold for the climate, there was no mail come to camp. Isaiah Shafer and myself bunk together in the camp. All the feast that Isaiah and I had was hardtack and sowbelly and sugar and coffee. We could get a good meal at a private house for a dollar a meal, other things sell accordingly around Chattanooga. I put in the best part of the day writing home and other places, New Years night passed very dry in camp.

Monday, January 2, 1865

The morning was cold, the day was pleasant. The mail did not come in. It does not come in regular now. There was nothing of importance occurred today. We are drilling twice a day now. My health is very good now. The boys are all in fine spirits. We are short of rations now on account of the obstructions in the [Savannah] river so that the boats cannot come up with supplies.

Tuesday, January 3, 1865

The morning was cold and the day was pleasant. There was nothing worthy of note occurred today. My health is good at this time and the boats are beginning to come up more every day. The mail does not come in regular yet. We have to buy rice from the citizens yet or go hungry. The town of Savannah is being cleaned up in style so it will be healthy for us next summer. They have started up a paper styled the Savannah Republican.

Wednesday, January 4, 1865

The morning was cold and the day was warm. No mail today. I have not heard from home for some time. We are having tolerable good times here. We have been on picket once since we have been here. We drill though every day. Company drill once a week. We drill brigade drills twice a week so the rest of the time we can go to town and walk around and look at the girls and other things fancy.

Thursday, January 5, 1865

The morning was cold, the day was warm. Nothing of importance transpired in camp today. The grub line is slim yet. The mail does not come in yet as it used to in the last campaign with Hood at Atlanta. The mail comes by New York and it takes from four to seven days to run from here with sail vessels to that point. We are receiving the news that General Thomas has defeated Hood and is pursuing his enemy.

Friday, January 6, 1865

The morning was cold and the day was pleasant. The mail did not come in, the news is that General Butler is pounding away at Fort Fisher on Cape Fear River in South Carolina. Grub is somewhat plentier than it has been for some time. The roads are very good now, the river has been very muddy since recent rain. We continue to drill company drills and have no good ground to drill on here.

Saturday, January 7, 1865

The morning was cold, the day was warm. The mail did not come in today. I have not heard from home since we left Kingston [November 14, 1864]. They have put up a bakery at government expense and are baking bread for us now. We still drill, I am tired of it. My health is good now, the health of the company is very good. We have only one man at the hospital and he is getting well as fast as he can I believe.

Sunday, January 8, 1865

The morning was cold and the day was warm. The mail come in and I received a letter from home. The folks were all well. Bill [Charles' brother] was out of the service, his time was out. My health is very good and the diarrhea has come back on me but is not very bad and does not hurt me as it did before. The time goes very slow. My old watch is not running, the matter is it is so dirty it can't run.

Monday, January 9, 1865

The morning was cold and the day warm. I wrote a couple of letters home and the mail come in and went out. It goes out every day. The rations are getting alright once more. My health is tolerably good and the diarrhea has not been very hard on my person yet. I have received several papers from Isaiah Shafer from Indianapolis. He was well the last I heard from him. The troops are all preparing to move at short notice. The clothing has come at last.

Tuesday, January 10, 1865

The morning was cold, the day the same. We did not drill today. We had inspection of arms at ten o'clock. I and the Boys put on all the style they could with dirty guns and old clothes. The clothing has come but not enough to supply the demand for it is almost impossible to get enough. Every man wants a new suit. He ought to have it for the time has come that men cannot stand everything. This is a long day to me.

Wednesday, January 11, 1865

The morning was cold and the day the same. The mail did not come in today. We had orders to draw two days rations and march at 7 o'clock in the morning. Just our brigade, we are going out about 8 miles to guard cattle. We do not like it very well. My health is good. Now the weather is the prettiest I ever saw in winter. The frogs are heard hollowing at various times through the day something unusual for me to hear them.

Thursday, January 12, 1865

The morning was cold, the day was the same. We marched out to where the cattle were and before we had our bunks fixed it set in and rained until dark then it turned cold and the night was very disagreeable being cold and windy. The mail did not come in. My health was good. I am now bunking with John Walker and he is alright for that purpose.

Friday, January 13, 1865

The morning was cold and windy. The mail did not come in. We move out on picket about one mile from the main road. We had a tolerably good time our time away while not on duty. We had an old darky to sing songs in the evening. He was a gay nigger and sure the time went fast. My health is good and my appetite is all right. Nothing is heard of the movements of [General] Thomas for a few days past.

Saturday, January 14, 1865

The morning was cold and the day was pleasant. We were relieved about 11 o'clock in the forenoon, we marched into camp and I was hungry. We drew rations, the mail did not come in. We had orders to be ready for picket by 8 o'clock in the morning. That made me mad. Just come off of duty and had to go on picket the next day. The time has been short since we took this ************** ----------.

Sunday, January 15, 1865

The morning was cold and the day was warm. The mail come in and I received a letter from Logansport from Isaiah Shafer. He sent me several since he left the company. We were out on picket and I had a good time of my part of the task. The day passed away and there was nothing of importance transpired. Thus another day has passed and gone and time swiftly speeds along. How true this is and how little it is thought of by mankind. So it is with better things.

Monday, January 16, 1865

The morning was cold and the day was warm. The mail did not come in. The whole regiment was on fatigue working on the fortifications around Savannah in its rear for its defense from land and water. Battery D. was up in town today. There was more business done than I ever saw in this, yet one day we had orders to be ready to march on the 18th and the boys first went bathing.

Tuesday, January 17, 1865

The mail come in. The morning was cold and the day was pleasant. I was well and was busy all day writing and booking up my diary. We had orders to march tomorrow but I think we would not move so soon. We got the news that [General] Butler was bombarding Fort Fisher on the Cape Fear River. He failed to take the fort and took the troops all back to Fortress Monroe, there was new troops moving at this point. I was not very well and that is not so good.

Wednesday, January 18, 1865

The morning was cold and the day was warm. The mail did not come in nor did we march either. I was well and had plenty to eat. I went to town to pass the day walking all over the place giving her a mere farewell view before I shall leave as I know we shall soon. We do not know where we will go yet or not. I do hate to leave out little bunks and warm fireplace in them. The boys are all right.

Thursday, January 19, 1865

The day was warm and the morning was cold. The mail did come in. I did not get any letters. I was well. Nothing of importance transpired in Com. C. today, only we had marching orders at 7 o'clock in the morning. That is what I dread is this campaign as it is now raining and the wet part of the season may set in now. If it should we would suffer some from the cold weather. I was at town and got dinner for $1.25. A meal that is not much for a soldier to pay.

Friday, January 20, 1865

The morning was cold and the day was warm. We marched out about 9 miles from the city and went into camp for the night. We received a very large mail but I did not get anything from it. Along in the afternoon it commenced raining and rained all the rest of the day and all night. I had a dry bed and rested very well and we drew rations about daylight and had orders to move at 7 o'clock but did not march.

Saturday, January 21, 1865

The morning was very foggy and dark and slowly passed. The rain continued to fall all day. The weather has set in very disagreeable and wet. The mail come in but brought nothing for me. We look for more mail soon. We are camped on a very dry place but firewood is very scarce. It is rumored that we will stay here for a few days. Rations are plenty now. My health is good. The day was long to me as we had to stay in our tents all the day long.

Sunday, January, 22, 1865

The morning was cold and wet. It rained all day. The mail came in and I received a letter from Bill. The folks were all well at home. There has been more rain in the last few days than there has been for a long time. My health is good. There was one of our recruits was hurt very bad by rassling [wrestling]. The sun came out for a short time then hid his face from view. The day was a dry one to me sure.

Monday, January 23, 1865

The morning was cold and the day was cold and cloudy and very disagreeable. The mail come in and I did not get any mail from home. I wrote a letter to Bill today. My health is good. The time passes way very fast with me. The weather turned colder. We think it will stop raining now for a while. We have no signs of moving soon now as everything is dubious. We are using pond water here to cook with and it is not very good for our health.

Tuesday, January 24, 1865

The morning was cold and the day was the same. The mail did not come in today. May health is good. Some of our boys were to town today. There was nothing of interest. The weather is turning colder. I could not sleep any on the account of being cold. The boys are all well and in good spirits. Nothing of importance transpired in camp. The time was passed away very quick this day with me.

Wednesday, January 25, 1865

The morning was cold and the day was chilly. We marched a seven o'clock and marched about 8 miles and went into the camp for the night. It was very cold and windy. We camped on an old Rebel's farm. His steam saw-mill was burnt down. He had some sorgum molasses. The boys there went for them. My bunkmate got enough to last us for several days. He had everything hid that he had.

Thursday, January 26, 1865

The morning was very cold and windy and continued all day. We marched out of camp at half past 7 o'clock. Our regiment and the 105th Ohio was train's guards. Today we marched about 9 miles and went into camp for the night. We have had no news of any importance from the city since. Still cold and windy.

Friday, January 27, 1865

The morning was cold and the day was windy. The mail did not come in. We broke camp at Springfield [GA] about 3 o'clock P.M. We crossed a very muddy slough and camped for the night. The night was cold. I was well but did not sleep much for it was very cold sleeping where I was sure. We have had no newspapers for a week or more. The forage is becoming plenty with all kinds of hogs and sheep.

Saturday, January 28, 1865

The morning was cold and the day was warm. There was a detail come from the regiment to cross the river and build a road across a very large and mean swamp. There was also a detail sent out for forage. The mail did not come in. I had my clothes washed today. Nothing can be learned of the Rebs movement around here nor any place else. My health is good.

Sunday, January 29, 1865

The morning was cold and the day was windy. We did not march, we laid in camp. The mail did not come in. No news from the north. Nothing of importance transpired in camp today. Forage is tolerably plenty. The country is very poor here in places. The times are good now. We do not suffer very much with the cold. The weather is changing warmer today. We are here cleaning up camp as if we would stay here some time.

Monday, January 30, 1865

The morning was cold and the day was very windy and cold. We had marching orders to march and we moved out about 9 o'clock and marched in the direction of the Savannah River. We marched about nine miles and went into camp at Sisters Ferry about 35 miles above the City of Savannah. The mail did not come in. The night is cold and I did not rest very well. My health is good.

Tuesday, January 31, 1865

The morning was cold, the day was warm. The mail did not come in yet nothing of importance occurred in camp today. The time was spent cleaning up camp and policing the grounds. The water here is pond water. It seems very healthy for the health of the company is good. I was down to the river today. There was a steamer laying there at the landing. The time wore away very slow.

Wednesday, February 1, 1865

The morning was cold and the day was warm. The mail come in but I did not receive anything from home. Nothing of interest occurred in camp. My health is very good. We had squad drill today. The old soldiers did not drill. We have heavy fatigue duty at this time. The boys are in fine spirits and ready for the ensuing campaign. The mail did not go out today.

Thursday, February 2, 1865

The morning was cold and the day was warm. The mail come in and I received a letter from Isaiah Shafer. He was well and he sent me an Indianapolis paper. I was very glad to hear from him. He is well. We had company drill today. The regiment was nearly all on fatigue down at the river unloading rations and forage, expecting to move soon. My health is very good.

Friday, February 3, 1865

The morning was cold and the day was warm and showery. It clouded up and rained in the after part of the day. The mail did not come in today. We had a Savannah paper in camp today. The rumor is prevalent that the port of Wilmington [N.C.] had been evacuated by the Rebels. Nothing of importance occurred in camp today of note. My health is excellent at the present time.

Saturday, February 4, 1865

The morning was cold and the day was cloudy. The mail did not come in. The talk in camp is that we will cross the river soon. My health is good. The order came around in the evening that we would cross in the morning at 6 o'clock probable. We had company drill today. The boys do not like to drill as their time is so near out. We have had no news from any source for some time. All is quiet here.

Sunday, February 5, 1865

The morning was damp, it had rained during the night. The day was pleasant. We pulled up stakes and marched across the river on pontoons. We saw some of the torpedoes[53] that our men had found and had stuck up a sign so our men would not run on them. I saw the worst road I ever saw in my life. The swamps had to be corduroyed before we could get over. We marched about two miles from the ferry and went into camp.

Monday, February 6, 1865

The morning was cold and the day was windy. The mail did not come in today. We drew one days rations. We laid in camp all day. Along in the after part of the day it set in and rained until night and all night the wind kept blowing all the time and it was very cold and disagreeable. We had plenty of rations and my bunkmate went out a foraging today. He brought in a fine lot of meat. He was very tired and wet, but the trip paid him sure.

Tuesday, February 7, 1865

The Morning was cold and raining. We had orders to march at 7o'clock but the road was the worst. We marched about eight miles and then went into the camp for the night. We passed through a small town by the name of Crawfordsville and we passed another by the name of Brighton. It rained all forenoon, then turned cold. The roads were very muddy, as bad as I ever saw in my life. The mail did not come, we can send no more mail out now.

Wednesday, February 8, 1865

The mail come in this morning. I received a letter from father and said they were all well at home. The morning was cold and windy and the day the same. I received an Indianapolis paper sent by Isaiah Shafer. Our regiment was detailed as train [guards] today. We moved out of camp at about 8 o'clock and marched about 6 miles and went into camp for the night. We were in camp by one o'clock P.M. We had all the forage we wanted to carry and use for one day sure.

---

53 A torpedo during the Civil War was a stationary submerged naval mine, not a self-propelled explosive.

Thursday, February 9, 1865

The morning was cold and the day was warm. We marched out of camp about eight o'clock A.M. and marched about 18 miles and went into the camp for the night. I was very tired. It was a very bad march as with the train. Yet our company and H were detailed to help the wagons over the mudholes and bad swamps. The men stand the cold weather very well but we nearly all have a bad cold. Myself for one has got the worst cold I ever had in the service I believe.

Friday February 10, 1865

The morning was cold and the day was windy. We marched about six miles and went into camp. The road was tolerably good, the sand is nearly shoemouth deep in the road. The wind blew and it was very cold on account, a tolerable good night's rest. We had orders to march at 7 o'clock A.M. The forage was plenty chickens were brought into camp for all were out. I had a very bad cold and sore eyes

Saturday, February 11, 1865

The morning was cold and the day was windy. I was well excepting a bad cold. We crossed a stream of some size, the name I did not learn. We passed through a town by the name of Barnwell and took dinner there. We laid in the town for several hours, then moved out about three miles and went into camp for the night. The country is very level here and tolerably good, the soil is too sandy here for wheat.

Sunday, February 12, 1865

The morning was cold and the day was warm. We marched out of camp at about half past eight o'clock and marched all day very hard. We crossed the Charleston Road and it had all been taken up and destroyed. We went into camp about sundown on a side hill and had a good night's sleep. I had a very bad cold and the boys all have it very bad. The weather has been very bad for laying out in the woods on this trip sure.

Monday, February 13, 1865

The morning was cold and the day was pleasant. We had orders to march at 7 A.M., and did not until about noon; then we crossed a river by the name of the South Edisto and went into camp. There was a detail made out of our regiment to help the teams through the swamps and cross the river. Our regiment is train guard, yet our division come back to act as train guards and so forth.

Tuesday, February 14, 1865

The morning was cold and the day was pleasant until about noon, then it set in and rained all the rest of the day and froze ice on the timber, the water froze on my gun as it fell. The road was tolerably good. We crossed the North Edisto River and went into camp for the night. I was in camp about one hour before the Company got in and had a lot of wood and a good fire for them. I was ringing wet sure.

Wednesday, February 15, 1865

The morning was cold and wet, the day was cloudy. We marched at 7 o'clock and on the way we saw a man that had been accidentally shot. We passed over a very hilly and rugged country. The road was down hill all the day long. We marched all day very hard and went into camp after dark. We drew rations, one days rations to do three days. The forage is plenty, we live fat off the country.

---

[54] The regiment was already burning its way through South Carolina.

Thursday, February 16, 1865

The morning was cold and the day was warm. We are train guards yet. Companies C. and I. went out a foraging and the rest was put along the trains at various points as guards. We passed through a town by the name of Texington [Lexington, SC]. We laid here long enough to get dinner then took up our line of march for Columbia, the Capital of the state. We went into camp about 7 miles from the city. We had all the potatoes we wanted to eat.

Friday, February 17, 1865

The morning was cold, the day was warm. We marched about ten miles and crossed a river by the name of Salude and passed by Columbia to the right. The roads were very bad. The country is, have been covered with pine, cedar and oak timber. It is not so sandy here as it was in Georgia away very fast with me. I saw more fires since I have been in this State than I in the service.

Saturday, February 18, 1865

The morning was cold, the day was warm. We marched out of camp at noon and marched until after dark and went into camp. I was very tired, my health was good. We drew three days rations of Coffee and sugar but no bread. We are living off the country. Hogs and bacon are plenty and forage of every kind is here in abundance. We had a mess of flapjacks for supper and fresh pork also. Everything is going off fine with all of us.

Sunday, February 19, 1865

The morning was cold the day was warm. We marched out of camp about noon and marched to the river and crossed on the pontoons, the name of the river was Broad River. It was a very large stream. We camped on a large plantation and he had a large crib of corn which our mules needed very much and they got it too. We had orders every night to march at 7 o'clock. We are train guards yet no more.

Monday, February 20, 1865

The morning was cold and the day was warm. We marched at 9 o'clock A.M. and marched about 7 miles and went into camp at 3 o'clock for the night. We had plenty to eat, we drew some clothing here. Forage is very plenty here. The country is very rugged and hilly, more so than I have seen any where for a year. The soil is not so sandy but more clay. The roads are tolerable bad and if it would rain it would stop us.

Tuesday, February 21, 1865

The morning was cold and the day was warm. We marched about 12 o'clock P.M. and went into camp for the night. I did not rest very well, the night was cold; and a heavy dew fell. We are train guards yet. The country is very hilly yet and the forage is not so plenty. Hogs, bacon and beef are plenty but flour and meal are scarce. My health is good at this time. I am better of my cold.

Wednesday, February 22, 1865

The morning was cold and the day was warm. We marched at 8 o'clock A.M. and marched about 7 miles and went into camp for the night. We had very bad and rough roads to pass over. The country is very hilly. We drew one day's rations to last until we get more. The forage is tolerable plenty here. My health is good. We have some of the gayest letters that I ever saw. We captured them from the citizens around here.

Thursday, February 23, 1865

The morning was cold, the day was cloudy; and along in the evening it set in and rained all night. Our company did not get in until 7 o'clock at night. I did not get in until morning. It was so bad, that is the roads, that the boys had to push all the wagons up the worst hill in the business. I sleep on three rails with my rubber blanket over me. It was rough. Sure it rained all the time straight down.

Friday, February 24, 1865

The morning was wet and the rain was falling and kept it up all day. I went to camp about daylight. We had tolerable plenty of rations but the signs are good for a scarce time. We marched out of camp and went up another hill and went into camp for the night. It stopped raining enough to get supper then it set in and rained all night. We had a tolerable good place to sleep but did not sleep much.

Saturday, February 25, 1865

The morning was wet and cold, the rain was yet falling. The roads were horrible. We had to carry rails a half mile to bridge the road so the trains could pass over it. We cross the Pataco River on the pontoons. It was a large stream here. We went through the muddiest road I ever saw, we had to bridge the road all the way with poles and rails and brush and the men tore old houses down and put them on the track.

Sunday, February 26, 1865

The morning was clear, the day was dry and warm. The mud dried up some. We laid in camp all day. I was well and very glad to get a days rest. The river raised very fast and washed our pontoons down the river. We had orders if we did not get across in such a time we should burn our trains and come on with the mules. We are train guards yet we are very scarce of grub and forage is hard to find. We are in good spirits and hope for the better.

Monday, February 27, 1865

The morning was cold, the day was cloudy. We laid in camp, we drew rations and had something to eat. Company C. went out foraging for corn. I was well. The roads are not much better and it is beginning to rain again. This evening, the wagons are all over now and we will line out tomorrow. Expect we have put things through all the time until we got into this country. We are in clay and hills.

Tuesday, February 28, 1865

The morning was cold and the rain was falling, the day was very foggy. Companies H and E went out after forage. The rumor is in camp that Charleston is evacuated and that General Grant had cleared out old Lee again but we can not hear anything reliable about anything that happens out of our sight. We are with the train, we are assisted by the 82 Ind. Vols. to get the train along the roads almost impassable for man or beast.

Wednesday, March 1, 1865

The morning was cold and wet, the rain was falling. We had orders to march at daylight. We took up our line of march about 7 o'clock A.M. and went in an eastern direction. We traveled over very bad roads. Today we went into camp at Hanging Rock on the old battlefield of Hanging Rock where the British were defeated.[55] We had a good dry place to camp. It rained all day until the afternoon then it quit raining, once more.

---

[55] The Battle of Hanging Rock was fought on August 6, 1780, one mile south of Heath Springs, South Carolina.

Thursday, March 2, 1865

The morning was cold and the day was cold and the rain fell by showers all day. We marched over some bad roads and some very good roads for this country. We marched about 16 miles and went into camp after dark. We had a tolerable good camp and I rested very well. We had nothing hardly to eat. We have been delayed at the river, that is our corps, and the other troops got the start of us for the next river.

Friday, March 3, 1865

The morning was cold and the day was cold and the rain fell by showers all day until evening. We marched all day and until 9 o'clock at night. We marched about 14 miles. The road was tolerable good and we made good head way. The country here in places is very sandy and the roads are good here but where the soil is clay then the roads are horrible. We had but little to eat for supper. The night was windy and I did not rest very well.

Saturday, March 4, 1865

The morning was cold and windy. The day was rainy and the roads were very bad. The country here is covered with little black oak, grubs and the soil is clay. We crossed the State line into North Carolina. We camped about five miles from the line. We marched about 12 miles and until after dark. We had a good camp and I rested fine. The sky was clear and it was moonlight. We went to bed at 11 o'clock at night.

Sunday, March 5, 1865

The morning was cold and the day was warm. We marched at about 10 o'clock A.M. and marched within 1 mile of the Big Pedee River and went into camp for the night. I was well and in fine spirits. We are train guards yet. The pontoon bridge is not down yet, the river is very wide and swift. The Rebels had some large shells in store for us, having no occasion to use them on us we found them and blowed them up entirely.

Monday, March 6, 1865

The morning was cold and the day was warm. We laid in camp today. The bridge was not completed until near dark. I washed my clothes today, that was a shirt and pocket handkerchief. I did not run about much today but sleep nearly half my time. The weather has been very nice for several days now. The time passes away very slow now with me as the marching is so hard and so much of it.

Tuesday, March 7, 1865

The morning was cold and the day was warm. We crossed the Pedee river in North Carolina about 10 miles from the State line. We went into camp about nine miles east of the river. The roads are very good and we marched very fast. Forage is not very plenty in this part of the country as the land is too poor to produce well. It is all nearly sand, it is the poorest state we have been in since we started from Nashville, Tennessee, I do believe.

Wednesday, March 8, 1865

The morning was cold and the day was warm and it rained along in the afternoon and continued to rain until 10 o'clock at night. We were very much fatigued. The roads were very good. We got into camp at 9 o'clock. I was very much out of humor. We had several foragers captured a few days ago among them was a member of Company C. He was Phillip Coon, of Mexico [Miami Co. Indiana]. He is missed in the Company.

Thursday, March 9, 1865

The morning was cold and the day was cold and it rained nearly all the afternoon and for two hours after dark. Our company was out foraging. We did not get into camp until about 9 o'clock at night. We had very bad roads and the train did not get into camp at all. I had crackers, coffee and meat for supper. Grub is tolerable scarce. I can see here how they tap the pine trees for turpentine, tar and pitch.

Friday, March 10, 1865

The morning was cold and the day was wet and the rain fell in torrents upon us. We marched about 7 miles and went into camp about 11 o'clock for the night. We had a good rest. We are on the Fayetteville plank road within 14 miles from the town we expect to go to tomorrow if things go right. The Cape Fear River is at this town. I am well and hearty, the men are in good health.

Saturday, March 11, 1865

The morning was cold and the day was fine. We marched to town. Our men drove the Rebels out of the place today and hoisted the stars and stripes over the courthouse in the city. We are camped in the edge of the place, it is a large place and the steamboats run up to it all the time the year round. We have all the sweet potatoes we want for supper. I am well and sound. The time goes fast.

Sunday, March 12, 1865

The morning was cold and the day was warm. Our foragers brought in a large amount of hens and chickens and two Johnnies as prisoners. We laid in camp today. The day was passed away in sleeping and resting our weary bones. The City of Fayetteville is a large town and has a great number of plank roads running into it. The Cape Fear River here is very narrow, but deep. Small steamers run up here all the time.

Monday, March 13, 1865

The morning was cold and the day was warm. We marched at 7 o'clock A.M. and crossed the river Birring first through the city, which was about 1½ miles long. We crossed and went into camp close by the supply trains. We are train guards yet, the division, that is the 3rd, is doing provost duty in the city. The people are very friendly. Our company went out foraging today and they all got drunk on cider that they found on their way.

Tuesday, March 14, 1865

The morning is cold, the day was warm and pleasant. We laid in camp. The convalescents were all sent down the river to Wilmington. We had all the forage we wanted to eat at this time. The Fifteenth and Seventeenth Army Corps are crossing the river today. The river is falling very fast. There were two or three steamboats come up the river since we have been here. I am well and in good health. The boys are all well in Company C.

Wednesday, March 15, 1865

The morning was cold and the day was warm, along in the afternoon it commenced raining and while it was at that the bugle sounded, strike tents, in less time than a half and hour we was on the road for Goldbara [Goldsboro, NC]. We went into camp after dark and it was still raining. Yet we come about six miles and the road was very bad. The whole way had to be bridged with poles and fence rails. The Twentieth Corps is ahead of us with the train.

Thursday, March 16, 1865

The morning was very disagreeable and wet. The rain ceased in the night sometime but the sky was yet cloudy and it rained during the day. We marched out of camp at daylight and marched about two or three miles and went into camp at 3 P.M. We struck tents and marched until dark. Afterwards it rained very hard but quit before bed time. We camped in a very bushy place.

Friday, March 17, 1865

The morning was cold and the day was clear. We marched out of camp very early and traveled until 9 o'clock at night. The roads were passable, the ambulances and empty wagons went to the South River to bring our wounded as there had been some hard fighting done. We were so far that we could not hear the cannonading. We do not know at this time the troops that were engaged in it. I am yet well and hearty.

Saturday, March 18, 1865

The morning was cold and the day was warm. We marched across South River and marched about 6 miles from the river and went into camp for the night. Company C. went out foraging. They had a very hard tramp of it. The road is very bad and swampy. It has to be all bridged before we can get our trains over. We are train guards yet. We can hear from the front of a hard fight but cannot anything authentic.

Sunday, March 19, 1865   [The Battle of Bentonville]

The morning was cold and the day was warm. The train moved out at about 9 o'clock A.M. and we marched about 8 or 9 miles and went into camp for the night. The roads were some better. I was well and in good health. The foragers have not come in for several days. The Rebels are now in front in force. There has been some very hard fighting, but we were so far off that we could not hear it from where the train was.

Monday, March 20, 1865

The morning was cold and the day was warm. The foragers come in with all the corn meal they could carry on their horses. We marched at 7 o'clock and crossed a very bad slough and went into camp for the night but moved out at about noon and marched all day. It clouded up and rained very hard until dark. We camped on a knoll and field.

Tuesday, March 21, 1865

The morning was cold and the day was pleasant. We marched out of camp very early and marched all day. We are with the supply train yet. Some of the boys have seen men from the Twenty-third Army Corps. They said we would go into camp and rest for a while at Goldsbara 10 miles from here. There has been very hard fighting in the campaign along South river. The time passes very fast with me. I am well and healthy.

Wednesday, March 22, 1865

The morning was clear and cold, the day was warm. We moved out of camp at 2 o'clock in the morning and crossed a very bad slough for a beginning, we marched until about three o'clock in the afternoon. We went into camp about 8 miles from the town. We had some corn meal, our mess had some old corn bread. We were ordered to stay here for six days and do guard duty.

Thursday, March 23, 1865

The morning was cold and the day was very windy and we could hardly keep our tents from blowing down. It was very disagreeable, the air being full of fine sand. We are laying in camp now guarding the things that the train left here. It went to Kingston [Kinston, NC] *after rations 30 miles from this place. The troops have commenced coming into town. The Rebels have retreated toward Raleigh in haste.*

Friday, March 24, 1865

The morning was cold and the day was very windy. We laid in camp until after dark, then about 7 o'clock we pulled up stakes and crossed Ruse River [Neuse River?] and went into camp for the night. We crossed on the pontoons. The night was very cold and a very heavy frost fell. We were 3 miles from town. I am well and feel alright.

Saturday, March 25, 1865

The morning was cold and the day was warm and pleasant. We marched into town and went into camp on the north side of the place. Goldsboro [spelled correctly this time in the diary] *is a very nice place. It has two railroads and one river running but it and tolerable good country. The town is surrounded by the Yanks. The cars come in already. We have not got our mail yet but it will be not long coming now as the cars are alright.*

Sunday, March 26, 1865

The morning was cold and the day was pleasant. We were very busy building up comfortable bunks as we expect to stay here for some time. The mail come in. I received a letter from father. They were all well at home, also received one from my old schoolmate. My health is good at this time. The mail will come in now regular as the cars will run in every day.

Monday, March 27, 1865

The morning was pleasant and the day was warm. I wrote a letter to father, the mail come in. The day was spent in washing our old dirty clothing. We have not drawn any clothing yet but will draw tomorrow. It is very pleasant to be in camp once more. We have roll call twice a day and no drill yet. The water is very good here and handy to camp. Our wood is green pine and oak, it burns poorly.

Tuesday, March 28, 1865

The morning was warm and pleasant. The day was cloudy and warm. The mail come in. Had a buggy ride for the first time I have been in the service. We rode all over the City of Goldsboro in fifteen minutes, the came back to camp. I am in good health. We have plenty to eat now. We drew clothing today but not enough for all of us lads.

Wednesday, March 29, 1865

The morning was cool and the day was warm. We were busy doing nothing all day. The mail come in, the time passes away very fast with me. We have not got very good bunks here. The boards were very scarce. We can not get any late papers to read here. The news is in camp that we will be paid off here before we start out on another campaign. That would suit me very much indeed to have some monies once more. We are in fine spirits and health.

Thursday, March 30, 1865

The morning was cold and the day was warm and pleasant. I wrote a letter to a friend. The mail come in but I did not receive any mail. My health is good and I hope to the almighty God that it may remain so and that I may be permitted to return home again. There was nothing of importance transpired in camp today worthy of note. The weather remains very fine and warm. The boys are lively and full of fun.

Friday, March 31, 1865

I witnessed a sight today I never wish to see again, that was the shooting of a soldier for inhuman conduct. The court sentenced him to be shot for the third offence. There were a great many lookers on and one brigade of infantry formed three sides and he was shot in the center. The boys did not like to see it, although it may be for the best. It is not for me to decide.

Saturday, April 1, 1865

The morning was cold and the day was warm and pleasant. The mail come in but I did not receive any letters or papers. The boys were telling one another all the day the old rig of April Fool's day on hand. Plenty to eat and we drew rations today, 5 days ahead. The rations are being run in here very fast on the river as far as Kinston and on the railroad to this place the wagon trains are kept in motion all the time from here to Kinston.

Sunday, April 2, 1865

The morning was cold and the day was pleasant. The mail come in. Nothing of note occurred in camp today.

Monday, April 3, 1865

The morning was pleasant. The mail come in. Nothing of importance occurred today except Isaiah Shafer come up.

Tuesday, April 4, 1865

The morning was cool and the day was warm and fine. General Schofield reviewed our division today. The mail come in.

Wednesday, April 5, 1865

The morning was fine and the day was pleasant. We commenced drilling two hours a day.

Thursday, April 6, 865

The morning was pleasant. We had one drill. The mail come in, nothing for me. My health is fine at present.

Friday, April 7, 1865

The morning was fine and the day was pleasant. We drilled our two hours. The mail come in. The news here is that Richmond is taken and 25, 000 prisoners are captured and a great number of guns. The time goes fast.

Saturday, April 8, 1865

We remained in camp. The mail come in. Nothing for me. We had orders to be ready to go on picket in the morning. All quiet.

Sunday, April 9, 1865

We went on picket and were relieved at dark. The Twenty-third Corps camped on the picket line.

Monday, April 10, 1865

We marched at 5 A.M. about 12 miles and camped. We skirmished with the Rebel all day. It was very windy and it rained all day.

Tuesday, April 11, 1865

The morning was wet. The rain was falling in the morning. We marched at daylight. Our brigade was in the front. The 75th Indiana Vols. skirmished with the Rebel cavalry all day. We took the town of Smithfield and camped there 1 night. The Rebels burned the bridge. We put down pontoons to cross.

Wednesday, April 12, 1865   [Receives news of General Lee's surrender]

We received a dispatch from Grant that Lee had surrendered his whole force to him. We marched about 14 miles and went into camp for the night. We're within 13 miles of Raleigh. The time goes fast.

Thursday, April 13, 1865

We marched through the city of Raleigh and camped at this place one night. It was a fine place. It rained all day. The roads were muddy.

Friday, April 14, 1865

We marched out of camp and marched about 10 miles from Raleigh. I wrote a letter home to father.

Saturday, April 15, 1865

We marched about 5 miles and went into camp for the night. The roads were bad.

Sunday, April 16, 1865

We marched about 8 miles and went into camp.

Monday, April 17, 1865

We laid in camp, nothing of importance.

Tuesday, April 18, 1865   [Receives news of President Lincoln's assassination]

We laid in camp. Company C. went out foraging. They brought in all the sweet potatoes we wanted to use and sorghum molasses also and other things. We received the orders that President Lincoln had been assassinated in a theater and the other officials had been fixed upon for the same fate.

Thursday, April 20, 1865

Nothing of note.

Friday, April 21, 1865

All is quiet in camp.

Thus ends the wartime diary of Charles F. Wallick.

Appendix II

Orders of Battle
for the Wallick Soldiers

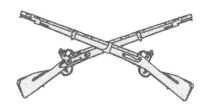

This appendix is to assist the reader in following the movements of the Wallick soldiers when visiting a Civil War battlefield or historic site. An order of battle tells how an army is organized and who the commanding officers are for each unit. Below is a list of major battles and events of the American Civil War where Wallick soldiers were present. To trace their foot-steps on a battlefield it is necessary to know (from the smallest unit to the largest) the soldier's regiment, brigade, division, corps and/or army group. A typical Civil War regiment found itself reorganized into different units many times throughout the war, so the order of battle for a regiment may not be the same for two different engagements, even though the battles were only weeks apart. During an engagement a change in command could happen at a moment's notice due to illness, a wound or the death of the commanding officer. Some command replacements are included in this appendix, but not all. States are in alphabetical order.

Georgia

Chickamauga SEP 19-20, 1863

Charles F.   87th IVI. - Col. Newell Gleason
              3rd Brig. - Col. Ferdinand Van Derveer
              3rd Div. - Gen. John Brannan
              XIV Army Corps - Gen. George Thomas

Charles F. was wounded in the left hand in this battle. He spent one month in a Chattanooga hospital then was given a furlough home to recuperate. He rejoined his regiment on Christmas Day, 1863.

Isaiah   49th OVI. - Maj. Gray & Capt. Luther Strong
              1st Brig. - Gen. August Willich
              2nd Div. - Gen. Richard Johnson
              XX Army Corps - Gen. Alexander McCook

Levi   44th IVI. - Lt. Col. Simeon Aldrich
              2nd Brig. - Col. George Dick
              3rd Div. - Brig. Gen. Horatio Van Cleve
              XXI Army Corps - Maj. Gen. Thomas Crittenden

Atlanta Campaign MAY 5 - Sept. 8, 1864

Michael   27th IVI. - Col. Silas Colgrove
              2nd Brig. - Gen. Thomas Ruger
              1st Div. - Gen. Alpheus Williams
              XX Army Corps - Maj. Gen. Joseph Hooker/ Maj. Gen. Henry W. Slocum
              Army of the Cumberland - Maj. Gen. George Thomas

Charles F.   87th IVI. - Col. Newell Gleason
              2nd Brig. - Col. Ferdinand Van Derveer/ Col. Newell Gleason
              3rd Div. - Gen. Absalom Baird
              XIV Army Corps - Gen. John Palmer/ Gen. Richard Johnson/ Gen. Jefferson C. Davis
              Army of the Cumberland - Maj. Gen. George Thomas

Resaca MAY 13-15, 1864

Michael 27th IVI. - Col. Silas Colgrove
2nd Brig. - Gen. Thomas Ruger
1st Div. - Gen. Alpheus Williams
XX Army Corps - Maj. Gen. Joseph Hooker

Michael was wounded in the left hip and sent to hospitals in Jeffersonville, IN, and Madison, IN. He rejoined his regiment in Atlanta on SEP 1, 1864.

Charles F. 87th IVI. - Col Newell Gleason
2nd Brig. - Col Ferdinand Van Derveer
3rd Div. - Gen Absalom Baird
XIV Army Corps - Gen. John Palmer

Kennesaw Mt. JUN 27, 1864

Michael 27th IVI. - Col. Silas Colgrove
2nd Brig. - Gen. Thomas Ruger
1st Div. - Gen. Alpheus Williams
XX Army Corps - Maj. Gen. Joseph Hooker

Michael was not present. He was still recuperating from the wounds he received at Resaca.

Charles F. 87th IVI. - Col. Newell Gleason
2nd Brig. - Col. Ferdinand Van Derveer
3rd Div. - Gen. Absalom Baird
XIV Army Corps - Gen John Palmer

March to the Sea NOV 15-DEC 21, 1864

Charles F. 87th IVI. - Lt. Col. Edwin Hammond
2nd Brig. - Col Newell Gleason
3rd Div. - Gen Absalom Baird
XIV Army Corps - Gen Jefferson C Davis
Army of Georgia, Left Wing - Maj. Gen. Slocum (General Sherman accompanied this wing)

Kentucky

Perryville OCT 8, 1862

Charles F. 87th IVI. - Col. Kline G. Shryock
3rd Brig. - Gen. Steedman
1st DIV. - Gen.Albin Schoepf
III Corps - (acting) Maj. Gen. Charles C. Gilbert

William 51st IVI. - Abel D. Streight
20th Brig. - Col. Charles G. Harker
6th Div. - Gen. Thomas J. Wood
II Corps - Maj. Gen. Thomas L. Crittenden

Perryville, cont.

Levi   44th IVI. - Col. Hugh B. Reed
                  14th Brig. - Col. Pierce Butler Hawkins
                  5th Div. - Gen. Horatio Van Cleve
                  II Corps - Maj. Gen. Thomas Crittenden

Louisiana

Red River Campaign   APR 26 - MAY 22, 1864

Charley   16th OVI. - Lt. Col. Philip Kershner
                  2nd Brig. - Michael K. Lawler
                  1st Div. - Michael K. Lawler to May 1, then James Keigwin
                  13th Army Corp - Gen. Thomas Ransom to APR 8, Gen. Robert Cameron to APR 27,
                  Gen. John McClernand to MAY 1.

Maryland

Antietam   SEP 17, 1862

Michael   27th IVI. - Col. Silas Colgrove
                  3rd Brig. - Gen. George H. Gordon
                  1st Div. - Gen. Alpheus S. Williams
                  XII Army Corp - Maj. Gen Joseph K. Mansfield/ Gen. Alpheus S. Williams

                  Michael missed this battle because he was still a POW, however, his regimental brothers performed
                  heroically and sustained heavy casualties in "The Cornfield."

Monocacy   JUL 9, 1864

Elias   126th OVI. - Col. Ebright
                  2nd Brig. - Gen. Matthew McClennan
                  3rd Div. - Gen. James Ricketts
                  VI Army Corps - Gen. Horatio Wright

Mississippi

Chickasaw Bayou   DEC 27-29, 1862

Charley   16th OVI. - Co. B Capt. Eli Botsford/ Maj. Milton Mills
                  3rd Brig. - Col. John F. DeCourcy
                  3rd Div. - Gen. George W. Morgan
                  Sherman's Yazoo Expedition - General William T. Sherman

Port Gibson   MAY 1, 1863

Abraham
    22nd IVI (Iowa) Col. William M. Stone
    2nd Brig. Michael K. Lawler
    14th Div. Eugene A. Carr
    XIII Army Corps – Maj. Gen. John McClernand

Charley
    16th OVI. - Capt. Eli Botsford/ Maj. Milton Mills
    2nd Brig. - Col. Daniel Lindsey
    9th Div. - Gen. Peter Osterhaus
    XIII Army Corps - Maj. Gen. John McClernand

    Charley was said to be wounded in the ankle in this battle. Account not verified in the official records.

Daniel
    20th OVI. - Col. Manning Force, Capt. Francis Shaklee
    2nd Brig. - Gen. Mortimer Leggett
    3rd Div. - Gen. John Logan
    XVII Army Corps - Maj. Gen. James McPherson

Champion Hill MAY 16, 1863

Abraham
    22nd IVI (Iowa) Col. William M. Stone
    2nd Brig. Michael K. Lawler
    14th Div. Eugene A. Carr
    XIII Army Corps – Maj. Gen. John McClernand

Charley
    16th OVI. - Co. B- Capt. Eli Botsford/ Maj. Milton Mills
    2nd Brig. - Col. Daniel Lindsey
    9th Div. - Gen. Peter Osterhaus
    XIII Army Corps - Maj. Gen. John McClernand

Daniel
    20th OVI. - Col. Manning Force, Capt. Francis Shaklee
    2nd Brig. - Gen. Mortimer Leggett
    3rd Div. - Gen. John Logan
    XVII Army Corps - Maj. Gen. James McPherson

Vicksburg   MAY-JUL 4, 1863

Abraham
    22nd IVI (Iowa) Col. William M. Stone
    2nd Brig. Michael K. Lawler
    14th Div. Eugene A. Carr
    XIII Army Corps – Maj. Gen. John McClernand

Charley
    16th OVI. - Co. B - Capt. Eli Botsford/ Maj. Milton Mills
    2nd Brig. - Col. Daniel Lindsey
    9th Div. - Gen. Peter Osterhaus
    XIII Army Corps - Maj. Gen. John McClernand,

    McClernand relieved of command June 22. Gen. Edward Ord became the new corps commander.

    JUN 22, 1864 - Charley's brigade was detached from Osterhaus' 9th Division and temporarily assigned to Gen. Alvin Hovey's 12th Division as part of Sherman's Exterior Line at Vicksburg.

Daniel   20th OVI. - Col. Manning Force, Capt. Francis Shaklee
2nd Brig. - Gen. Mortimer Leggett/ after June 3, 1863, Manning Force
3rd Div. - Gen. John Logan
XVII Army Corps - Maj. Gen. James McPherson

North Carolina

Battle of Bentonville   MAR 19, 1865

Charles F.   87th IVI. - Lt. Col. Edwin Hammond
2nd Brig. - Lt. Col. Thomas Doan
3rd Div. - Gen. Absalom Baird
XIV Army Corps - Gen. Jefferson C Davis
Army of Georgia - Maj. Gen. Slocum

Hewit   38th IVI. - Col. David H. Patton
3rd Brig. - Lt. Col. David Miles & Arnold McMahan
1st Div. - Gen. William Carlin
XIV Army Corps - Gen. Jefferson C. Davis
Army of Georgia - Maj. Gen. Slocum

General Johnston's Surrender   APR 26, 1865

Charles F.   87th IVI. - Lt. Col. Edwin Hammond
2nd Brig. - Lt. Col. Thomas Doan
3rd Div. - Gen. Absalom Baird
XIV Army Corps - Gen. Jefferson C Davis
Army of Georgia - Maj. Gen. Slocum

Hewit   38th IVI. - Col. David H. Patton
3rd Brig. - Lt. Col. David Miles & Arnold McMahan
1st Div. - Gen. William Carlin
XIV Army Corps - Gen. Jefferson C. Davis
Army of Georgia - Maj. Gen. Slocum

Pennsylvania

Gettysburg   JUL 1-3, 1863

Michael   27th IVI. - Lt. Col. John Fesler/Col. Silas Colgrove- temporary brigade commander
3rd Brig. - Gen. Thomas Ruger - temporary division commander
1st Div. - Gen August Williams - temporary corps commander
XII Army Corps - Army of the Potomac, Maj. Gen. Henry Slocum - temporary army commander
until Gen. George Meade arrived.

South Carolina

Ft. Wagner   JUL 11-18, 1863

Henry M.   67th OVI. - Col. Alvin C. Voris/ report by Maj. Lewis Butler
2nd Brig. - Gen. Haldimand Putnam- KIA in attack
Gen. Seymore's Division
Dept. of the South - Gen. Gillmore/Gen. Alfred Terry

Sherman's Carolinas Campaign   FEB 1- APR 14, 1865

Charles F.   87th IVI. - Lt. Col. Edwin Hammond
2nd Brig. - Lt. Col. Thomas Doan
3rd Div. - Gen Absalom Baird
XIV Army Corps - Gen Jefferson C. Davis
Army of Georgia - Maj. Gen. Slocum (Sherman accompanied this wing of the army)

Hewit   38th IVI. - Col. David H. Patton
3rd Brig. - Lt. Col. David Miles & Arnold McMahan
1st Div. - Gen. William Carlin
XIV Army Corps - Gen. Jefferson C. Davis
Army of Georgia - Maj. Gen. Slocum (Sherman accompanied this wing of the army)

Tennessee

Ft. Donelson   FEB 16, 1862

Levi   44th IVI. - Col. Hugh B. Reed
1st Brig. - Gen. Charles Cruft
3rd Div. - Gen. Lew Wallace
General Ulysses S. Grant commanding officer

Shiloh   APR 6-7, 1862

William   51st IVI. - Col. Abel D. Streight
20th Brig. - Gen. James A Garfield
6th Div. - Gen. Thomas J. Wood
Army of the Ohio - Gen. Don Carlos Buell

Isaiah   49th OVI. - Col. Gibson /Lt. Col. Albert M. Blackman
6th Brig. - Col. William H. Gibson
2nd Div. - Gen. Alexander McCook
Army of the Ohio - Gen. Don Carlos Buell

Levi   44th IVI. - Col. Hugh B. Reed
3rd Brig. - Gen. Jacob G. Lauman
4th Div. - Gen. Stephen A.Hurlbut
Army of the Tennessee - Maj. Gen. Ulysses S. Grant

Stones River   DEC 31, 1862-Jan. 3, 1863

William   51st IVI. - Col. Silas Colgrove
             3rd Brig. - (late 20th) Col. Charles Harker
             1st Div. - (late 6th) Gen. Thomas Wood
             Left Wing - Maj. Gen. Crittenden
             XIV Corps - Army of the Cumberland, Maj. Gen. William Rosecrans

Isaiah   49th OVI. - Col. William H. Gibson
             1st Brig. - (late 6th) Gen. August Willich
             2nd Div. - Gen. Richard Johnson
             Right Wing - Maj. Gen. Alexander McCook
             XIV Corps - Army of the Cumberland, Maj. Gen. William Rosecrans

Levi   44th IVI. - Col. William Williams
             2nd Brig. - (late 14th) Col. James Fyffe
             3rd Div. - (late 5th) Col. Horatio Van Cleve
             Left wing - Maj. Gen. Crittenden
             XIV Corps - Army of the Cumberland, Maj. Gen. William Rosecrans

Chattanooga & Missionary Ridge NOV-DEC, 1863

Charles F.   87th IVI. - Col. Newell Gleason
             2nd Brig. - Col. Ferdinand Van Derveer
             3rd Div. - Gen. Absalom Baird
             XIV Army Corps - Gen. John Palmer

Isaiah   49th OVI. - Maj. Samuel Gray
             1st Brig. - August Willich
             3rd Div. - Gen. Thomas Wood
             IV Army Corps - Maj. Gen. Gordon Granger

Isaiah died NOV 27, 1863, of the wounds he received in the assault on Missionary Ridge.

Levi   44th IVI. - Lt. Col. Simeon Aldrich
             Post of Chattanooga - Col. John Parkhurst
             Div. - Chattanooga Garrison, Brig. Gen. James Steedman
             Army of the Cumberland - Maj. Gen. George Thomas

The 44th was assigned provost duty in Chattanooga and did not participate in the assault on Missionary Ridge.

Battle of Franklin NOV 30, 1864

William   51st IVI. - Capt. William W. Scearce
             1st Brig. - Col. Abel Streight
             3rd Div. - Gen. Thomas Wood
             IV Corps - Gen. David Stanley/Maj. Gen. John M. Schofield

Battle of Nashville DEC 15-16, 1864

William   51st IVI. - Capt. William W. Scearce
                   1st Brig. - Col. Abel Streight
                   3rd Div. - Brig. Gen. Samuel Beatty
                   IV Corp - Brig. Gen. Thomas Wood
                   XIV Corps Army of the Cumberland - Maj. Gen. William Rosecrans
                   Commander - Maj. Gen. George H. Thomas

Virginia

First Kernstown MAR 22-23, 1862

Henry M.   67th OVI. - Col. Alvin C. Voris
                   1st Brig. - Gen. James Shields/ Gen. Nathan Kimball
                   Shields Div. - Gen. James Shields
                   V Army Corps - Gen. Nathaniel Banks

William F.   13th IVI. - Lt. Col. Robert S.Foster
                   2nd Brig. - Col. Jeremiah C Sullivan
                   2nd Div. - Gen. James Shields
                   V Corps - Gen. Nathaniel Banks

Buckton Station MAY 23, 1862,

Michael   27th IVI. - Col. Silas Colgrove
                   3rd Brig. - Gen. George Gordon
                   1st Div. - Gen. Alpheus Williams
                   V Corps - Gen. Nathaniel Banks

Michael was wounded, captured and became a POW. He rejoined his regiment on SEP 18, 1862.

Chancellorsville MAY 2-4, 1863

Michael   27th IVI. - Col. Silas Colgrove
                   3rd Brig. - Gen. Thomas Ruger
                   1st Div. - Gen. August Williams
                   XII Corps - Army of the Potomac, Maj. Gen. Henry Slocum

Wilderness MAY 5, 1864

Elias   126th OVI. - Col. Benjamin Smith
                   2nd Brig. - Gen. Truman Seymour
                   3rd Div. - Gen. James Ricketts
                   VI Army Corps - Maj. Gen. John Sedgwick/Maj. Gen. Horatio Wright

Chester Station   MAY 10, 1864

Henry M.   67th OVI. - Col. Alvin C. Voris
                   1st Brig. - Gen. Joshua B. Howell
                   1st Div. - Gen. Alfred Terry
                   X Corps - Gen. Quincy Gillmore

                   Henry was killed in action at this battle.

Spotsylvania "The Bloody Angle"   MAY 12, 1864

Elias   126th OVI. - Col. Benjamin Smith
                   2nd Brig. - Gen. Truman Seymour
                   3rd Div. - Gen. James Ricketts
                   VI Army Corps - Gen. Horatio Wright

Cold Harbor   JUN 3, 1864

Elias   126th OVI. - Col. Benjamin Smith
                   2nd Brig. - Gen. Truman Seymour
                   3rd Div. - Gen. James Ricketts
                   VI Army Corps - Gen. Horatio Wright

Petersburg   JUN 9, 1864

Elias   126th OVI. - Col. Benjamin Smith/ Col. Ebright
                   2nd Brig. - Col. Benjamin Smith
                   3rd Div. - Gen. James Ricketts
                   VI Army Corps - Gen. Horatio Wright

Second Kernstown   JUL 24, 1864

Edward   34th OVI. - Lt. Col. Luther Furney
                   2nd Brig. - Col. Daniel Johnson
                   2nd Div. - Col. Isaac Duval
                   Army of the Kanawha - Maj. Gen. George Crook

Opequon Creek   SEP 19, 1864

Elias   126th OVI. - Lt. Col. Aaron Ebright - KIA - Capt. George Hoge
                   2nd Brig. - Gen. Warren Keifer
                   3rd Div. - Gen. James Ricketts
                   VI Army Corps- Gen. Horatio Wright

                   Elias died on SEP 23, 1864, of wounds he received during the battle.

Edward   4th OVI. - Lt. Col. Luther Furney
                   2nd Brig. Col. Daniel Johnson, wounded - Lt. Col Benjamin Coates
                   2nd Div. - Col. Isaac Duval, wounded - Col. Rutherford B. Hayes
                   Army of West Virginia - Bvt. Maj. Gen. George Crook

Fisher's Hill   SEP 22, 1864

Edward
34th OVI. - Lt. Col. Luther Furney (Piatt's Zouaves)
2nd Brig. - Lt. Col. Benjamin Coates
2nd Div. - Col. Rutherford B. Hayes
VIII Army Corps - Army of W.V. Bvt Maj Gen. George Crook

Cedar Creek   OCT 19, 1864

Edward
34th OVI. - Lt. Col. Luther Furney (Piatt's Zouaves)
2nd Brig. - Lt. Col. Benjamin Coates
2nd Div. - Col. Rutherford B. Hayes
VIII Army Corps - Army of W.V. Bvt Maj Gen. George Crook

Washington, D.C.

Grand Review of the Union Army   MAY 23-24, 1865

Charles F.
87th IVI. - Lt. Col. Edwin Hammond
2nd Brig. - Lt. Col. Thomas Doan
3rd Div. - Gen Absalom Baird
XIV Army Corps - Gen Jefferson C Davis
Army of Georgia - Maj. Gen. Slocum

Hewit
38th IVI. - Col. David H. Patton
3rd Brig. - Lt. Col. David Miles & Arnold McMahan
1st Div. - Gen. William Carlin
XIV Army Corps - Gen. Jefferson C. Davis
Army of Georgia - Maj. Gen. Slocum

Appendix III

Descendants of the Wallick Soldiers

Descendants of the Wallick Soldiers

Family patriarchs are **bold**.
Those who served in the Civil War are **bold and underlined**.
Preceding each name is a number representing that person's generation in the Hans Michael Wallick lineage.
The + symbols are for those who married into the Wallick family.

Son of George Jr.

.... **5 Elias B. Wallick** b:13 Aug 1838 Wayne, Tuscarawas, OH,
d:23 Sep 1864 Winchester, Frederick, VA - No descendants

Son of "Boat Builder" George

.... **5 Benjamin Wallick** b:Jan 1828 Dover, Tuscarawas, OH,
d:20 Jun 1920 Stark Co., OH
.... + Anne Winters b:Bet. 1821-1843, m: 27 Sep 1860
Tuscarawas Co., OH, d:Aft. 1865
.... 5 Margaret Wallick b:Oct 1830 Dover, Tuscarawas, OH,
d:18 Aug 1910 Tuscarawas Co., OH
.... + Joshua F. Hensel b:Sep 1834 Tuscarawas Co., OH, m: 06 Sep 1855 Tuscarawas Co., OH, d:06 Sep 1910
New Philadelphia,
Tuscarawas, OH
.... 5 Mary Anne Wallick b:21 Jan 1835 Dover, Tuscarawas, OH,
d:27 Feb 1914 Dover, Tuscarawas, OH
.... + William Andreas b:21 Jul 1835 Dover, Tuscarawas, OH,
m: 27 Sep 1860 Dover, Tuscarawas, OH,
d:30 Aug 1901 Dover, Tuscarawas, OH
.... 6 Carrie C. Andreas b:23 Jun 1861 Dover, Tuscarawas, OH,
d:29 Jul 1891 Dover, Tuscarawas, OH
.... + Charles Cline b:16 Jan 1858 OH, m: 01 Jun 1882,
d:28 Oct 1940
.... 6 Elmer E. Andreas b:Abt. 1875, d:18 Jan 1942

Son of Zachariah

.... **5 Jeremiah Wallick** b:28 Nov 1830 Dover, Tuscarawas, OH,
d:04 Jun 1903 Peru, Miami, IN
.... + Mary Alida Demeyre b:11 Dec 1840 OH, m: 11 Sep 1859 Miami, IN, d:31 Jul 1914 Peru, Miami, IN
.... 6 James M. Wallick b:05 Sep 1860 Peru, Miami, IN, d:17 Jul 1900
.... 7 Mabel Wallick
.... 7 Florence Lida Wallick
.... 6 Frank Wallick b:1866 Peru, Miami, IN, d:06 May 1881

Sons & grandsons of "Peru" Benjamin Wallick Senior

.... **4 "Peru" Benjamin Wallick Junior** b:08 Jun 1804 Tuscarawas Co., OH,
d:05 Dec 1884 Peru, Miami, IN
.... + Elizabeth Shalter b:1812 Stark Co., OH, m: 15 Jan 1832
Tuscarawas Co., OH, d:08 Apr 1882 Miami, IN
.... 5 James M. Wallick b:Bet. 1826 -1853, d:Bef. 1887

.... **5 Cpt. William Wallick** b:04 Nov 1832 Tuscarawas Co., OH,
d:31 Aug 1892 Peru, Miami, IN
.... + Mary Elizabeth Burns b:07 Nov 1838 OH, m: 11 Jun 1855,
d:25 May 1905 Miami, IN
.... 6 Flora M b:Abt. 1861 Pipe Creek, Miami, IN,
d:21 Apr 1876 Miami, IN
.... 5 Joseph Wallick b:20 Dec 1833 Tuscarawas Co., OH,
d:13 Aug 1871 Miami, IN
.... + Margaret York b:Abt. 1846 IN, m: 22 May 1862 Miami, IN,

.... 6 Carrie Wallick b:Abt. 1866 Pipe Creek, Miami, IN
d: Aft. 1865
.... 5 Emma Anna Wallick b:27 Jan 1837 Tuscarawas Co., OH,
d:15 Nov 1909 Fulton, IN
.... + Andrew Jackson Ewing b:23 Jan 1828 Greene, OH, m: 07 Oct 1855 Miami, IN, d:11 Oct 1883 Fulton, IN

.... **5 John Wesley Wallick** b:08 Aug 1843 Butler Twp., Miami, IN,
d:21 Jun 1888 Miami, IN
.... + Rebecca A. Buskirk b:Abt. 1854 IN, m: 22 May 1874 Miami, IN,
d:01 Dec 1943 Peru, Miami, IN, m: 05 Feb 1893 Miami, IN
.... 6 Rutherford B. `Ford' Wallick b:02 Mar 1877 Peru, Miami, IN,
d:08 Mar 1962 Peru, Miami, IN
.... + Dora M. Shively b:Dec 1875 IN, m: 30 Apr 1899 Miami, IN,
d:27 Dec 1967 Miami, IN
.... 7 unknown Wallick b:Bef. 1910

.... **5 Charles F. Wallick** b:08 Aug 1843 Butler Twp., Miami, IN,
d:03 Mar 1904 Lafayette, Tippecanoe, IN
.... + Lucy A. Search b:Abt. 1860 IN, m: 10 Nov 1876 Miami, IN,
d:Bet. 1885 -1954
.... 6 Charles Milo Wallick b:Dec 1877 Pipe Creek, Miami, IN,
d:11 Aug 1958 Miami, IN
.... + Mamie Schrock b:Bet. 1885 - 1886, m: 23 Apr 1902 Miami, IN, d:Bet. 1920 - 1979
.... 7 Female Wallick b:07 Jan 1903 Miami, IN,
d:07 Jan 1903 Miami, IN
.... 7 Charles Solomon Wallick b:06 Oct 1904 Peru, Miami, IN, d:Aug 1972
.... + Viola Rabe
.... 8 Charles "Bud" Wallick
.... + Dorothy unknown
.... 9 Randy Scott Wallick
.... 10 Brittany Wallick
.... 8 William Frederick Wallick
.... 9 Brenda Wallick
.... 9 Tim William Wallick
.... 9 Shirley Jean Wallick
.... + Frank Midola
.... 7 Elizabeth Elnora Wallick b:Bet. 1910 - 1911
.... + Clarence Lloyd Gouch
.... 7 Roy E. Wallick b:Bet. 1913 - 1914
.... 7 John E. Wallick b:21 Jun 1916 Peru, Miami, IN, d:Jan 1987
.... 7 Juanita Evelyn Wallick b:15 Oct 1918 IN
.... + Oscar R. Faulkner m: 09 Jan 1936 Miami, IN
.... 8 Mamie Kathleen Faulkner Varga
.... 7 Mary Ann Wallick
.... 6 William Custer Wallick b:Dec 1878 Pipe Creek, Miami, IN,
d:18 Apr 1956 Miami, IN
.... + Mary Angie Miles b:Abt. 1889 IN, m: 18 Oct 1909 Miami, IN,
d:Bet. 1915 - 1983
.... 6 Emma G. Wallick b:Abt. 1881, d:Bet. 1895 - 1975
.... + John E. Miles b:Bet. 1864 -1884, m: Bet. 1895 - 1928,
d:Bet. 1898 - 1970

.... **4 Christopher Wallick** b:06 Oct 1810 Tuscarawas Co., OH,
d:11 Mar 1876 Peru, Miami, IN
.... + Elizabeth Black b:Abt. 1814 PA, m: 14 Dec 1834 Tuscarawas Co., OH, d:Bet. 1851 - 1909
.... 5 Orintha Wallick b:Abt. 1837 Tuscarawas Co., OH, d:Bet. 1866 - 1931
.... + Henry Diebert b:Bet. 1814 - 1840, m: 10 May 1860 Miami, IN,
d:Aft. 1865

.... **5 William F. Wallick** b:Bef. 03 Nov 1875 Tuscarawas Co., OH,
d:Bef. 1929
.... + Anna Elizabeth Hagee
.... 6 Maude Groff Wallick b:21 Mar 1870 Peru, Miami, IN,
d:02 Aug 1940 CO Springs, El Paso, CO
.... + William Walter Flora m: 21 Aug 1892
.... 6 Pearle Wallick b:Aft. 1860

.... 5 Elmira Wallick b:Abt. 1843 Tuscarawas Co., OH, d:Bet. 1844 - 1937
.... + Carrier
.... 5 Henry C. Wallick b:Abt. 1845 Tuscarawas Co., OH,
d:Aft. May 1850 Tuscarawas Co., OH
.... 5 Mary A. Wallick b:Abt. 1848 Tuscarawas Co., OH, d:Bet. 1849 - 1942
.... + Frank E. Kingsbury m: 07 Apr 1869

.... **4 Wesley Wallick** b:04 Feb 1821 Tuscarawas Co., OH, d:07 Jul 1890
.... + Mary Ann Fisher b:Abt. 1826 OH, m: 19 Dec 1843 Miami, IN,
d:Bet. 1851 - 1920
.... 5 Susan Wallick b:Abt. 1846 Peru, Miami, IN, d:Bet. 1875 - 1940
.... + Leander Hoover b:Bet. 1823 - 1850, m: 18 Oct 1870 Miami, IN, d:Bet. 1875 - 1936
.... 5 Maria Wallick b:Abt. 1847 Peru, Miami, IN, d:Bet. 1848 - 1941
.... + unknown Houser

Sons of "Guthrie" Michael

.... **5 Charles "Charley" Wallick** b:08 Jul 1843 Holmes Co., OH,
d:02 Jul 1926 Victor, Iowa, IA
.... + Mary J Gray b:19 Jan 1846 Holmes Co., OH, m: 09 Feb 1865
Holmes Co., OH, d:05 Nov 1865 Victor, Iowa, IA
.... 6 Ada Mary Wallick b:04 Nov 1865 Victor, Iowa, IA,
d:29 Jan 1948 San Antonio, Bexar, TX
.... + George William Morrison b:20 Jun 1863, m: 26 Apr 1887
Stuart, Guthrie, IA, d:12 Sep 1932 San Antonio, Bexar, TX
.... + Mary E. Shaull b:17 Aug 1846 Hopewell, Seneca, OH, m: 17 Apr 1867 Holmes Co., OH, d:09 Aug 1919 Victor,
Iowa, IA
.... 6 Charles Edgar Wallick b:15 Jul 1869 Warren Twp, Poweshiek Co., IA, d:20 Aug 1880 Allison Twp.,
Decatur, KS
.... 6 William P Wallick b:17 Aug 1872 Victor, Iowa, IA,
d:14 Jan 1873 Victor, Iowa, IA
.... 6 Fairy Belle Wallick b:07 Jul 1874 Ladora, Iowa, IA,
d:26 Mar 1946 Victor, Iowa, IA
.... 6 Estella S. Wallick b:28 Feb 1877 Warren Twp, Poweshiek Co., IA, d:12 Nov 1942 Los Angeles, Los
Angeles, CA
.... + Charles Marble b:Abt. 1857 Iowa, IA, m: 04 Mar 1902
Warren Twp, Poweshiek Co., IA
.... 6 Frederick S Wallick b:13 Oct 1878 Victor, Iowa, IA,
d:03 Jun 1927 Carnforth, Poweshiek, IA
.... + Ida Sparrowgrove b:1871 Belle Plaine, Benton, IA, m: 30 Jun 1909 Iowa, IA, d:1955 Poweshiek, IA
.... 6 John William Wallick b:19 Dec 1881 Warren Twp, Poweshiek Co., IA, d:25 Sep 1971 Red Oak,
Montgomery, IA
.... + Anna Maude Rodgers b:15 Apr 1885 Clinton, Henry, MO,
m: 12 Jul 1905 MO, d:31 Aug 1986 Red Oak, Montgomery, IA
.... 7 John R. Wallick b:05 Dec 1906 MO, d:10 Nov 1965
.... + Madeline C Akeson b:Abt. 1908 NB, m: 12 Nov 1932 Omaha, Douglas, NB,
.... 8 John T. Wallick
.... + Joyce
.... 9 Thomas John Wallick
.... 9 James Timothy Wallick
.... 8 Larry D. Wallick
.... + Judy S unknown
.... 9 Scott Alan Wallick b:1966 d: 1966

```
.............................. 8  Helen M. Wallick b:14 Mar 1909 NB
.............................. + Charles Burns m: 30 Jul 1930 Red Oak, Montgomery, IA
.............................. 7  Helen M. Wallick b:14 Mar 1909 NB, d: Benson, Douglas, NB
.............................. + Charles Burns m: 30 Jul 1930
.............................. 6  Bertha Rebecca Wallick b:13 Aug 1884 Warren Twp, Poweshiek Co., IA, d:05 Oct 1974 Victor, Iowa, IA
.............................. + William Henry Sherwood b:13 Mar 1884 Elkader, Clayton, IA,
m: 19 Aug 1908 Warren Twp, Poweshiek Co., IA,
d:29 Sep 1927 Warren Twp, Poweshiek Co., IA
.............................. + George Weisskopf b:19 Jul 1875 Homestead, Iowa, IA,
m: 30 Jun 1940 Homestead, Iowa, IA, d:27 Jun 1957
.............................. 6  Charles M. Wallick b:19 Oct 1886 Warren Twp, Poweshiek Co., IA, d:Bef.
.............................. 6  Pearl Virginia Wallick b:15 Sep 1889 Warren Twp, Poweshiek Co., IA, d:19 Jul 1969 NV, Story, IA
.............................. + Harvey Amos Wheeler b:29 Jun 1888 Brooklyn, Poweshiek, IA,
m: 08 Jan 1908 Brooklyn, Poweshiek, IA,
d:27 Feb 1946 Cambridge, Story, IA
.............................. 7  Harold R. Wheeler b:1925 Elkader, Clayton, IA,
.............................. 6  Virgil Wallick


.............................. **5 William D. Wallick** b:1846 Holmes Co., OH,
d:26 Feb 1862 Cumberland, Allegany, MD - No descendants
```

Son of "Kansas" Benjamin

```
.............................. **6 Benjamin Franklin Wallack** b:10 Sep 1844 Tuscarawas Co., OH, d:11 May 1897 Effingham, KS
.............................. + Ellen Green b:Dec 1846 Tuscarawas Co., OH,
m: 26 Dec 1871 WA, OH
.............................. 7  Mark Green Wallack b:Nov 1872 Atchison, KS
.............................. + Hattie Sun b:Sep 1874 KS
.............................. 8  Walter Wallack b:04 Oct 1896 Effingham, Atchison, KS, d:Aug 1973 Ulster, NY
.............................. + Loretta Townsend
.............................. 9  Paul Wallack
.............................. 9  Mary Susan Wallack
.............................. + Donald Simmons
.............................. 8  Paul C. Wallack b:1904 KS
.............................. + Hazel Crawford b:1902 OK
.............................. 8  Constance Wallack b:1904 KS
.............................. + Carroll H. Smith b:1903 KS
.............................. 7  Mary Ellen Wallack b:Oct 1876 Atchison, KS
.............................. + Harold Horr
.............................. 7  Lucy Bertha Wallack b:Oct 1876 Atchison, KS
.............................. + William Babbager
.............................. 7  Benjamin Wallack b:1879 Atchison, KS
.............................. 7  John W. Wallack b:Mar 1887 Atchison, KS
.............................. 7  Dorthea Wallack b:Sep 1891 Atchison, KS
```

Sons of Samuel

```
.............................. **5 Isaiah Wallick** b:Abt. 1840 Crawford Twp, Coshocton Co., OH,
d:27 Nov 1863 Chattanooga, Hamilton, Tennessee - No descendants


.............................. **5 Edward Wallick** b:Dec 1844 Crawford Twp, Coshocton Co., OH - No descendants
d:20 Oct 1918 Portland, Multnomah, OR
.............................. + Jennie Hannah Stroud b:14 Jul 1848 Kenton, Hardin, OH, m: 03 Jul 1872 Ada, Hardin, OH, d:16 Jan 1914
Portland, Multnomah, OR,
.............................. 6  James Louis Henry Wallick b:27 Nov 1872 Liberty Twp.,
Hardin, OH, d:14 Nov 1939
.............................. + Emma A. Schaffer b:Abt. 1881 OH, m: Abt. 1902 Hardin Co., OH
.............................. 7  Treva LaVella Wallick b:10 Sep 1903 Ada, Hardin, OH,
d:11 Nov 1991 Summit Co., OH
.............................. + Elmer Galbraith b:Bef. 1991, m: Bef. 1926
.............................. 8  Ronnie Galbraith b:24 Jan 1936, d:11 Sep 2010
.............................. 7  Robert E. Wallick b:19 Nov 1909 Liberty Twp., Hardin, OH, d:13 Oct 1965
.............................. + Magdalena Merkhoffer b:16 Aug 1912 Akron, Summit, OH,m: 01 Sep 1934, d:01 Jul 1968
```

.... 8 James Joseph Wallick
.... + Karen
.... 9 Jeffrey Alan Wallick
.... + Tari Lynn
.... 10 Corey Jay Wallick
.... 10 Cody Alan Wallick
.... 9 Kriss Ann Wallick
.... 9 James Patrick Wallick
.... + Haslee Jo
.... 10 Jared Maxwell Wallick
.... 10 Jaden Keller Wallick
.... 10 Jana Nicole Wallick
.... 9 Jason Andrew Wallick
.... 8 Mary Emma Wallick
.... + Fred Steirhoff
.... 8 Robert Edgar Wallick Jr.
.... 7 Willis Kennard Wallick b:15 Jun 1914 Ada, Hardin, OH,
d: 31 Jan 1992 Hillsborough Co., FL
.... + Mae Louise Boughton b:02 Jan 1919 Copley, Summit, OH,
m: 30 Nov 1939 Copley, Summit, OH,
d:16 Mar 1994 Brandon, Hillsborough, FL
.... 8 Kennard Earl Wallick
.... + Patricia Sue
.... 9 Jeffery Kennard Wallick
.... + Stacie Topougis
.... 10 Robert Jeffery Wallick
.... 9 Brian Edward Wallick
.... 9 Kristin Kay Wallick
.... 8 Donald Eugene Wallick
.... + Anna Marie
.... 9 Donald Eugene Wallick Jr.
.... 9 Margaret Ann Wallick
.... 9 Julie Andrea Wallick
.... 9 Monica Louise Wallick
.... 6 Clarence Leroy Wallick b:18 Feb 1874 Liberty Twp., Hardin, OH, d:01 Sep 1918 Allen Co., OH
.... + Clara A. Poling b:17 Jul 1883 Alger, Hardin, OH,
d:01 Jan 1967 Lima, Allen, OH
.... 7 Paul W. Wallick b:06 Oct 1906 Liberty Twp., Hardin, OH
d:02 Jul 1988
.... + Virginia B Burton b:Abt. 1913, d:02 Nov 2009 Lakeland Highlands, Polk, FL
.... 8 Susan Wallick b:30 Jan 1942, d:12 Jan 1984
.... 7 Clara Ladonna Wallick b:27 Apr 1909 Liberty Twp.,
Hardin, OH
.... 7 Jennie Ruth Wallick b:01 Aug 1910 Ada, Hardin, OH
.... 7 Theodore Roosevelt Wallick b:01 Sep 1911 Ada, Hardin, OH, d:23 Oct 1993 Bedford, Bedford, VA
.... 7 Helen Irene Wallick b:01 Mar 1913 Ada, Hardin, OH,
d:01 Sep 1991 Beavercreek, Greene, OH
.... + Bowlus b:Bet. 1903 - 1923
.... 6 Laurel Elden Wallick b:13 Mar 1875 Liberty Twp., Hardin, OH, d:22 Jul 1962 Portland, Multnomah, OR
.... + Nellie Slater b:Jan 1878 OH, m: Abt. 1897,
d:04 Mar 1952 Portland, Multnomah, OR
.... 7 Gladys Huston Wallick b:Abt. 1903 OR
.... 6 Lola Alma Wallick b:05 Nov 1876 Liberty Twp., Hardin, OH
.... 6 Laura Nora Wallick b:08 May 1878, d:Portland, Multnomah, OR
.... 6 Daisey I. (Reany) Wallick b:05 Sep 1879 Liberty Twp., Hardin, OH, d:Portland, Multnomah, OR
.... + Arthur Christopher b:14 Jun 1875 Delaware, OH,
m: 24 Dec 1901 Hardin Co., OH

Son & grandson of "Bunker Hill" Michael

.... **4 "Daviess" Michael Wallick** b:06 Mar 1817 Bedford, PA,
d:12 Feb 1905 Odon, Daviess Co., IN
.... + Nancy Jane Booth b:17 May 1818 OH, m: 29 Aug 1839 Wayne, Tuscarawas, OH, d:15 May 1899 Daviess Co., IN

.... 5 Sarah E. Wallick b:Abt. 1844 Wayne, Tuscarawas, OH
.... + Dunlap m: 31 Jul 1862 Daviess, IN

.... **5 William "Hewit" Wallick** b:10 May 1845 Tuscarawas Co., OH,
d:02 Jan 1910 Madison Twp, Daviess Co., IN
.... + Sarah Elizabeth Taylor b:07 Apr 1851 Odon, Daviess, IN,
m: 23 Feb 1871 Daviess Co., IN, d:26 Aug 1925 Odon, Daviess, IN
.... 6 Oscar M. Wallick b:09 May 1872 Madison Twp, Daviess Co., IN, d:15 May 1924 Daviess Co., IN
.... + Ida Dean Ketcham b:04 Dec 1873 IN, m: 26 Mar 1898
Daviess Co., IN, d:21 Dec 1968 Elnora, Daviess, IN
.... 7 Owen Michael Wallick b:29 May 1899 Madison Twp, Daviess Co., IN, d:09 Aug 1900 Madison Twp,
Daviess Co., IN
.... 7 unknown b:21 Feb 1901 Daviess Co., IN,
d:21 Feb 1901 Daviess Co., IN
.... 7 W Gleason Wallick b:31 Oct 1903 Madison Twp, Daviess Co., IN, d:05 Nov 1923 Daviess Co., IN
.... 7 Michael W. Wallick b:29 May 1909 Madison Twp, Daviess Co., IN, d:Abt. 1909
.... 7 Verna Emerine Wallick b:01 Sep 1911 Madison Twp, Daviess Co., IN, d:02 Jul 1982 Daviess Co., IN
.... + Sheldon Wilbur Eubanks b:17 Aug 1909 Elnora, Daviess, IN, m: 23 Apr 1938 Odon, Daviess, IN,
d:23 Apr 1938 Elnora, Daviess, IN
.... 6 Nancy J. Wallick b:23 Jun 1875 Daviess Co., IN,
d:31 Oct 1875 Daviess Co., IN
.... 6 Ada G. Wallick b:25 Aug 1877 Madison Twp, Daviess Co., IN, d:Feb 1964 IN
.... + Daniel Rufus McCarter b:02 Jun 1872 Daviess Co., IN,
m: 31 Dec 1898 Daviess Co., IN, d:Oct 1942 Daviess Co., IN
.... 6 Ray Byron Wallick b:21 Nov 1880 Daviess Co., IN,
d:03 Jan 1936 Odon, Daviess, IN
.... + Josephine Maggie Hasler b:Abt. 1882 IN, m: 25 Dec 1904
Greene Co., IN, d:04 Feb 1926
.... 7 George Hasler Wallick b:23 Mar 1906 Daviess Co., IN,
d:06 Jul 1968 Akron, Summit, OH
.... 8 Jim R Wallick
.... 9 James Samuel Wallick
.... 9 John Michael Wallick
.... 9 Thomas Hasler Wallick
.... 9 Peter Frederick Wallick
.... 7 unknown Wallick b:23 Mar 1908 Daviess Co., IN,
d:Bef. Jun 1910
.... 7 Hazel Roberta Wallick b:02 Oct 1909, d:1966
.... + Marley A. Hamm
.... + John T. Vance
.... 7 Harold William Wallick b:09 Sep 1912 Daviess Co., IN
.... + unknown
.... 8 unknown Wallick
.... 8 unknown Wallick
.... 6 Lola Ellen Wallick b:01 Jan 1884 Daviess Co., IN, d:1941
.... + William Thomas Summerville b:15 Mar 1883 Martin, IN,
m: 02 Apr 1908
.... 6 Henry Bruce Wallick b:28 Feb 1886 Odon, Daviess Co., IN,
d:07 Dec 1977 Bloomington, Monroe, IN
.... + Susan Lydia Ledgerwood b:30 Sep 1890 Scotland, Greene, IN,
m: 29 Jul 1910 Daviess Co., IN, d:01 Aug 1977
Odon, Daviess Co., IN
.... 7 William Ledger Wallick b:04 Mar 1912 Daviess Co., IN,
d:08 Aug 1990 Bloomington, Monroe, IN
.... + Martha Marie Overton b:19 Feb 1917 Van Buren Twp, Daviess Co., IN, m: 29 Feb 1940 Evansville,
Vanderburgh, IN
.... 8 Randy Ledger Wallick
.... + Donna Lee
.... 9 Bryan Wallick
.... 9 Brent D. Wallick
.... 7 Ledger Wallick

.... 6 Jennie M. Wallick b:Aug 1888 Daviess Co., IN
.... + Iden Love b:Bef. 1920, m: 02 Jun 1935
.... 6 infant
.... 5 Nancy Wallick b:Abt. 1848 Tuscarawas Co., OH
.... 5 Harvey N. Wallick b:1849 Wayne, Tuscarawas, OH, d:Bet. 1861 - 1865
.... 5 Rachael A. Wallick b:1851 Tuscarawas Co., OH,
.... + George Correll
.... 5 Mary Ellen Wallick b:Feb 1855 Tuscarawas Co., OH, d:
.... + Whitlock

Son of "Coshocton" Philip

.... **4 Levi Wallick** b:Abt. 1820 Coshocton, OH, d:Aft.1 Feb 1875 - No known descendants

Sons of Jacob

.... **4 Daniel Wallick** b:21 Oct 1823 Goshen Twp., Tuscarawas, OH,
d:03 Mar 1906 Wallowa, Wallowa, OR
.... + Sarah Catharine Hasbrook b:03 Nov 1832, m: 27 Apr 1851 Tuscarawas Co., OH, d:14 Apr 1893 New Philadelphia,
Tuscarawas, OH
.... 5 Edward J. Wallick b:15 Jun 1852 Tuscarawas Co., OH, d:11 May 1929 Cleveland, Cuyahoga, OH
.... + Isabella Bell b:Abt. 1855, m: 28 Dec 1872 Tuscarawas Co., OH,
d:28 Feb 1875 Tuscarawas Co., OH
.... 6 John Henry Wallick b:11 Jun 1873 Tuscarawas Co., OH
.... 6 Nora E. Wallick b:28 Feb 1875 Goshen Twp., Tuscarawas, OH, d:28 Feb 1875 Tuscarawas Co., OH
.... + Emma Grace Breyley b:19 Mar 1857 Cleveland, Cuyahoga, OH,
m: 30 Aug 1881 Cuyahoga Co., OH, d:07 May 1936 Cleveland, Cuyahoga, OH,
.... 6 William James Wallick b:07 Jan 1882 OH, d:07 Aug 1902 Monroeville, Huron, OH
.... 6 Ralph Edgar Wallick b:06 Oct 1883 Cleveland, Cuyahoga, OH, d:07 Aug 1886 Cleveland, Cuyahoga, OH
.... 6 Clinton Leroy Wallick b:01 Mar 1886 Mantua, Portage, OH,
d:24 Jul 1943 Cleveland, Cuyahoga, OH
.... + Virginia C. Gross b:Abt. 1888 OH, m: Abt. 1907
.... 7 unknown Wallick b:13 Jun 1908 OH
.... 6 Maud Marie Wallick b:01 Mar 1889 Geauga, OH, d:05 Jun 1971
.... + Myron R. Monroe b:Abt. 1888 Shiawassee, MI,
m: 19 Jun 1907 Huron, Erie, OH
.... + David Cook b:22 Mar 1885 Richland, OH, m: 18 Dec 1909
Huron, Erie, OH, d:29 Jun 1971 Shelby, Richland, OH
.... 6 Sybil Priscilla Wallick b:04 Oct 1890 North Baltimore, Wood, OH, d:09 Aug 1989 Cleveland,
Cuyahoga, OH
.... + Henry Glendon Smith b:09 Apr 1885 Baltimore, MD,
m: 12 Feb 1919 Delaware, IN
.... 6 Elizabeth Alice Wallick b:10 Jun 1892 Republic, Seneca, OH,
d:26 Aug 1987 Cleveland, Cuyahoga, OH
.... + Hubert W.Fassett b:07 Oct 1891 Medina, Orleans, NY
.... 6 Catherine May Wallick b:12 May 1894 Huron, Erie, OH,
d:19 Apr 1988 Cleveland, Cuyahoga, OH
.... + Charles William Fassett b:Abt. 1893 Medina, Orleans, NY,
m: 09 May
.... 6 Arnold Edwin Wallick b:27 Aug 1897 Huron, OH,
d:23 Oct 1990 Muncie, Delaware, IN
.... + Ethel Marie Alexander b:20 Feb 1909 Saratoga, IN,
m: 23 Jun 1927, d:08 Nov 1997 Greenville, Darke, OH
.... 7 Betty Jean Wallick
.... + Glen Darrell
.... 8 Jennifer Diane
.... + David Alan Rice
.... + Edith K. Leonard b:21 Mar 1903, m: 22 Sep 1918,
d:26 Feb 1925 Cleveland, Cuyahoga, OH
.... 5 Elizabeth Wallick b:10 Jan 1855, d:10 Apr 1862
.... 5 Henry Wallick b:11 Aug 1858 26 dec 1860
.... 5 Emma Catharine Wallick b:23 Mar 1862, d:02 Apr 1862

244

.... **4 David Wallick** b:21 Nov 1827 Tuscarawas Co., OH,
d:24 May 1911 York Twp, Van Wert Co., OH

.... + Mary Ann Smith b:01 Feb 1825 Harrison, OH, m: 26 Mar 1851 Tuscarawas Co., OH, d:02 Oct 1896 York Twp, Van Wert Co., OH

.... 5 John Wesley Wallick b:03 Jun 1853 Tuscarawas Co., OH,
d:13 Jul 1929 Van Wert Co., OH

.... + Sarah A. Cook b:30 Jun 1855 OH, m: 08 Sep 1878 Van Wert Co., OH, d:08 Feb 1905

.... 6 Wilbur Wallick b:25 Sep 1879 Liberty Twp, Van Wert Co., OH, d:1919

.... 6 Edna V Wallick b:16 Feb 1884 Van Wert Co., OH,
d:13 Feb 1946 Norwood, Hamilton, OH

.... + Robert Lamond Bush b:24 Apr 1876 Flint, Genesee, MI, m: 23 Mar 1910 Van Wert Co., OH, d:Abt. 1933 Rockford, Winnebago, IL

.... 6 Vera B. Wallick b:14 Mar 1890 Van Wert Co., OH,
d:27 Jun 1943 Rockford, Winnebago, IL

.... + William Earl Bothwell b:18 Jul 1896 Cincinnati, Hamilton, OH,
m: 30 May 1918, d:13 Jul 1954 Van Wert Co., OH

.... + Rachel A. Deuman b:29 Feb 1856 Licking, OH,
d:17 Jul 1921 Van Wert Co., OH

.... 5 James Harvey Wallick b:Aug 1854 Liberty Twp, Van Wert Co., OH

.... + Martha Jane b:Nov 1860 Mishawaka, St Joseph, IN, m: Abt. 1875

.... 6 Albert Perry Wallick b:15 Jul 1879 Van Wert Co., OH, d:1970

.... + Adilia Mary b:1877, m: Abt. 1901 OH,
d:1942 Mishawaka, St Joseph, IN

.... 6 Curtis Leroy Wallick b:15 Aug 1880 Van Wert Co., OH, d:1958

.... + Minnie Peterson b:1878, m: 1906, d:1980

.... 7 John Wilbur Wallick b:Abt. 1912

.... 7 Annabelle Marie Wallick b:Abt. 1918 IN

.... + unknown Hoover

.... 6 Otto Clyde Wallick b:29 Dec 1885 OH, d:Abt. 1946

.... + Bertha unknown d:1942

.... 5 Mary Elizabeth Wallick b:Abt. 1855 Liberty Twp, Van Wert Co., OH

.... + Jacob Profitt

.... + unknown Doenges

.... 5 David Henry Wallick b:12 Oct 1861 Liberty Twp., Van Wert, OH,
d:22 Apr 1938 Skiatook, Osage, OK

.... + Sarah Jane Foss b:Abt. Aug 1865 Grant, IN, m: 23 Apr 1891 Van Wert Co., OH, d:Abt. 1906

.... 6 Cora Foss b:Jul 1887

.... 6 Emma Grace Wallick b:Abt. May 1895 OH,
d:05 Apr 1929 Jenks, Tulsa, OK

.... + James Madison Dunn b:Abt. Feb 1878 Ozark Co., MO,
m: Abt. 1912, d:19 Jan 1935 OK

.... 6 David H Wallick

.... 5 Willes Leroy Wallick b:Abt. Aug 1863 Liberty Twp, Van Wert Co., OH, d:1935 Van Wert Co., OH

.... + Anna Margaret Beeler b:Abt. Sep 1867 IN, m: Abt. 1893, d:1948

.... 6 Wayne B. Wallick b:30 Nov 1902 OH, d:03 Apr 1981 IN,

.... + Ethyl L Thompson b:30 May 1904 IN, m: 1934, d:22 Dec 1986

.... 7 Willaim D. Wallick

.... 7 Betty L. Wallick

.... 5 Emma C. Wallick b:26 Jul 1866 Liberty Twp., Van Wert, OH,
d:03 Mar 1926 KS

.... + Dalton Dunn m: 20 Nov 1895 McDonough, IL

.... + Lamach D Wheeler b:Abt. 1874

.... 5 Roscoe Wallick b:Abt. 1868 Liberty Twp, Van Wert Co., OH

.... 5 Viole Wallick b:Abt. 1874 Liberty Twp, Van Wert Co., OH, d:

.... 6 Ralph Kiggins b:Jun 1890 OH

Son of Andrew

.... **4 Elijah Wallick** b:Apr 1831 Kilbuck Twp., Holmes Co., OH,
d:08 May 1922 Ladora, Iowa, IA

.... + Olive A. Gibbons b:1854 Williams Co., OH, m: 07 Mar 1872 Williams Co., OH, d:22 Feb 1926 Ladora, Iowa, IA

.... 5 Rosa Wallick b:24 Nov 1873 Paulding Co., OH, d:12 Sep 1892

.... + Francis Elias Whitlock m: 13 Sep 1891 Ladora, Iowa, IA

Sons of "Holmes" Henry

.... **4 David H. Wallick** b:07 Aug 1832 Holmes Co., OH,
d:01 Dec 1909 Olathe, Johnson, KS
.... + Sarah Emeline Moore b:12 Apr 1845 OH, m: 10 Apr 1862 Holmes Co., OH, d:20 Jul 1912 Johnson, KS
.... 5 Margaret Elzora Wallick b:May 1863 OH, d:1954 Johnson, KS
.... + Gilbert. H. Sinnett b:Dec 1858, m: 17 Dec 1890 Johnson, KS,
d:1946 Johnson, KS
.... 5 Delbert Lazell Wallick b:17 Jan 1866 Millersburg, Hardy Twp, Holmes Co., OH, d:09 Oct 1957 Fresno, CA
.... + Grace Alice Bee b:22 Nov 1867 Provo, Utah, UT, m: 08 Jun 1891 Provo, Utah, UT, d:13 Jul 1947 Provo, UT
.... 6 Bert Bee Wallick b:01 May 1892 Logan, Cache, UT,
d:11 Feb 1953 Riverside, CA
.... + Genevieve Marie Howard b:Abt. 1898 Salt Lake Co., UT,
m: 01 Oct 1916 Salt Lake Co., UT, d:
.... 7 Neil Lazell Wallick
.... 8 Barney Neil Wallick
.... + Patricia unknown
.... 9 Brandon Wallick
.... + Heidi
.... 9 Natalie Wallick
.... + Joshua J. White
.... 9 Megan Wallick
.... + unknown Wiscombe
.... + Gianni Jewkes
.... 9 Bethany Wallick
.... + Gary Robert Bown
.... 9 Brittany Wallick
.... + Benjamin Skousen
.... 5 Franklin (Freddie) Wallick b:30 Apr 1871 Johnson, KS,
d:01 May 1871 Johnson, KS

.... **4 Henry M. Wallick** b:Abt. 1838 Holmes Co., OH,
          d:10 May 1864 Chester Station, VA - No descendants
.... + Ellen E. Wells b:1845 Holmes Co., OH, m: 17 Mar 1864 Holmes Co., OH

Bibliography

Military Records

National Archives, Washington, D.C., Compiled Military Service Records of Abraham Wallick, 22nd IA.

National Archives, Washington, D.C., Compiled Military Service Records of Benjamin Wallick, 162nd, OH.

National Archives, Washington, D.C., Compiled Military Service Records of Benjamin F. Wallick, 17th KS.

National Archives, Washington, D.C., Compiled Military Service Records of Charles F. Wallick, 87th IN.

National Archives, Washington, D.C., Compiled Military Service Records of Charles Wallick, 16th OH.

National Archives, Washington, D.C., Compiled Military Service Records of Daniel Wallick, 20th OH.

National Archives, Washington, D.C., Compiled Military Service Records of David Wallick, 139th OH.

National Archives, Washington, D.C., Compiled Military Service Records of David H. Wallick, 102nd OH.

National Archives, Washington, D.C., Compiled Military Service Records of Edward Wallick, 34th & 36th OH.

National Archives, Washington, D.C., Compiled Military Service Records of Elias B. Wallick, 126th OH.

National Archives, Washington, D.C., Compiled Military Service Records of Elijah Wallick, 102nd OH.

National Archives, Washington, D.C., Compiled Military Service Records of Henry M. Wallick, 67th OH.

National Archives, Washington, D.C., Compiled Military Service Records of Isaiah Wallick, 49th OH.

National Archives, Washington, D.C., Compiled Military Service Records of John W. Wallick, 138th & 151st OH.

National Archives, Washington, D.C., Compiled Military Service Records of Levi Wallick, 44th IVI.

National Archives, Washington, D.C., Compiled Military Service Records of Washington Wallick, 71st PA.

National Archives, Washington, D.C., Compiled Military Service Records of Michael Wallick, 27th IN.

National Archives, Washington, D.C., Compiled Military Service Records of Wesley Wallick, 138th IN.

National Archives, Washington, D.C., Compiled Military Service Records of William Wallick, 51st IN.

National Archives, Washington, D.C., Compiled Military Service Records of William D. Wallack, 67th OH.

National Archives, Washington, D.C., Compiled Military Service Records of William F. Wallick, 13th & 151st IN.

National Archives, Washington, D.C., Compiled Military Service Records of William H. Wallick, 38th IN.

Pension Files

National Archives, Washington, D.C., Civil War Bureau of Pensions - Abraham Wallick, 22nd IA.

National Archives, Washington, D.C., Civil War Bureau of Pensions - Charles F. Wallick, 87 IN.

National Archives, Washington, D.C., Civil War Bureau of Pensions - Elijah Wallick, 102nd OH.

National Archives, Washington, D.C., Civil War Bureau of Pensions - Levi Wallick, 44th IN.

National Archives, Washington, D.C., Civil War Bureau of Pensions - Michael Wallick, 27th IN.

National Archives, Washington, D.C., Civil War Bureau of Pensions - Washington Wallick, 71st PA.

National Archives, Washington, D.C., Civil War Bureau of Pensions - William Wallick, 51st IN.

Newspapers/Manuscripts

Advertisement for Wesley Wallick, Western Hotel Proprietor: Peru Chronicle, Peru, Indiana, 1857.

Articles about Wesley Wallick in the California Gold Rush: Peru Chronicle, Peru, Indiana, 1852.

Editorial by William Wallick: Indianapolis News, Indianapolis, Indiana, 1880.

Obituary for Charles F. Wallick: Peru Republican, Peru, Indiana, 1904.

Obituary for Michael Wallick: Odon Journal, Odon, Indiana, 1905.

Obituary for William Wallick: Peru Chronicle, Peru, Indiana, 1892.

Obituary for William F. Wallick: Peru Chronicle, Peru, Indiana, 1873.

The Hans Michael Walck/Wallick Family Lineage- Researched by Jeffery Andrew Wallick

Books

Arnold, James R. *Grant Wins the War*. New York: John Wiley & Sons, Inc., 1997.

Boaz, Thomas M. *Libby Prison and Beyond- A Union Staff Officer in the East, 1862-1865*. Shippensburg PA: Burd Street Press, 1999.

Bowers, John. *Chickamauga & Chattanooga- The Battles that Doomed the Confederacy*. New York: Harper Collins, 1994.

Brown, Dee Alexander. *Morgan's Raiders*. New York: Konecky & Konecky, 1959.

Bryant, William O. *Cahaba Prison and the Sultana Disaster*. Tuscaloosa, AL: University of Alabama Press, 1990.

Catton, Bruce. *This Hallowed Ground*. Garden City, NY: Doubleday & Co., 1958

_____. *Terrible Swift Sword*. Garden City, NY: Doubleday & Co., 1958

_____. *Grant takes Command*. Boston: Little, Brown & Company, 1969.

_____. *Grant Moves South*. Little, Brown & Company, 1960.

Coddington, Edward B. *The Gettysburg Campaign- A Study in Command*. New York: Simon & Schuster, 1968.

Cozzens, Peter. *Shenandoah 1862*. Chapel Hill, North Carolina: University of North Carolina Press, 2008.

Dyer, Frederick H. *A Compendium of the War of the Rebellion*. New York, New York: Thomas Yoseloff, 1959.

Egger, Donald. *Holmes County- Flashes from the Past*, page 32-33. Self-published, 1963.

Flood, Charles Bracelen. *Grant & Sherman- The Friendship that Won the Civil War*. New York: Farrar, Straus and Giroux, 2005.

Foote, Shelby. *The Civil War: A Narrative*. Vols. 1-3. New York: Random House, 1958-1974.

Freehling, William W. *The Road to Disunion*. Vols. 1&2. Oxford & New York: Oxford University Press, 2007.

Fugiitt, Greg. *Fantastic Shadows Upon the Ground, The Thirty-fifth Ohio Volunteer Infantry in the Civil War.* Milford, Ohio: Little Miami Publishing, 2011.

Furguson, Ernest B. *Chancellorsville 1863: The Souls of the Brave.* New York: Alfred A. Knopf, 1992.

Garten, James. *Clarksburg and Early Odon.* May, 1981

Gilson, J. H. *History of the 126th Ohio Volunteer Infantry.* Huntington, West Virginia: Blue Acorn Press, 2000.

Goodwin, Doris Kearns. *Team of Rivals.* New York, NY: Simon & Schuster, 2005.

Gottfried, Bradley M. *Brigades of Gettysburg: The Union and Confederate Brigades at the Battle of Gettysburg.* Da Capo Press, 2002.

Griffith, Paddy. *Battle Tactics of the Civil War.* New Heaven & London: Yale University Press, 1989.

Grundlesperger, James. *Escape from Libby Prison.* Shippensburg PA: Burd Street Press, 1996.

Hartpence, William R. *History of the Fifty-First Indiana Veteran Volunteer Infantry.* Robert Clark Printers Co., 1894.

History of Antietam National Cemetery including A Descriptive List of All The Loyal Soldiers Buried Therein. John W. Wood Steam Printing, 1869

Hughes Jr., Nathaniel Cheairs. *Bentonville- The Final Battle of Sherman & Johnson.* Chapel Hill, North Carolina: University of North Carolina Press, 1996.

Jones Jr., Wilber D. *Giants in the Cornfield, The 27th Indiana Infantry.* Shippensburg, PA: White Mane Publishing Co., 1997.

Leckie, Robert. *None Died In Vain.* New York, NY: Harper Collins, 1990.

Library of Congress Civil War Desk Reference. Edited by Margaret E. Wagner, Gary W. Gallagher and Paul Finkelman. New York: Grand Central Press, Simon & Schuster Paperbacks, 2002.

Mann, Richard F. *The Buckeye Vanguards: The Forty-Ninth Ohio Veteran Volunteer Infantry.* Milford, Ohio: Little Miami Publishing Company, 2010.

McPherson, James. *Battle Cry of Freedom.* New York, Oxford: Oxford University Press, 1988.

_____. *Drawn with a Sword- Reflections on the American Civil War.* New York & Oxford: Oxford University Press, 1996.

_____. *For Cause and Comrades.* Oxford: Oxford University Press, 1997.

_____. *Tried By War.* New York, NY: The Penguin Press, 2008.

McDonough, James Lee. *Stones River- Bloody Winter in Tennessee.* Knoxville: The University of Tennessee Press, 1980.
_____. *Shiloh - In Hell Before Night.* Knoxville: The University of Tennessee Press, 1980.

McKenna, Thomas P. *From Vicksburg to Cedar Creek, The 22nd Iowa Volunteer Infantry in the Civil War.* Iowa City, Iowa: Camp Pope Publishing, 2014.

Moore, Mark A. *The Battle of Bentonville.* Da Capo Press, 1996.

Mushkat, Jerome. *A Citizen-Soldier's Civil War, The Letters of Brevet Major General Alvin C. Voris.* Dekalb, Illinois: Northern Illinois Press, 2002.

Myers, L. Rex. *Daviess County, Indiana, History.* May 1988.

Nosworth, Brent. *The Bloody Crucible of Courage.* New York: Carrol Groff Publishing, 2003.

Oates, Stephen B. *The Whirlwind of War: Voices of the Storm, 1861-1865.* New York, NY: Harper Collins Publishers, 1998.

Official Records. *The War of the Rebellion: A Compilation of Official Records of the Union and Confederate Armies.* 70 vols.,128 books. Washington, D.C: Government Printing Office, 1881-1900.

The Official Military Atlas of the Civil War. Washington, D.C.: Government Printing Office, 1891-1895.

Official Roster of Soldiers of the State of Ohio in the War of the Rebellion, 1861-1866. Vols. 1-12. Ohio Valley Publishing and Manufacturing Co., 1886.

Oldroyed, Osborn H. *A Soldier's Story of the Siege of Vicksburg, from the Diary of Osborn H. Oldroyed.* Springfield IL: Published by Author,1885.

Overmyer, Jack. *A Stupendous Effort- The 87th Indiana in the War of the Rebellion.* Bloomington: Indiana University Press, 1997.

Pfanz, Harry W. *Gettysburg- Culp's Hill and Cemetery Hill. Chapel Hill*: The University of North Carolina Press, 1993.

Potter, Jerry O. *The Sultana Tragedy: America's Greatest Maritime Disaster.* Gretna: Pelican Publishing Co., 2006.

Pryce, Samuel D. *Vanishing Footprints, The Twenty-Second Iowa Volunteer Infantry in the Civil War*, edited by Jeffry C. Burden. Iowa City, Iowa: Camp Pope Publishing, 2008.

Reid, Whitelaw. *Ohio In The War: Her Statesmen, Generals and Soldiers.* Vol. 2, *The History of Her Regiments and Other Military Organizations.* New York, New York. Moore, Wilstach & Baldwin,1868.

Report of the Adjutant General of the State of Indiana, 7 vols. Indianapolis: Alexander H. Conner, State Printer, 1869.

Rerick M.D., John H. *The Forty-Fourth Indiana Volunteer Infantry, History of its Services in the War of the Rebellion,* Ann Arbor MI: The Courier Steam Printing Co., 1880.

Roster and Records of Iowa Soldiers in the War of the Rebellion, and, *Historical Sketches of Volunteer Organizations, 1861-1866.* Des Moines: E.H. English, State Printer, 1908-11.

Schmutz, George. *History of the 102nd Ohio Volunteer Infantry.* Wooster, OH: Published by Author, 1907.

Sears, Stephen W. *Chancellorsville.* Boston & New York: Houghton Mifflin Co., 1996.

____. Stephen W. *George B. McClellan- The Young Napoleon.* New York: Tickner & Fields, 1988.

Simpson, Brooks D. *Ulysses S. Grant- Triumph over Adversity, 1822-1865.* Boston & New York: Houghton Mifflin Co., 2000.

Smithsonian's Great Battles & Battlefields of the Civil War. New York: William Morrow Co. 1997.

Soman, Jean Powers & Frank L. Byrne. *A Jewish Colonel in the Civil War, Marcus M. Spiegel of the Ohio Volunteers.* Lincoln & London: University of Nebraska Press, Bison Books, 1995.

Stevens, Joseph E. 1863- Rebirth of a Nation. New York: Bantam Books, 1999.

The Sixty-Seventh Ohio Veteran Volunteer Infantry, a Brief Record of its Four Years of Service in the Civil War:1861-1865. Written by Regimental Committee. Ohio Print & Publishing Co. Massillon, Ohio. 1922.

Time-Life Books. *The Civil War- Decoying the Yankees: Jackson's Valley Campaign.* Alexandria, VA: 1984.

_____. *The Civil War- War on the Mississippi: Grant's Vicksburg Campaign.* Alexandria, VA: 1984.

_____. *The Civil War- Road to Shiloh: Early Battles in the West.* Alexandria, VA: 1984.

_____. *The Civil War- The Fight for Chattanooga: Chickamauga and Missionary Ridge.* Alexandria, VA: 1984.

_____. *The Civil War- The Struggle for Tennessee: Tupelo to Stones River.* Alexandria, VA: 1984.

_____. *The Civil War- The Killing Ground: Wilderness to Cold Harbor.* Alexandria, VA: 1984.

Trudeau, Noah Andre. *Bloody Roads South: The Wilderness to Cold Harbor, May-June 1864.* Boston: Little, Brown & Company, 1989.

_____. *Southern Storm- Sherman's March to the Sea.* New York: Harper Collins: 2008.

Wallick, Scott Alan. *Hans Michael Wallick's Descendants in America- 1732-2012,* Self-published: ISBN-13: 978-1466433076   ISBN-10: 1466433078, 2012.

Welcher, Frank J. *The Union Army, 1861-1865, Organization and Operations. Vols. 1&2.* Bloomington and Indianapolis: Indiana University Press, 1993.

Wiley, Bell I. *The Life of Johnny Reb- The Common Soldier of the Confederacy.* New York: The Bobbs-Merrill Co., 1943.

_____. *The Life of Billy Yank- The Common Soldier of the Union.* New York: The Bobs-Merrill Co., 1952.

Willett, Robert L. *The Lightning Mule Brigade- Abel Streight's 1863 Raid into Alabama.* Lexington, KY: ISBN 1-4392-1996-6, 1999.

Made in the USA
Middletown, DE
01 September 2023

37722014R00150